ESL RESOURCE BOOK FOR ENGINEERS AND SCIENTISTS

ELAINE CAMPBELL, PHD

JOHN WILEY & SONS, INC.

New York   Chichester   Brisbane   Toronto   Singapore

Publisher: Katherine Schowalter
Editor: Theresa Hudson
Managing Editor: Robert S. Aronds
Text Design & Composition: Irving Perkins Associates

Designations used by companies to distinguish their products are often claimed as trademarks. In all instances where John Wiley & Sons, Inc. is aware of a claim, the product names appear in initial capital or all capital letters. Readers, however, should contact the appropriate companies for more complete information regarding trademarks and registration.

This text is printed on acid-free paper.

This publication is designed to provide accurate and authoritative information in regard to the subject matter covered. It is sold with the understanding that the publisher is not engaged in rendering legal, accounting, or other professional service. If legal advice or other expert assistance is required, the services of a competent professional person should be sought.

ISBN 0-471-12172-X (paper)
ISBN 0-471-12171-1 (cloth)

Printed in the United States of America
10 9 8 7 6 5 4 3 2 1

*To John Campbell
who supports my every effort
and
to Woody Cunningham
who encouraged my new studies*

ABOUT THE AUTHOR

Until recently, Dr. Elaine Campbell was in charge of training and education for employees at the 63 domestic and overseas sites of a federally funded research and development center. She is now a partner in Campbell Consulting. She teaches technical communications at the Massachusetts Institute of Technology (MIT) where she has been a member of the faculty for the past 10 years.

Her doctorate is in English with a specialization in Third World Culture and Literature. She has published chapters of books, reviews, and articles in professional and academic journals in many countries. She recently completed a Master of Education degree from Boston University (BU) with a specialization in TESOL (Teaching of English to Speakers of Other Languages). For her work at MIT and BU, Dr. Campbell has been initiated into Pi Lambda Theta, the international honors society for education. She is listed in *Who's Who in American Education, Who's Who in the World, Who's Who in the East*, and *Who's Who of American Women*.

For over 25 years, Dr. Campbell lived in the British Caribbean to which she returns frequently. She is the co-editor of a forthcoming anthology of writing by Caribbean women, *The Whistling Bird* (Three Continents Press), and is working on a collection of Caribbean folklore and herblore for Virago Press in London.

CONTENTS

ESL
RESOURCE BOOK
FOR
ENGINEERS
AND
SCIENTISTS

1

VERBAL

COMMUNICATIONS

Scientists and engineers are almost always people with preferences and skills that lead them naturally to technology. They are the thinkers and the doers of the world. Their aptitude for mathematics and their skill in analysis usually take precedence over verbal skills. Often practical, shy, and reliable, they are not as likely to be outgoing or idealistic. Developing interpersonal relations is not high on their list of things to do.

If this description sounds like you, the Resource Book will help you. It has been written specifically for engineers and scientists, and is full of practical exercises that will help you strengthen your communications skills. In addition to technical writing materials, it includes a chapter on "Speaking and Listening," and one on working in a collaborative setting, "The Group Experience." Throughout the book, you'll find down-to-earth tips and suggestions. And at the end, you'll find a short chapter on survival strategies.

Keep in mind that engineers and scientists want to know the why of things. In working with one another, you must go beyond the mere report of "this is the status of my project." Your audience will want to learn how your project got to where it is, what problems you encountered on the way, how you resolved the problems, and so on. All this inquisitiveness works on your behalf. It forces you to communicate more and better. Out of necessity, you learn to explain, support, describe, and justify. You will never be at a loss for what to write or say. Writer's block doesn't exist for laborers in the vineyard of technology. If for one moment you're at a loss for what to write next, give your draft document to a colleague and ask for reactions. Your draft will be returned with questions and comments filling the page margins.

The Resource Book recognizes that *you* want to know the reason for things. Just learning a rule of grammar is really not good enough for a researcher. As you go through the chapters that follow, you'll find lots of explanations about the why of what's included. Rules of grammar, or rules of physics for that matter, are essential foundations, but you also need to know how a rule was formulated, what led to its acceptance, and how you can bend it, if possible. You also ought to know what to do when you find yourself in territory that's not governed by a rule. Even though English is a rule-based language, there are evolving areas where you have to pick your own path. Furthermore, not everything in a language responds to grammar; a large area falls into the less well-charted territory of style. Because the Resource Book is a self-help resource for experienced professionals, it's written to satisfy your need to know.

Perhaps it should be a requirement that anyone writing a book with an English as a second language (ESL) orientation come from a different country. Not enough authors of ESL books do. Knowing the struggle of learning English provides invaluable insight into the process of language acquisition. It also ensures sympathy for anyone undertaking the task. Closely related to learning English as a second language is the experience of coming to the United States from a different country and learning how to get along in a different culture. As you progress through the Resource Book, you'll find that it's informed by a knowledge of what it's like to see life from a different cultural perspective. For that reason, those of you who were born overseas, who first knew the conventions of a different culture, and who first spoke a different language should feel at home with this book.

The Methodology

A four-dimensional figure would best represent how this book has been written. In terms of relativity theory, we think of the universe as being four-dimensional: the three spatial dimensions plus time. If you take a cube—having length, width, and depth—and add the fourth dimension of time, you'll see the shape of the ESL Resource Book. This diagram illustrates the methodology behind the book's creation.

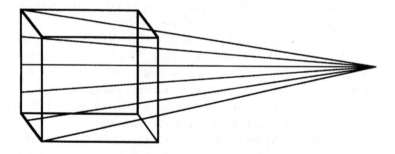

The first dimension is that of general writing practices. Some general grammar problems that occur every day in everyone's writing are reviewed. But the Resource Book goes beyond issues of grammar to include information on the aspects of style: What constitutes style? How do you make style work for you? Further, a chapter on tone will aid you in controlling the attitudes expressed in your writing—attitudes toward your reader and about your material. These are attitudes that often emerge undetected to injure an unsuspecting writer.

Discussions about general writing practices offer a point of departure for the second dimension: technical writing. The largest portion of the Resource Book describes the special requirements for technical documentation in the United States. Many peculiarities of technical writing style are illustrated with practical examples. These descriptions are placed in a real-world context of commercial laboratories, federal research centers, and civilian companies, both for-profit and not-for-profit.

English as a second language (or third or fourth) is the third dimension that informs the other two. You'll find distinctions made between British English and American English because many mathematicians and scientists from overseas have been schooled in traditional British systems. Documents produced in the American[1] workplace are expected to reflect the American dialect of English. There are exercises to help you meet that expectation. Also included is advice on identifying the cultural norms of the American technological workplace. How you respond to those norms affects the success of your career in this country.

Time—the fourth dimension—is an ever-present consideration in the Resource Book. Its target audience is the professional worker, someone who has graduated from a university and is engaged in the daily encounters of the workplace. To use the vocabulary of the training industry, the target audience of the Resource Book is the adult learner. The adult learner has the patience and maturity to undertake a time-consuming self-help program. If you are from overseas, you'll know that self-help programs are more widely practiced in the third world than in the first. Consequently, the self-help aspect of the book intersects with both the third and fourth dimensions.

The World of Work

A typical engineering student believes that brilliant performance in an engineering program guarantees not only a job but also subsequent promotion through the ranks. With native intelligence and lots of hard work, undergraduates in engineering and the sciences earn high grades. High grades are academia's marks of success. The high grades, in turn, attract job offers whether the market is competitive or not. Going from graduate or undergraduate school into the workplace, recent students are fresh and eager to make a mark in the world. Their expectation is to be happy and successful in the laboratory or research center whose offer they've accepted.

As an experienced employee, you've discovered that it's not as easy as that. In the commercial laboratory or the research and development center, brilliant performance is not sufficient. If you labor alone, designing increasingly elegant systems, you will succeed as a scientist but not necessarily as an employee. If your life goals include substantial promotions, appropriate raises, and national recognition, you've got to communicate. Rarely does the lone scientist have a private publicity agent who will advertise the significance of his or her accomplishments. You must plan to be able to do it for yourself.

The avenues of communication are all around you. They are waiting to be used. Learn to recognize their existence and use them to your very best

[1] The words America and American are sometimes used in the *Resource Book* in place of the United States. The author is aware that the United States is not all of America and that technically North America is a more suitable term. To readers from Mexico, Canada, and the countries of South America, note that this was done in the interest of economy in writing.

personal advantage. Many of these avenues of communication are not merely available; they are required. An example is your monthly activity report. If you consider your monthly report drudgery to write, you're probably ignoring it or at best writing a brief and boring summary of the month's activities. Granted, your supervisor will only take bits and pieces of subordinates' reports to integrate into his or her own monthly report. However, if your report is interestingly written, some of your accomplishments will be chosen to be passed up the management ladder.

Staff meetings are a burden for all of us who work in what is being called knowledge-based industry. They are a burden because they consume valuable development and implementation time. They are sometimes called to convey officially information we already know from the grapevine, thus wasting precious time better used for product design. Often, however, they are convened for very important reasons: to work out the problems of an experiment, or to discuss an upcoming deadline. Regardless of the merit of any particular meeting, how you act in staff meetings will eventually influence your career. If you are too uncomfortable to break into a rapid-fire discussion, your presence will be overlooked. If you never participate in meetings, you'll not be seen as a member of the team.

Monthly reports and staff meetings are only two in an array of communication modes you'll be expected to use. Formal briefings, technical documents, trip reports, roundtable discussions, informal conversations, and scientific conferences are some of the other modes that you can look upon as either threats or opportunities.

For the engineer or scientist from overseas, it may seem that in the United States too much time is spent in communicating. Remember, too much time cannot be spent in communicating with one another. Unfortunately, for the professional from overseas, assertive communication practices may be even more difficult than for an American engineer. The combination of frequent communication incidents plus expectations for unfamiliar (and often uncomfortable) behavior can make the workplace a nightmare for someone from a different culture. Although the electronic information highway will ease the pain of communications for nonnative speakers of English, face-to-face meetings and briefings will continue to exist. You have no alternative but to develop your verbal communication skills and to learn tactics for using them successfully.

What Are Verbal Communications?

First, let's resolve the confusion between *oral* and *verbal*. The two words are sometimes used interchangeably. If you are alert to the subtleties of English, you'll know they aren't interchangeable. Simply, *oral* means by mouth whereas *verbal* means by word. *Oral communication* includes anything that's spoken. Briefings, meetings, office conversations, telephone conversations, and lectures are oral. Everything that involves words is *verbal*. All your written products—reports, documents, fax messages, electronic mail, letters and memos, policies and procedures—are included, plus all the spoken forms of communication. Unless you are told differently, most references are to verbal communication.

Verbal communication includes everything except nonverbal communication. Nonverbal communication provides a fascinating way of conveying meaning. Every living creature engages in nonverbal communication. Communication is essential for survival, but some creatures don't have the capability of speech. They must nevertheless be able to tell one another where to find food, how to avoid threats to life, and when it's time to mate. They can often communicate to other species as well. They can signal a potential enemy that he or she is under surveillance, that lethal methods of defense are ready to be launched, or that the interloper must stay away from a nest or hive. These forms of communication are signals. That's what nonverbal communication is composed of: signals. Many species can both speak and signal. Humans are one such specie. We speak and we use signals such as body space, body language, mime, facial expressions, hand movements and finger gestures, among others, to either augment speech or substitute for it. Watch for human signals during your next staff meeting!

Verbal communication includes writing and speaking (the message-sending skills). It also includes a command of reading and listening (the message-receiving skills). Scientists and engineers from overseas almost always have a high level of proficiency in reading, whereas listening skills usually need cultivation. In fact, both United States-born and foreign-born professionals need to pay more attention to listening carefully and patiently to the speech of others. The communications skills most needy of development—for both native English speakers and ESL professionals—are writing and speaking.

Meaning Conveyed through Speaking and Writing

What are some of the ways we convey meaning in writing and speaking? Regardless of what you may have learned in elementary school, the two skills are not expressed in an identical manner: we do not write the way we speak. Conversational speech (or *discourse* as it's called by linguists) contains many elusive meaning markers. Although creative writing, in simulating dialogue, can sometimes suggest these meaning markers, they certainly aren't conveyed in technical writing. So forget what you ever learned about punctuating your writing to match the way you speak.

Meaning in both speaking and writing is conveyed by *semantics*, *syntactics*, and *prosody*. Ordinarily, you read or listen to the meaning of a sentence by a combined search of all three factors. It's possible, however, to separate the factors and decode a sentence one factor at a time, focusing specifically on its words, its structure, or its rhythm.

- Semantics refers to words, specifically, the meaning of words. How you select your words, which words you select, the meaning of the words, their connotative (or implied) meanings are all aspects of semantics. Put another way, semantics equates word choice. Engineers and scientists must choose their words with great precision. As a scientist, your greatest concern regarding word choice is finding the most accurate word possible to describe a phenomenon. Engineers searching for specificity often rely too heavily on enhancing their choice of a word with multiple qualifiers. A careful, sometimes time-consuming search for the best word can minimize the need for extravagant qualification. Words are the first level for conveying meaning. Consequently, you'll find several sections in the Resource Book that focus exclusively on word choice.
- Syntax refers to sentence structure. When words are placed into sentences, they can exert their greatest power. They achieve their full significance through context. The context can be arranged into hundreds of different patterns. English sentence structure is relatively flexible, and you can manipulate meaning to a significant degree by how you arrange the words in the context of their sentence. The same words can have different meanings according to whether they're placed into dependent or independent clauses, for example. Or punctuation within a sentence can intensify the meaning of a word or alter it. Sentence structure is usually treated under grammar in any textbook you might use for reference.
- Prosody refers to the rhythm of the prose. We aren't referring to poetry, but to either speaking or writing. This may be the rhythm of individual sentences or of whole paragraphs. Prosody is probably the most neglected aspect of decoding meaning in communications. Engineers, scientists, and technical editors don't pay much attention to prosody because it isn't as easy to discuss as sentence structure or word choice. It's a subtle factor that doesn't fall under the rubric of grammar. It does, however, fall under the purview of style. It involves stress, intonation (in speaking), and positioning of information, among other elements. Prosody is often influenced by linguistic or cultural factors. For example, the sound of a sentence in English may be different when written by someone whose mother language is Arabic. Some of these issues are discussed in the chapter about style.

A Focus on Writing

Human communications includes reading, listening, writing, and speaking, as well as signals. Hence, it involves both verbal and nonverbal communication. Verbal communications—a somewhat narrowed span of communication competency—are the more frequently used modes of conveying meaning in the workplace. Nonverbal communication is used less often and is usually involuntary. As an example, finger tapping that conveys impatience during a meeting might be intended or not.

Speaking and writing, the two message-sending skills, are characterized by semantics, syntax, and prosody. Narrowing your focus even more enables you to concentrate on writing. Writing can be analyzed in terms of style, tone, and grammar. You'll find that the longest chapters of the Resource Book are about these three aspects of writing. Exercises and examples are included to help you adopt the appropriate tone, acceptable style, and correct grammar for professional writing.

You'll find that the Resource Book focuses most fully at the level of technical writing. It would be possible to narrow the lens even further to look at the types of technical writing—specifications, feasibility studies, proposals, and so on. However, types are usually the subject matter of technical writing textbooks that abound in college bookstores. Because the *ESL Resource Book for Engineers and Scientists* is written to provide information not easily available elsewhere, the types of technical writing are not covered. Instead, the generality of technical writing is the point at which the book's information converges. A diagram illustrating the context of technical writing would look like a pyramid, as shown in Figure 1.2.

FIGURE 1.2 Diagram of technical writing.

Now that you are equipped with diagrams for both the methodology of the *Resource Book* and its content, you might start to think about how you can graphically illustrate your own progression through the book. Will you create a milestone chart to help you see how far you've progressed? Or will you draw a Gantt chart to show the different topics you'll be covering? Perhaps you can create a mapping graphic that will help you see the interconnections of the information in the book. The information is quite diverse, and you might enjoy mapping out bubbles showing relationships. The choice is yours. There are no examinations to pass at the end of the book; there are some exercises, but for most of them the answers have been provided. One requirement is that you share with the author her delight in the language you are about to explore. The rewards are limitless.

2

ESL AND TECHNICAL WRITING STYLE

Business English and Technical English

English has become the international language of business and of technology. The current need for men and women throughout the world to learn business English is so widespread that commercial companies have sprung up across the United States to fill it. In Boston alone, 15 companies offer English as a second language (ESL) with year-round programs in business English. One of the larger companies has 23 teaching centers across the United States and enrollment offices in 54 countries.

Paralleling the worldwide emergence of business English is the growth of English as the international language for science and technology. In fact, worldwide use of English for technical communications probably emerged first. Just as businessmen and businesswomen from overseas need to learn American-style patterns of business communication, so must engineers working in the United States learn American-style documentation standards.

In the past, an engineer had to be a good draftsman; his or her drawings told the story. Now, engineers are expected to write the story and supplement it with graphics. Drafting is becoming a lost art with computer packages taking its place. Today, engineers are expected to be able to write good technical reports (as well as many other types of reports), and write them quickly. For many companies, especially research and development centers, the technical report is the only product delivered to the client to fulfill a contract. The technical report has become the single most important document in technical companies, both for-profit and not-for-profit, across the United States.

On-Site Technical Writing Courses

The United States is also absorbing a greater number of engineers, scientists, physicists, and mathematicians from abroad than ever before. These new members of the technical workplace are expected to produce technical documentation in the same manner as their colleagues whose first, and often only, language is English. To help all employees with their technical writing, most companies provide technical writing seminars in the workplace.

These seminars are very useful even though they're designed primarily for employees who speak and write English as their native language. They are especially useful for learning how to produce a report or a proposal in a standardized manner. For example, the instructor will teach how to structure the overall report and also how to structure internal sections of the report. If the seminar is long enough, you'll learn how to compose specialized sections such as the abstract or the executive summary. The seminar may also provide information on constructing the materials that follow the body of the report. But because in-house seminars are restricted by how much time employees can take away from their jobs, they have serious limitations. They can rarely offer practice in writing and revising text of an actual report, and there isn't enough time to explore the subtleties of style. Despite these shortcomings, however, the seminars are valuable.

If classes in technical report writing are not offered at your company, consider asking a co-worker if you may use his or her reports as a model. But first make sure that your friend has a reputation for writing good reports! Once you've learned how to design a technical report, either from classes or from models, you hold the key for structuring reports that will meet your management's expectations.

Documentation Standards

Most laboratories and high-tech companies have a Manual of Documentation Standards for employee use, although some younger companies haven't yet codified standards because they're still concentrating on product and service lines, staffing, and organizational necessities. But one sure sign of an established technical center is its documentation manual. This is an extremely helpful resource that you mustn't overlook. Sometimes it offers suggested guidelines; more often it states required standards. These recommendations and requirements explain the details of a company's expectations for a professional-looking document. Capitalization, punctuation, typographic choices (font sizes and styles), letter and memo formats, heading formats, placement of page numbers and footnotes are some of the many items included in corporate writing manuals.

Technical Report Writing Style

After taking classes, adopting good models, and familiarizing yourself with your company's documentation manual, you'll find you've mastered the mechanical aspects of technical report writing. The next challenge is mastering technical writing style.

First of all, *style* is a difficult concept to understand. There is no one official definition for *style*, and writing experts differ widely over how to define the concept. Because style is an abstraction, it remains a vague idea. More than a decade ago, Robert Rathbone, Professor Emeritus of Communications at MIT, grappled with the notion of style, and especially technical writing style, in his book *Communicating Technical Information*.

> Broadly defined, "style" is the element in a piece of writing that distinguishes one writer's way of saying something from the way someone else might say the same thing. In so-called creative writing, this difference can be most pronounced. . . .

> In technical writing, style also plays an important role, but in a different sense than in nontechnical prose. The writer's personality must not interfere with the clear and efficient transmission of a message. In this sense, then, a good style in technical writing is one that does its work quietly in the background without calling undue attention to itself. In no way is this an absence of style; rather it is one that centers on satisfying the reader both psychologically and materially.[1]

Rathbone is suggesting that style has a lot more to it than simply selecting short words rather than long words. Most rhetoric books try to address the issue of style by talking about word choice and sentence structure. These two aspects are very important, but they really don't sum up the nature of style. Despite the mysterious nature of good technical writing style, it's assumed that engineers and scientists somehow imbibe it. In fact they do, but what isn't well understood is that the characteristics of good technical writing style are based as much on cultural as on rhetorical factors.

SIX CHARACTERISTICS OF TECHNICAL STYLE

For practical and immediate purposes, let's look at some of the characteristics of technical writing style as practiced in American English. Michael Markel offers an excellent list of six basic characteristics that he considers necessary for a piece of effective technical writing.[2]

Clarity: The document must convey a single meaning that the reader can understand easily.
Accuracy: The facts must be recorded carefully.
Comprehensiveness: The document must include all the information that the reader will need.
Accessibility: The readers can easily locate the information they seek.
Conciseness: The document must be just long enough to be clear.
Correctness: The writing displays correct grammar, punctuation, and usage. It also follows designated format standards.

[1] Robert R. Rathbone. *Communicating Technical Information*. Reading, Massachusetts: Addison-Wesley Publishing Co., Inc. Second Edition, 1985, p. 25.

[2] Michael H. Markel. *Technical Writing Situations and Strategies*. New York: St. Martin's Press. Third Edition, 1992, p. 5.

Markel's list identifies the specific features expected in a technical document written in English. These characteristics, when skillfully controlled by the writer, combine to create the elusive technical style. But some of these characteristics run counter to the writing conventions of other cultures.

OTHER CULTURAL WRITING STYLES

Whereas conciseness is highly esteemed in technical documentation in English, repetition and digression are valued as aids to explanation in other writing traditions. In the interest of multicultural awareness, let's consider a paragraph written in English by an engineer whose first language is Arabic.

> Software engineering, which suffered from the contempt of hardware engineers for decades, is now admitted to be an honorable profession that has attracted many MTS (members of the technical staff) who are women, coming into the profession along with computer scientists. These women form a growing proportion of students in university programs in software engineering, a discipline that didn't exist 10 years ago, but which now constitutes an important specialty at such an esteemed university as Carnegie-Mellon in Pennsylvania.

This paragraph displays considerable content unity, but a technical editor would certainly fault the sentences as too long. In addition to their length, the sentences are quite complex from the point of view of structure. The intricate sentences reflect what it's possible to do in Arabic, a highly flexible language. When the possibilities of Arabic are somehow transferred into technical English, they encounter prohibitions that are, in fact, the reflection of a different language structure.

A second example will help establish that other cultures have different logic structures as well as different writing conventions. Knowing alternative logic structures and different ways of expressing ideas will certainly influence a writer. Here's the introductory paragraph of a document written in English by an engineer from Europe.

> The purpose of this paper is to give the technical reader who is not a systems engineer a good working understanding of the Systems Approach. Key concepts of the Systems Approach are developed, and systems-type activities are traced historically since before engineering became a structured discipline up to the recently emerged concept of systems architecture. *If the importance of the Systems Approach in our future is not better understood, it stands in danger of possible demise unless we figure out a better way of handling conflict resolution than the way we are handling it today.* It is also important to address both civil and military systems at some length because in combination they illustrate many essential points about the Systems Approach.

This paragraph might almost serve as an abstract for the paper, but the italicized sentence is hardly abstract material. The italicized sentence is a digression within the paragraph. It has logical justification—the writer refers to the past and the present of systems engineering before making his comments about the future. But it drifts into the beginning of an argument about conflict resolution. This sort of drift is found in student papers and even in unedited working papers, but this sample is from a published document that passed through several reviews. The fact that the author is from Europe is significant. The acceptance of digressive material in French writing, even technical writing, may explain the inclusion of the digression which is disturbing in English.

The paragraph is not simply an example of a lack of conciseness or even a failure in paragraph unity. It represents a clash of cultures: Sentences one, two, and four reflect an English model, whereas sentence three reflects a way of writing that forgives digression. An alert technical editor would identify the digression, but not necessarily know its cultural reason: that French, Spanish, and other languages allow much greater freedom to digress.

SELF-HELP PROGRAM

The point of these two examples is that technical writing style is not derived from a universal absolute although that may seem to be the case as you go about your writing tasks. But there aren't many secretaries and technical editors who can be expected to appreciate the many cultural reasons influencing writing style. Consequently, as an ESL professional you need to undertake a self-help program to supplement on-site technical writing courses, peer models, and help from technical editors. This self-help program is based on a contrastive method that goes beyond a single language view of technical writing.

First, approach the issue of technical writing style from the viewpoint of what's culturally familiar to you. Think about what a sample of technical writing might be like written in your own language and in your home environment. In your first language, write a paragraph or two on a technical subject that you know well, and then put it aside so that you can distance yourself from it. Return to the paragraph a day or so later and analyze it as objectively as possible. Here are some questions you might ask yourself; you may think of others.

- How does this writing relate to the reader?
- Does it express any relationship to the reader?
- What is the level of formality in the writing?
- What makes it formal, informal, neutral?
- How long are the sentences?
- Can you describe the structure of some of the sentences?
- Is the writing embellished? If so, how much?
- What is the overall logical pattern used?

- Can you trace the shape of the logical pattern?
- Is the writing elegant?
- If so, are you proud of the elegance?
- Why is it elegant?
- Are there digressions?

Some of these questions will seem strange to an American editor, but these are considerations that writers in other language traditions might entertain. The purpose of the exercise is to help you understand how you write in your first language. This is the first part of the contrastive analysis.

Second, turn to a sample of technical documentation in American English. Make sure it's a good example. Try to analyze the style based on the sort of factors Markel suggests: clarity, accuracy, comprehensiveness, accessibility, conciseness, correctness. The more important characteristics for your purposes are clarity, comprehensiveness, and conciseness. Let's assume that you present your facts accurately in any language, you've already learned the formatting devices that ensure accessibility, and you can always get editorial help for correct grammar. Here are some questions you might ask yourself.

- Are the sentences short?
- Is the subject of each sentence easy to identify?
- What is the attitude of the writer toward the reader?
- Is the attitude evident?
- Does the writing avoid digressions?
- Is the logic of presentation inductive or deductive?
- Is there an identifiable level of formality?
- How does the sample achieve clarity?
    by modifiers and prepositional phrases?
    by carefully selected words?
    by closely related sentences?
    by coordination and subordination?
    by other methods?

SIMPLE STYLE

These are some of the concerns of documentation style in the United States. These questions are different from the first-language questions because cultural concerns are often different. By contrasting the concerns (and their related questions), you can move toward understanding the hidden factors that may be influencing your writing style. The contrastive analysis will illustrate that technical writing in English has some predictable characteristics that may be at odds with the first-language product. The analysis will also show that the primary characteristic of technical writing in English is simplicity. Further, you'll see that a simple style isn't difficult to produce. To help you produce a simple style in your own writing, make sure that you review your draft document to see if you've used:

- More short sentences than long sentences
- Minimal or no digressions
- Mixed sentence structure
- Minimal embellishment
- Nonacademic tone
- Disinterested approach to the reader
- Careful word choice: as specific as possible
- Simple word choice: few syllables, if possible
- Linear logical structures: inductive or deductive

After several self-directed exercises in contrast analysis, you'll be ready to move from a dual approach to a single focus. Accept the fact that different writers make the transition at different rates of speed, and that you may even develop a temporary inter-language style at some point along the way. You will gain increased understanding and self-confidence as you get closer to your target style. As you progress, keep in mind the following tips for success.

- Accept that American documentation style is highly standardized.
- Participate in technical writing courses, but don't become frustrated by their limitations.
- Learn required formats to enhance your documents.
- Use the services of technical editors, but understand that some will over-correct.
- Imitate good peer models of technical writing if they're available.
- Underwrite rather than overwrite, but consider moderating this position as your documentation fluency improves.
- Obtain a copy of your company's style manual for documentation.
- Create a writing-editing partnership with your secretary.
- Request corporate training designed for ESL employees.
- Motivate yourself to achieve second-language proficiency.

The final tip is the most important of all. Many studies of second-language acquisition conclude that the subject's motivation is far more important than the method of acquiring language skills: self-teaching, classroom learning, or total cultural immersion.

THE TARGET STYLE

Having advanced to the stage where you can concentrate exclusively on the target style, you need to get a firm grasp of the paragraph convention in English. After that, you might plan to take another, more advanced, seminar in technical documentation. This second seminar will reinforce what you've learned on your own and also refresh what you learned in basic documentation coursework.

SUBTITLE 1: SEE THE FOLLOWING EXERCISE

In English, the paragraph is the basic building block of an entire piece of writing. Words are critical, but they have limited use outside the context of the sentence. Sentences and the countless ways of structuring them are fascinating. But it's only when sentences converge into a paragraph that they can bear the weight of a technical writing task.

SUBTITLE 2: SEE THE FOLLOWING EXERCISE

At risk of repeating what you already know, paragraphs in English are expected to include a keystone sentence: the topic sentence. Most readers will look for an explicit (expressed) topic sentence. As a matter of fact, a well-written paragraph can contain an implicit (understood) topic sentence instead of one that's stated. This is often the case in academic writing. But for the purposes of technical writing and its simple style, always write out your topic sentence.

SUBTITLE 3: SEE THE FOLLOWING EXERCISE

In general writing, the placement of the topic sentence is the writer's choice. It may be the first sentence, announcing the topic of the paragraph; it may be the last sentence, summarizing the paragraph's message; or it may be anywhere within the paragraph. Again, the simplicity of the technical writing style eliminates the need to make a decision about where to place the topic sentence; a rule of thumb is to place it at the beginning of the paragraph. Strict interpretation of this rule places the topic sentence in the first sentence position, but you're working with a rule of thumb, something that's approximate. So it's realistic to place the topic sentence among the first few sentences of a paragraph.

SUBTITLE 4: SEE THE FOLLOWING EXERCISE

Placing the topic sentence early in the paragraph contributes to clarity. The reader can't mistake the purpose of the paragraph. As a simple test of your own writing, after you've completed a document, see if you can underline the topic sentence of each paragraph. If you can't be sure which sentence is the topic sentence, then you need to rewrite the paragraph. Richard Marius, the director of composition at Harvard University, believes that all the underlined topic sentences should flow together into a sort of summary of the paper.

SUBTITLE 5: SEE THE FOLLOWING EXERCISE

You can try another mechanical test for identifying the topic sentence. See if you can write a short subtitle for each of the untitled paragraphs in this section. In this book you'll find boldfaced subtitles throughout each chapter. These are to help you find information that may be of special interest. Not every paragraph has a subtitle because that would be distracting. For your test of the topic sentence, try to write a subtitle of three or four words that equate a shorthand version of the topic sentence.

To illustrate, look at the paragraphs in this section, "The Target Style." There are five paragraphs following the introductory paragraph. As an exercise, create subtitles that echo each of the five topic sentences. Again, it's unlikely that every paragraph of a subsection would have its own subtitle in a real document. Here are some possible subtitles for the first four paragraphs.

Paragraph 1 **The Paragraph**
Paragraph 2 **The Topic Sentence**
Paragraph 3 **Topic Sentence Position**
Paragraph 4 **A Topic Sentence Test**

What subtitle did you write for the fifth paragraph?

PARAGRAPH LENGTH

The most frequent question asked in writing seminars is "How long should a paragraph be?" Briefly, there are no rules about correct length and incorrect length. In academic writing, paragraphs tend to be dense and quite long—perhaps 10 or 12 sentences. But in technical writing, paragraphs tend to be shorter. In creative writing, dramatically short paragraphs of one or two sentences exist, but in a technical paper, a two-sentence paragraph would probably be underdeveloped, leaving the reader with unanswered questions.

Don't try to make all paragraphs the same length. Variety in paragraph length helps relieve monotony, and we all have to work hard at making technical writing interesting.

PARAGRAPH CHARACTERISTICS

Teachers and practitioners of technical writing agree that three characteristics are necessary for a satisfactory paragraph: unity, completeness, coherence. Because your work in contrastive analysis has moved you to focus exclusively on the target language, resist the temptation of protesting that these three characteristics collide with the idea of a paragraph as it exists in different languages.

This warning isn't a digression. It alerts you as an ESL scientist to an awareness that you may be bringing communication experience to the task of paragraph writing that your English-only colleagues have never had. For example, Japanese paragraphs tend to define by eliminating what a subject is not. French and Spanish writing may include digressive material to support a topic sentence, and Semitic languages develop paragraphs by a set of parallel constructions. Writing in English, in contrast, remains dominantly linear.

At a recent international festival in Boston, the committee for the Arab world booth handed out an information sheet about Arab culture and language. The following paragraph from the information sheet offers a good example of the heavy parallelism that characterizes Arabic writing.

> Originators of the third monotheistic religion, beneficiaries of the other two, co-sharers with the west of Greco-Roman cultural tradition, holders aloft of the torch of enlightenment throughout medieval times, generous contributors to European Renaissance, the Arabic speaking peoples have taken their place among the awakened, forward marching independent nations of the modern world. With their rich heritage and unmatched natural resources, they should be able to make a significant contribution to the material and spiritual progress of mankind.

Although this paragraph was written in English and is not a translation from Arabic, it displays the influence of Arabic paragraph style. The series of five long parallel phrases builds up to a crescendo culminating in the final statement: . . . *the Arabic speaking peoples have taken their place among the awakened, forward marching independent nations of the modern world.* The artistic pattern of the paragraph is highly contrived and very effective from a rhetorical point of view. It would not be difficult to draw a graphical representation of this pattern.

Graphically, an Arabic paragraph would be a series of horizontal lines, each line either a bit longer or stronger than the last. Asian paragraphs would be spiral, and paragraphs in the Roman languages would be vertical with projections. The paragraph in English would be drawn as a single straight vertical line. This final representation is the form of the paragraph used in technical writing. Figure 2.1 shows all four graphical representations.

PARAGRAPH UNITY

Paragraph unity is the close relationship of all sentences in a paragraph to the topic sentence. The entire paragraph, regardless of its length, focuses on one aspect of one topic. The content of each sentence is closely related to the

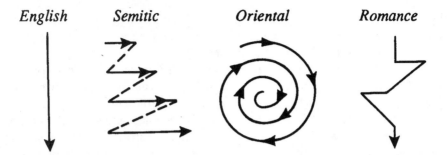

English   *Semitic*   *Oriental*   *Romance*

FIGURE 2.1   Graphical paragraph representations.

content of the topic sentence. If you find yourself engaged in developing a sub-unit of the topic announced in the topic sentence, that subunit needs its own paragraph. Often you won't catch a movement away from the announced topic until you proofread your paper after completing a major section. The following example of a unified paragraph of technical writing is from an unclassified document. It comes near the beginning of the document, but is not the opening paragraph. In contrast, the student paragraph that follows lacks unity.

Good Example
Large amounts of electric power are needed to run the pumps and compressors used in the gaseous diffusion process for the nation's uranium enrichment programs. The three diffusion plants would require about 7,800 megawatts of electricity to operate at their full capacity, or about three percent of total U.S. electric power generation. Primarily because of this large consumption of costly electricity, it is estimated that in the early 1990's the price the U.S. will have to charge for enrichment service will be uncompetitive in the world market.

Bad Example
There are many types of martial arts that fall under the heading of karate. The three most well known are judo, a Japanese art, and tae kwan do and hop ki do. These last two are Korean. Although we break up sections of the martial arts, it is rare for a person to know only one form. All forms use the same uniform known as gi and have a very similar belt system. The white belt is for the beginner up to the black belt which is advanced. The black belt "master" is the highest level of all types of martial arts.

You can exercise your editing skills on the opening paragraph from a freshman composition in any number of ways, but lack of paragraph unity is the issue here. The topic sentence is well placed at the beginning of the paragraph, but the paragraph splits in the middle. The first four sentences begin the task of defining martial arts, and the last three sentences start to discuss the uniforms used in the martial arts. All this material is fascinating, but both topics are shortchanged. Both are sadly underdeveloped, leaving the reader with a sense of wanting to know more. Each of the two topics needs its own paragraph—at least one paragraph.

Paragraph unity is easy to achieve. Write a strong topic sentence, place it very early in the paragraph, and make sure that every other sentence in the paragraph relates closely to it. Examples help to reinforce the topic sentence, but make sure they're really relevant. Because technical and scientific subjects require a lot of detailed support, it's important to guard yourself against drift. As long as the details support the announced topic, you are on track. If you find the details taking on a life of their own, it's time to harness them and give them their own space in a new paragraph.

PARAGRAPH COMPLETENESS

Paragraph completeness is the existence of sufficient evidence within a paragraph to prove the topic sentence or to support it satisfactorily. Lack of paragraph completeness is the writing consultant's "bread and butter." It's also the most frequent flaw of paragraphing. A simple test for completeness is to ask if the reader will come back to the writer with questions about the announced topic of the paragraph. It might be helpful to have a colleague read your draft document paragraph by paragraph to see if he or she can come up with any outstanding questions about the content. It's better to be challenged by a friend than by a stranger who may be hostile. Remember that as a technical writer, you must fulfill all the reader's expectations in every paragraph. Creative writing permits unanswered questions, but not technical writing.

In addition to not providing enough information to prove your topic sentence (just writing it doesn't make it so), there are other ways of failing to deliver. Consider the following paragraph from an unclassified document about systems engineering.

Bad Example
The concept of the systems approach is simple. Systems are complex products or processes. Whether something is a product or a process or both, if it is sufficiently large and complex, it may qualify as a system. In an oversimplified fashion, the approach of applying numerous, highly disparate enabling mechanisms to the creation of complex and large products or processes is what we call the systems approach. There are dozens of overlapping terms floating around to define *systems*, but we choose to define it as a large or complex product or process that relies on a number of enabling mechanisms to bring it into being.

This wordy and repetitious paragraph provides another opportunity for you to exercise your own editing skills. Setting aside other issues, consider the paragraph's completeness. The reader is deluged by a torrent of words and feels as if he or she is drowning. All the words are intelligible, so why is the result so unsatisfactory? This is the sort of paragraph that appears when a writer can't progress with an idea. The paragraph doesn't go anywhere. It's undeveloped (rather than underdeveloped). In this case, the writer has negated the problem by merely saying the same thing over and over. Entire papers can be written in this manner.

PARAGRAPH COHERENCE

Paragraph coherence is the holding together of sentences within a paragraph by more than sequence on the page. Even though a paragraph looks like a paragraph (it's indented, has unity, and contains sufficient information about a single topic), it still may not pass as a good paragraph. Not only must the sentences all relate to a single topic, they should also have interconnectivity—to use a systems word. The sentences shouldn't stand like toy soldiers in a row. They need to touch one another in some way. This requirement comes as a surprise to a lot of writers, especially to those for whom English is an only language. This reaction of surprise may be caused by the fact that coherence is the most subtle of the three requirements for a successfully rendered paragraph. Because paragraph structure in English doesn't have the intricate parallel sets of Semitic languages or some of the flexibility of other languages, this need for coherence is often filled by mechanical devices. The most easily used mechanical devices are

- transitional words and phrases
- pronoun reference
- repeated key terms

TRANSITIONAL WORDS AND PHRASES

Using transitional words and phrases is the basic way of relating one sentence to another. These words and phrases are used all the time in all levels of writing. They can be used within a sentence, between sentences, and between paragraphs. They can be found in any grammar book and in most writing manuals. Usually, they are separated into groups according to their general meaning. The following list includes many transitional expressions appropriate for technical writing.

To add an idea	also, and, first, moreover, too, next, similarly, furthermore
To compare an idea	like, likewise, similarly, equally, correspondingly
To contrast an idea	but, nevertheless, however, in contrast, instead, otherwise, on the other hand, unlike, contrary to
To concede	although, of course, at the same time
To illustrate	for example, to illustrate, for instance, in other words

To show result	therefore, thus, consequently, as a result, hence, accordingly
To show time	then, afterward, later, meanwhile, now, earlier, immediately, before, soon, finally
To show frequency	often, frequently, sometimes, now, then

In addition to these expressions, you can use ordinal numbers (first, second, third) to indicate steps in a process or parts of a plan. Ordinal numbers are commonplace signals of transition, helping readers move more quickly through the text.

All these expressions are useful, but don't overuse them. Because they're useful, it's easy to rely too heavily on them. In fact, of all the transitional devices, they're the least sophisticated way of achieving paragraph coherence.

The following selection from a sole source selection (a document required to justify procuring a product or service without competitive bidding) illustrates good use of transitional expressions to relate one idea to another. It doesn't overuse the transitional expressions but it takes advantage of their availability.

There are two other considerations that favor sole source procurement from this company. **First**, the nonrecurring engineering costs of this purchase order are justified and reasonable as it will require engineering modification to combine three of the single-axis probes into one 3-D Delta configuration. **In addition**, the construction process itself will be modified so that future probes can be purchased as "off-the-shelf" items by medical researchers in and out of government. **Second**, Narda has quoted delivery time on these new 3-D Delta probes to be 16 weeks. Narda has a reputation for delivering usable, reliable, and well-constructed products; **consequently**, the probe should require minimal time for acceptance testing.

Finally, there is no other company that could deliver these probes in 16 weeks. Should another company appear, acceptance testing would take at least one staff year, and commercial availability would not be a reality for yet another year. The end result would be an unnecessary delay in studies of the biological effects of nonionizing radiation, only possible with implantable probes.

PRONOUN REFERENCE

Pronoun reference is a more subtle way of achieving coherence. It sets up a dynamic relationship between nouns and pronouns. It ties together elements within a sentence and it also relates one sentence to another. Sometimes several patterns of reference can be operating simultaneously. This kind of writing results in richly textured prose. Note how the various kinds of pronouns in the following short selection echo the noun-subject *systems*.

Systems are complex products or processes. As a rule, **they** are also large in scope. A proper understanding of **them** leads to the systems approach which applies numerous and highly disparate enabling mechanisms to **their** creation.

The pronouns of the second and third sentences relate back to the noun that introduces the topic sentence, pulling the three sentences together.

> TIP: It's a good idea to reintroduce the noun at the beginning of a new paragraph. Your reader can forget the original reference or confuse it with another if there's too much space between the noun and its pronouns. In any case, start fresh with a new paragraph.

REPEATED KEY TERMS

For now-forgotten reasons, American school children have been taught for decades that they should not repeat the same noun in a paragraph. They are encouraged to use a thesaurus to find substitute words. These instructions have created a great problem because while the thesaurus offers many possible substitutions, few if any exactly match the meaning of the original word.

As adult learners and responsible writers, you can ignore that prohibition from an earlier era. Your task is to search for the very best word to express a concept. Having found that word, don't throw it away. Use it wherever it's needed. This advice applies especially to technical writing where vocabulary has great specificity. If you abandon the specific word that conveys a concept in favor of a feeble substitute, you weaken your writing. You may also confuse your reader.

Concluding Remarks

Sometimes, writers and editors forget that the paragraph is a completely artificial way of imposing order on thoughts. Different cultures have different ways of organizing thoughts. Robert B. Kaplan explains that, "The expected sequence of thought in English is essentially a Platonic-Aristotelian sequence. . . . It is not a better nor a worse system than any other, but it is different."[3] In English generally, and in technical English especially, paragraph creation is strictly circumscribed. The rules are many, but they're easy to follow. You've reviewed the most important ones by reading this chapter, and you're now equipped to apply the paragraph rule that stands above all others in technical English: One Thought, One Paragraph.

[3] Robert B. Kaplan. "Cultural Thought Patterns in Inter-Cultural Education," in *Towards Multiculturalism*, edited by Jaime S. Wurzel. Yarmouth, Maine: Intercultural Press, Inc., 1989, p. 208.

3

THE TECHNICAL

WRITER'S TONE

Relation of Tone to Style

Tone and style are so closely allied that it's possible to think of them as the same subject. However, they can be separated from one another, and doing so helps you understand an aspect of business or technical writing that's often overlooked. If you can distinguish between style and tone, you can exert better mastery over your writing.

As in the case of style, tones of writing can be influenced by different cultural perceptions of the purpose of a document. Later in this chapter, you'll see how various cultural assumptions about the reason for writing business letters affect their tones. You'll also see that the "you approach" of American communications is distinctive to the United States and is not an approach adopted naturally throughout the world. As an ESL businessman or scientist working in the United States, you will need:

- To recognize the range of tones used in North American communications.
- To select the ones appropriate for various tasks.
- To learn how to produce them.

DIFFERENCES BETWEEN STYLE AND TONE

In chapter 2, Rathbone's definition of *style* offers a wide-ranging view of the issue. It suggests that an author's individuality is more likely to be expressed through style than through any other factor of writing. But Rathbone also alerts us to the fact that technical writing admits fewer expressions of individualistic style than other forms of writing. On an elementary level, an author's style can be analyzed and defined by taking apart sentences to see how a particular author constructs them, looking at paragraphs to see what patterns they exhibit, and examining the author's choice of words. Word choice is frequently a clue to a writer's educational, social, or cultural background—important elements that contribute to the creation of a style.

Tone is simpler to define than style. Randall Decker offers a concise definition: "Tone is determined by the attitude of the writer toward his [or her] subject and toward his [or her] audience."[1] The thrust of tone is in the direction of the subject and the reader, often called *audience*, whereas the focus of style is on the writer and his or her way of creating prose. As an expression of

[1] Randall E. Decker. *Patterns of Exposition 8*. Boston: Little, Brown and Company. 1982, p. 419.

attitude, tone can take on all the colorations of how the writer feels about the audience he or she has in mind.

A Brainstorming Exercise in Tone

Brainstorming is a commonplace method of eliciting creative ideas in the workplace. (It, too, has cultural dimensions; for example, engineers from China and Japan might feel very uncomfortable in the free-for-all atmosphere of a typical brainstorming session.) The basic rule is that everyone in a brainstorming session calls out ideas, and all ideas are accepted and recorded without judging them. Only after everyone in the brainstorming session has contributed all their ideas does the process begin of sorting out more or less appropriate choices.

In a recent technical communications class exercise at MIT (Massachusetts Institute of Technology), students were asked to call out to the teacher all the writing tones they could think of. They were assured that no suggestions would be refused. The exercise began slowly but built up momentum until the entire blackboard was covered. One student volunteered to make a paper record of the suggestions on the board. The suggestions are listed here in the random order in which they were made.

Careful	Angry	Casual	Considerate
Arrogant	Concerned	Diplomatic	Condescending
Delicate	Factual	Critical	Enthusiastic
Firm	Distant	Gentle	Formal
Fussy	Persuasive	Friendly	Humorous
Thoughtful	Helpful	Insulting	Informal
Judgmental	Kind	Pleading	Instructional
Journalistic	Pessimistic	Neutral	Matter-of-fact
Praising	Objective	Sarcastic	Optimistic
Stilted	Practical	Somber	Sad
Pragmatic	Regretful	Serious	Brusque
Subtle	Tactful	Harsh	Understanding
Happy	Cheerful	Hurt	Straightforward

Because all these tones are not appropriate for every writing task, the students were then asked to choose from the list the tones they thought might be appropriate for business letters. They first thought about the kinds of business letters described in their textbook: order letter, inquiry letter, response to an inquiry letter, sales letter, and claim letter. Their teacher expanded the kinds of business letters to include college application letters, job application letters, and funding requests. By eliminating the tones that seemed inappropriate for these eight kinds of letters, the class came up with a shorter list.

You might enjoy joining in the exercise by filling in the empty box below with the tones from the first box that you think are appropriate for the eight kinds of letters named in the above paragraph. You may add tones that are missing from the list. Remember, the boundaries of range are determined by what is an appropriate attitude toward the subject and the audience for the designated tasks.

Appropriate Tones for Business Letters

_____   _____   _____

_____   _____   _____

_____   _____   _____

LIMITATIONS OF TONE

The range of tones used for business letters is far more limited than the range of tones for personal letters. And the range of tones used in business correspondence is, in turn, far *less* limited than the range of tones admissible to technical documentation. So if you've already reduced the number of tones acceptable in general writing in response to the needs of business writing, you'll find yourself again reducing your choices to meet the limitations of technical writing. Just as the range of styles acceptable for technical writing is small, so too is the range of tones used in technical documentation.

But before resizing the box to contain an even smaller number of appropriate tones—for technical documentation—let's first look at a few examples of tone in letters. Several short samples are offered to help you see the effect of varying tones. You, in the role of reader for these three sample letters, probably will find yourself responding to each letter with a different set of feelings.

Sarcastic Tone

To the Editor
The Detroit News

If the United States mayors' conventions were held at Cobo Hall [a conference hall in Detroit], Garden City would no doubt manage to have one delegate in attendance. However, with this year's event being held in Hawaii, it seems necessary that the city send not only the mayor but also all four councilmen.

Travel expenses will come out of our tax funds. If this doesn't win us the trophy for the Nation's Most Gullible City, we should run a close second.

Helpless Taxpayer
Garden City, Michigan

Officious Tone

Mr. Charles Grandy
President, City Bank

Dear Charles:

I've received your letter inviting me to serve as a member of City Bank's evaluation team for contractor proposals. I regret that I must decline the invitation. As you doubtlessly realize, this litigious era requires that large companies avoid any suggestion of conflict of interest. I fear that my acceptance of your invitation could be construed in a manner damaging to Emanon Corporation.

We, here at Emanon, plan to submit a proposal in response to City Bank's RFP for a financial reengineering plan. Consequently, it would be unseemly for me to participate in an effort to evaluate the services of competing companies. I trust you will understand my inability to assist you.

Yours very truly,

Chief Executive Officer
Emanon Corporation

Humorous Tone

Service Department
Orange Computers

Dear Sir or Madam:

I've recently purchased a new laptop Orange, and I need help with learning how to live with her. I've come to the conclusion that computers don't like me. I don't know why. I try to be friends with them; I clean their screens and cover them at night. Sometimes I even talk to them. A kind word now and then does wonders for people and even for plants. But computers in general, and your Orange laptop in particular, are different from people, and even from plants. They have no souls—only a disk drive.

Do you have a service representative here in the Atlanta area who can teach me how to set up a good relationship with my new Orange? I've reviewed all the documentation that came with her, but I believe my problems lie at a deeper level than covered by the user manuals.

Sincerely,

Michael McNally

Having responded to these three sample letters as a reader, now change roles and consider the writer's role in each case. Is the writer's sarcastic attitude in the letter to the editor directed toward the reader or to the subject matter? Here, the subject matter of political corruption is the target of sarcasm. In the second letter, the CEO's officious attitude is directed toward the reader of the letter, the President of City Bank. And in the third letter, the humorous attitude seems directed toward the designers of Orange laptop computers.

In passing, you might also notice that while these highly distinctive tones capture your attention, at the same time they divert your attention from the content of the letters to the tones themselves. This diversion is one very good reason for avoiding flamboyant tones when writing technical material. The element of distraction may make it more difficult for the reader to absorb important and perhaps complex technical information.

TONE IN THE TECHNICAL ENVIRONMENT

Because of the emphasis on clarity in technical documentation, you may wonder how a writer working in a technical environment can err in the area of tone. Interestingly, most reviewers and editors of technical documentation simply assume that tone is not a concern. Consequently, it's overlooked while editorial attention is directed toward the more mechanical issues of correct grammar, proper formatting, and acceptable style. At the same time that the documentation copy editor bypasses tone, the peer reviewer will also over-look tone because his or her focus is on the content.

Consider the situation in which a documentation consultant recently evalu-ated environmental reports in a Washington area research center. The cogni-zant department head felt that his scientists' reports suffered from awkward writing and imperfect grammar. Submitting a number of reports with their attached letters of transmittal, he asked the consultant to look over the reports and then organize a seminar to address their writing problems. Contrary to what she had been led to expect, the consultant found the reports contained rather good writing with some minor problems of organization and me-chanics. But the glaring flaw was in each of the department head's covering letters. In each case the flaw was one of tone. No one in the research center thought to fault the arrogant tone of the covering letters. How must the client have felt when the following letter arrived? Titles and names have been replaced with fictional ones.

Subject: Review of Draft Environmental Remediation Plan 94±2388/B

Dear Colonel [   ]:

Enclosed herewith is our review of the subject document as prepared by your staff and contractor team. The review was prepared under the direction of our Project Manager, Dr. Albert V. Reynolds, with support from our Remediation Technical Center headed by Dr. Sidney Weinberg.

As you know, our organization was tasked under Air Force Regulation 80/200 to provide expert, impartial assistance to environmental remediation projects associated with the closure of Air Force bases on a worldwide basis. Your project's plan is required by that Regulation to undergo our expert review before it can emerge from the Draft stage.

As you will see from reading our review of your draft planning document, we find it incomplete in many areas, inaccurate in several others, and lacking in understanding of basic environmental remediation technology. Examples of these deficiencies are:

- Your failure to identify the procedures to be employed to select and manage the contractor that will oversee the remediation project, or the criteria for proposal evaluation leading to contract award.
- Your inadequate characterization of the toxic materials on the Base, and failure to show expected concentrations in a graphical depiction.
- Your lack of understanding of the petroleum emulsification techniques for groundwater purification.

It is obvious to us that your efforts to date have not been supported by suitable technical expertise. To assist your staff to address the problems we found in your plan, and to produce a revision that will be complete and free of flaws, I suggest a meeting at your earliest convenience between your staff and a team that Dr. Weinberg and Dr. Reynolds will designate. We look forward to assisting you to proceed to a workable program. If you have any questions, feel free to contact me directly.

Very truly yours,

[   ], Ph.D.
Head, Evaluation Department

This writer's arrogant tone seems to be directed primarily toward the reader of the letter of transmittal, although it also attacks the draft remediation plan. You might say that the writer treats the plan with a tone of contempt, so that both the draft plan and the reader are victims of the writer's abuse. Granted that reviewers are expected to search for flaws, they will not contribute to a productive relationship if they report their findings in this manner. In sum, a good writer always maintains a polite tone.

An Exercise in Tone

Be alert to the fact that you must be sensitive to your tone if you're asked to evaluate a technical situation or critique a technical report. It's very easy to interpret a critiquing assignment as an exercise in negativism. If you find that your critique notes are consistently negative, there's the possibility that they may also be insulting. If they're insulting, they'll be counterproductive to whatever technical effort is in progress. Here are some tips that should help you protect yourself from slipping into a wrong tone.

TIP 1: Try to express each negative reaction in as positive a way as possible.

TIP 2: Avoid condescending expressions like "it is obvious" and "of course."

TIP 3: Move away from the "you approach" if you need to minimize personal-sounding criticisms.

TIP 4: Pay special attention to your word choice.

TIP 5: Be wary of using shall and should unless they are indicated in military regulations or agency specifications.

As an exercise, read the following paragraphs from another transmittal letter and decide why they also express an arrogant tone (the salutation and second paragraph have been omitted to save space). Identify the specific features that need rewriting or editing in order to replace the arrogance with a more straightforward tone.

Subject: Review of Software Modernization Plan for AN/QSS±33A

This letter transmits our Center's technical evaluation of the subject Modernization Plan.

Our review was performed by a team of software and electronic warfare experts headed by Dr. Alexander Carswell, supported by the Real-Time Software Laboratory which is under the direction of Dr. Stanley Taub. As you know, we have an extensive database that catalogs the experiences of other military programs in developing and modernizing software of the type you describe in the subject plan. This experience base has led us to conclude that your plan, if allowed to progress to the contract stage, will produce a badly flawed system that will be almost impossible to maintain and which will exceed cost and schedule by almost 75%.

There is no doubt that the software in the existing AN/QSS–33 electronic jammer is outdated, is based on obsolete equipment, and can no longer be efficiently maintained. The modernization, therefore, is badly needed. You should now be releasing specifications for the procurement of replacement software. We looked for evidence in your draft plan that you understood the concepts of reusability, modularity, object-oriented soft-ware design, configuration management systems, and tracking of design progress. Unfortunately, your plan falls short in all these areas.

We recommend that your current plan be terminated and a replacement document be developed by a joint effort between your staff and our experts. We would remind you that our experience will help you advance your development plan to the development stage. We will be glad to assist you in reaching this goal without the waste of any more time.

Very truly yours,

Paul V. Martin, Ph.D.
Chief, Evaluation Center

These two examples of technical transmittal letters exhibit certain attitudes that can creep into reviews, evaluations, and critiques. By eliminating tones that express excessively emotional attitudes, you automatically limit the tones admissible in technical writing to those that are unlikely to interfere with relaying the technical message as efficiently as possible, without distraction, and without creating negative reactions. By deemphasizing both authorial style and attitude, technical writers reduce the list of usable tones to a very small number. A reduced box of tones might now look something like this.

Careful	Factual
Instructional	Objective
Practical	Serious
Matter-of-fact	Straightforward

And of these, straightforward is the tone that will always serve you best.

Cultural Conventions in Communications

Because the "you approach" is used so widely in the United States for communications, it sometimes comes as a surprise to English-only writers that this rather direct, often friendly, and somewhat informal approach is not favored throughout the world. The truth is that there are many other approaches for relaying information. Some of these approaches are dictated by cultural attitudes that emerge in writing as different tones. These attitudes may relate to purpose or to the writer-reader relationship.

For example, in France a business letter is more often than not viewed as a document for file. In some respects, it's a legalistic form of protection to the writer: It verifies that a required action was taken or a contracted study delivered. It's an object for the archives of the writer's agency. The letter exists to protect the writer. In this situation, how the reader of the letter feels is of little interest to the writer, and the "you approach" would be unsuitable.

Further, in France, the format of business letters is strictly prescribed. The "Dear Henry" sort of salutation is not accepted, and the complementary close is expected to reflect the formality of the salutation: *Monsieur, Messieurs, Madame,* and so on. Body information is brief, impersonal, and formulaic. This, in almost every way, is the direct opposite of the business letter written in American English where the purpose is to try to influence the reader. Whereas chapbook phrases are routinely used in French business correspondence, business writers in the United States are urged to avoid using clichés. Earlier letterwriting in the United States was closer to the European mode, but the gap widens every year. Figure 3.1 is an example of a French business letter from *Le Français Economique et Commercial.*[2] Note the short paragraphs, abrupt tone, and absence of "you approach." Indeed, with its many references to *nous* (we) it demonstrates instead a "we approach." Thus, the French business letter is writer-focused rather than reader-focused.

Each of the first five paragraphs is remarkably short and to the point. Only the final paragraph ("We thank you for the interest you have shown in our publication, and beg you to believe in the sincerity of our devoted feelings.") seems somewhat more courteous, but it is really only a courtesy formula suitable for ending the letter. Were the writer of a technical information letter to reflect his or her French training in the United States, he or she would be thought cold and aloof and perhaps not a suitable partner for a team venture.

Even more removed from the American "you approach" and the French "we approach" are the Japanese business conventions for written communications. These conventions are rigid and complex, and they are neither you nor we based. As in direct encounters, the relationship *between* the writer and the reader is of extreme concern in Japanese interaction. A question like, "What is the position of the recipient in his or her organization compared to my position in my organization?" is important to the writer. "What is the context of our association?" might be another. As in the French cultural milieu, many formulas are available for covering these issues. While the Japanese formulas are very sensitive to degrees of relationship between parties, writers can easily find them in books of business writing.

---

[2] Mustapha K. Bénouis, *Le Français Economique et Commercial.* New York: Harcourt Brace Jovanovich, Inc., 1982, p. 115.

Aujourd'hui

765, rue Saint-Honoré
75009 Paris
Tél.: 046.22.63

Paris, le 4 Juin 1980

Dr. Mustapha K. Bénouis
Department of European Languages
and Literature
1890 East-West Rd., Moore 470
HONOLULU
HAWAII

JC/CG

Monsieur,

Nous vous accusons réception de votre chèque bancaire
de 43,71 $ que vous nous avez adressé en règlement de
votre abonnement à notre revue "Aujourd'hui".

Nous vous en remercions.

L'échéance en est maintenant au 1er décembre 1980.

Toutefois, l'acheminement par voie ordinaire étant
irrégulier, nous avons installé ce service par avion,
ce qui est plus adapté pour une revue d'actualité.

Nous vous serions donc reconnaissants de bien vouloir
nous faire parvenir en complément la somme de 91 FF
(coût de la taxe aérienne pour six mois).

Nous vous remercions de l'intérêt que vous portez à
notre publication et vous prions de croire a l'assurance de nos sentiments dévoués.

J. CARTIER
Administrateur

FIGURE 3.1   An example of a French business letter.

AN EXAMPLE

Here's an actual letter of appreciation received by the technical director of a research center in Massachusetts from a group of Japanese scientists who toured the center. Notice how aware the writer is of the relationship between the research center as host and the visitors as guests. This awareness is expressed in what may be an attempt to achieve the American "you approach." (The letter was written in English and is not a translation from Japanese.) Unfortunately, from an American point of view, the tone is too effusive. The recipient (reader), however, fully understood the intention of the writer as well as the cultural difference the letter exhibits. So while the tone is less than successful, the letter was well received. This is one of the occasions where a truly civilized relationship between communicators from disparate cultures worked. As technical editor Marcia Sweezey believes, "To Americans, a level of other-cultureness can be very charming."[3] Unfortunately, in the technical writing environment, the perimenters of such tolerance are narrow.

As a parting comment on this lovely letter, you might note the italicized comment about New England's crimson foliage. While this constitutes a digression in an American-style paragraph, someone familiar with Japanese letterwriting conventions would recognize echoes of the seasonal greeting that is a formulaic part of a Japanese business letter. Instead of a reference to "Spring season" or "the season of glorious cherry blossoms," Mr. Kashihara refers to the fall foliage.

So if you are one of the many Japanese technical staff members now working in the United States, you too may find yourself retrieving familiar formulas as you compose your prose. You can recognize the cultural significance of these formulas, and retain them to use if you have occasion to mediate between the two countries for business or personal reasons. In fact, this ability is one that isn't sufficiently advertised by our engineers and scientists from Japan and elsewhere. You have the skills to do a better job of representing your company in an expanding world market than English-only employees. In addition to technical know-how, you bring cultural and linguistic skills to the negotiation table.

THE REWRITTEN VERSION

So that you might have a good example of an American-style business letter for your use, the recipient of Mr. Kashihara's letter was asked to rewrite it as if it had been composed by an American guest to an American host. Notice that the letter really had to be rewritten rather than merely revised in order to achieve a style and tone congruent with United States custom.

[3] Marcia Sweezey to Elaine Campbell, manuscript notes, June 6, 1994.

HOKKAIDO/MASSACHUSETTS SOCIETY

C/O HOKKAIDO YOUTH & WOMEN'S INTERNATIONAL EXCHANGE CENTER
MAINICHI SAPPORO HALL BLDG., WEST-6, NORTH-4, CHUO-KU, SAPPORO, HOKKAIDO, JAPAN 060
PHONE: (011)231-6451   FAX: (011)231-3392

November 5, 1991

Mr. John B. Campbell
Associate Technical Director
Information Systems
The MITRE Corporation
Burlington Road
Bedford, Massachusetts 01730
U.S.A.

Dear Mr. Campbell,

On behalf of the members of the Hokkaido Trade Mission, I would like to express my deepest and sincerest thanks for your kind arrangements during our visit to Massachusetts. Your varied explanations on and kind arrangements for a company tour which covered the detailed actual operations on the occasion of our visit to your company were much appreciated. Thanks to your kind arrangements for the on-site tour of your company, we could gain a better understanding of the latest software technology in your company. We cannot have adequately express our heartfelt gratitude and thanks for everything you did for us.

We could appreciate Massachusetts more deeply and obtain very fruitful results through this visit. We also enjoyed seeing the beautiful crimson foliage peculiar to New England. I would like to express our appreciation for your kind helpfulness. Your continuing friendly support in promoting future mutual exchanges between Hokkaido and Massachusetts will be much appreciated.

Yours sincerely,

Yasuaki Kashihara

Yasuaki Kashihara
Leader
Hokkaido Trade Mission
President
Hokkaido/Massachusetts
Society

FIGURE 3.2   Example of a Japanese thank-you letter.

The rewritten letter has less of a "you approach" than might be expected from a business letter of appreciation, but because the writer of the Americanized version is completely familiar with the letterwriting conventions of a technical environment, his balanced use of first person and second person is in itself a useful lesson.

HOKKAIDO/MASSACHUSETTS SOCIETY

Mainichi Sapporo Hall Bldg., West-6, North-4, Chuo-Ku, Sapporo, Hokkaido, Japan 060

                                                                November 5, 1991

Mr. John B. Campbell
Associate Technical Director
Information Systems
The MITRE Corporation
Burlington Road
Bedford, MA 01730

Dear Mr. Campbell,

I am writing on behalf of my fellow members of the Hokkaido Trade Mission to thank you for spending time with us during our recent visit.

We were very impressed with the facilities we saw during the guided tour you organized and conducted. Thanks to the demonstrations you selected, we came away with an excellent understanding of the software technology that MITRE employs in its operations.

I hope there will be opportunities for us to meet again in the future and continue our information exchange. Thank you again for your generous assistance in making our visit a success.

                                        Yours sincerely,

                                        Yashuki Kashihara
                                        Leader
                                        Hokkaido Trade Mission

The paragraphs here are quite a bit shorter than in the original letter, and each paragraph is more clearly limited to one topic—a good example of paragraph unity. The overall length of the rewritten version is also significantly shorter: 98 words in the body of the letter in contrast to 154 in the original. Despite its brevity, however, there is no sense of abruptness or lack of courtesy.

The most apparent differences are in simpler sentence structure and less adjectival enhancement. There is also less repetition. And, of course, the seasonal greeting is missing. What other differences can you identify?

A FINAL EXERCISE IN TONE

You have just returned to the United States from a two-week fact-finding mission to Ukraine and Estonia. The purpose of your mission was to determine the status of computer software development in these two Baltic countries and to explore the possibility of technology exchange.

You are the leader of the three-member team that spent one week in each country. While in Tallinn, Estonia, your team toured the Tallinn Technical University. The Rector, Dr. Boris Tamm, personally conducted the tour and afterwards invited you and your colleagues to his home for dinner.

As the team leader, you are responsible for follow-up activities. You've written and submitted a trip report, and now wish to write thank you letters. Compose a letter to Dr. Tamm, thanking him for his hospitality. Compose your letter in the manner of an American engineer, adopting an appropriate tone and style. Remember that you received Dr. Tamm's personal attention at the university, and that your team spent the evening at his home. Further, you may wish to continue negotiating with him for a future exchange of research personnel and computer technology.

Your challenge is to develop a tone that is appreciative without being effusive. If you wish, you may be more "you-oriented" than in the written revision of Mr. Kashihara's letter, but you must keep in mind the conventions of U.S. communications. This task will be difficult because it requires you to mediate between technical and social environments.

Summary of Strategies for Successful Tone

When working in a single-culture environment, you need to move beyond your first-language communication habits, beyond the inter-language stage that the Hokkaido Trade Mission letter represents, and into the practices of your target language. As in the case of style, you can use as models for tone the letters of colleagues who are good writers. (A writer is not necessarily good simply because he or she composes in his or her first language.) While it's also possible to find business letter models in rhetoric books, this returns you to the European method of template writing, thereby building up a dependency on models from which you'll wish to liberate yourself as soon as possible. Working with a technical editor to improve your correspondence is a better alternative because you'll have the advantage of one-on-one help customized to your particular needs. And, again, don't overlook the immense amount of help that sympathetic secretaries can provide.

Your best ally will be your own ear. As you'll read later in the discussion of accent reduction, you must learn to listen to American-born speakers to pick up the cadences of the language. Writing is not the same as speaking, but there is a certain amount of transfer. The greatest roadblock to acquiring the cadences of another language—be it speaking or writing—is reinforcing your own sounds. You must break the out-of-mouth, back-into-ear cycle. If you hear only your own voice, you will reproduce only your own sounds.

The openness of the American culture is reproduced in the cadences of its speech and the tone of its writing. The trick is to not go overboard. But good writing requires constant judgment checks for *all* writers, regardless of their language background.

Here are some final tips for producing an appropriate tone for technical documentation in American English.

TIP 1: Recognize the limited number of tones used in technical writing.

TIP 2: Try to be as straightforward as possible without being blunt.

TIP 3: Remember that clichés (groups of prepackaged words) will give your writing a stilted tone.

TIP 4: Liberate yourself from emotional attitudes as you write; for example, anger, contempt, pride.

TIP 5: Identify a suitable tone for a writing task, adopt it, and remain consistent to it throughout your document.

TIP 6: If possible, picture your reader(s) as you write.

TIP 7: Think of your reader as a colleague; don't be overly concerned with your reader's social or business status.

TIP 8: Value the communications conventions of your own culture.

TIP 9: List the advantages to your company of your two-culture communication experience.

TIP 10: Explore how your company can use this experience.

As the vision of business, university, and research communities in the United States becomes more international, your knowledge of alternative modes of speaking and writing will become a significant factor in your personal success. Until you are given an opportunity to use this knowledge, write as if no conventions of style or tone exist other than those practiced in your own workplace.

4

SPECIAL STYLE

NOTES

Special Style Practices of U.S. Technical Documentation

Command of the style and tone of technical prose combined with knowledge of the documentation standards of a particular company will enable you to produce good technical writing. Once you've mastered these three factors—standards, style, tone—you've cleared your highest hurdle, and are ready to review a variety of documentation practices peculiar to the United States. Some of these practices, like the use of bullets and acronyns, are mechanical in nature and easy to learn. Some, however, like coined words and transferred terms, are perplexing for an employee who has recently acquired English as a second language.

Bullets and Vertical Writing

The use of bullets to create lists is a peculiarly American feature of technical documentation. Bullets are believed to have first been used in U.S. military briefings. Their original military use helps to explain both their shape and associated name. When the briefing charts were afterwards incorporated into longer documents, the bullets were also transferred into the general text. Civilian companies with military sponsors adopted the bullet format which has spread far beyond the military-related environment. You'll now see bulleted lists in medical and financial reports, in political analyses, and in management studies. They are used widely in seminar and workplace training descriptions and in user manuals. Bullets and their associated vertical lists are now becoming an aspect of technical reports throughout the world.

Although no one can name the exact time and place they first appeared, the small circles preceding entries in vertical lists do look like the blunt end of a bullet shell. They looked even more like a shell end or cross-section before engineers began filling them in. Originally, word processing software was not capable of producing a special character for the bullet. Consequently, secretaries typed the lowercase letter o (not the number). Graphic designers explain that engineers began to fill in the o's with ink to differentiate them from the letter o and to make them stand out from the running text. It presents an amusing picture to think of thousands of engineers across the United States busily filling in their lowercase o's to form bullets.

Eventually, software was written to produce a special character for the bullet. Wang was one of the first companies to provide it, and it was always easy to spot which departments had Wangs and which had other equipment. The format battle began: Would a company use open bullets or filled bullets? As more software was written to produce bullets, the filled bullet became an informal national standard. Now there are large filled bullets and small filled bullets.

Square bullets didn't exist until quite recently, and the term really is a contradiction of terms. Further, applications like Powerpoint provide filled diamond-shaped bullets as well as filled stars. And there are those who use boldfaced, filled apple symbols in place of bullets. Despite the existence of square, diamond, star, and apple bullets, format purists consider all these as design elements for use elsewhere.

Filled bullets are usually boldfaced for greater visibility. In fact, the reason for using bullets at all is to provide the easiest possible access to information in a document. With them and their vertical lists, you can break information out from the main text so that it's easier to find. Once you've isolated the information into the bullet-vertical list format, you need to arrange the data in parallel structure. Any information, whether written in conventional horizontal lines or in technical vertical lists, is easier to remember if parallel structure is used.

PARALLELISM

Parallelism means using the same grammatical structure for all items that have the same function. Parallel sentence structure contributes to clarity because it indicates parallel ideas. Parallelism has a long history; it was used by the ancient Greek rhetoricians to organize thoughts. It was later used by medieval musicians and story tellers because it helped them remember their long narratives, and it helped their listeners re-create the stories. And parallelism seems to satisfy a basic human love for symmetry. You'll note that orators and politicians today rely on parallelism to give their speeches a memorable quality: JFK's "Ask not what your country can do for you, but what you can do for your country" is perhaps the most famous example from modern American speechwriting.

Here are some examples of parallelism in conventional sentences.

Good Parallelism

Emanon Corporation report #9999 is out of print and out of stock.

Emanon personnel sometimes travel with laptop computers, electronic datebooks, and cordless telephones.

A good manager not only works well with people, but he or she also supports corporate goals.

You can get to M-building by taking either the tie corridor or the outdoor route.

The reviewer couldn't decide whether to ignore the report or to review it negatively.

Here are some examples of flawed parallelism in conventional sentences. If you read them aloud, you'll note how they disappoint your sense of symmetry.

Flawed Parallelism

Our client is not only well funded but also is very frugal.

Logical thought, coherent organization, and the ability to express ideas clearly are important aspects of good prose.

As the fact-finding mission leader, you are responsible for meeting appropriate scientists, collecting pertinent data, and you should also establish guidelines for future visits.

A corporate training unit must meet the educational needs of a company's technical staff, secretarial force, support service employees, and provide training for both middle and upper management.

The circuit board design incorporated four improvements: ease of maintenance, compatibility, reliability, and usability.

Often you can correct flawed parallelism simply by changing the incongruous element to match the other items in a series. In the last sentence, for example, you can change *ease of maintenance* to *maintainability*. In some cases, you need to revise the structure slightly. For example, in the first sentence, you need to create a more balanced pattern: *Our client is not only well funded but also very frugal.* Sometimes the balanced items come at the beginning of the sentence (the second sentence) and sometimes at the end (sentences three, four, and five). You'll find parallelism useful throughout paragraphs as well as within sentences. In larger blocks of writing, you must monitor it carefully.

In any case, when you create a parallel structure, you're writing in a studiously artificial manner. Consequently, in technical English, parallelism is used more frequently in lists than in sentences. In this way, you can use its qualities without disturbing the tone of your writing. You know that vertical lists are not a conventional way of writing a sentence in English. And as soon as you start to use them in your own writing, you're connecting ancient Greek parallelism with twenty-first century technology.

PARALLELISM IN BULLETED LISTS

The following bulleted list needs to be corrected for faulty parallelism. In this example, assume that the company documentation standards dictate that each new item in the list begin with a lowercase letter. Sometimes a documentation standard states that each item should begin with an uppercase letter. This isn't a matter of grammar; it's merely an arbitrary formula that one corporation decides to use to achieve visual consistency among all its documents.

Faulty List Parallelism

What Dr. Press proposed are actions that will be beneficial even if global warming does not exist. These actions include the following:

- reforestation
- energy conservation
- water conservation
- better coastal management
- replace CFC by other chemicals
- improved pollution control
- increased research in other forms of energy including redeveloping nuclear energy to make reactors safer and more reliable

PUNCTUATION IN BULLETED LISTS

This fairly simple list exemplifies vertical writing—writing in which the rules of punctuation used in conventional horizontal prose are suspended. You needn't punctuate after each item in the list because the physical separation of items into discrete lines replaces conventional separation by commas, semicolons, or periods. You may place a period at the end of the list if you believe that brings about better closure. Again, this period really isn't required.

Do be aware that this issue of punctuation in vertical lists is highly controversial. Traditionally oriented technical editors will use their red pencils to add punctuation to vertical lists while more recently trained editors will not. In general, older writers and editors are loyal to the heavy punctuation they were taught decades ago, while younger ones will recognize that English has moved in the direction of lighter punctuation and lighter capitalization.

THE FOLLOWING, PLUS COLON

Often, as in the example, a list will be introduced by a statement written in horizontal prose. This sample uses an introductory colon to launch the list. It's useful to remember the grammar rule that colons should not separate verbs from their objects; that's the reason for using the phrase *the following* after the verb *include*. A colon immediately following the verb is grammatically incorrect, although it's used so often that it has ceased to be a matter of great concern. A neat solution to the problem is simply to use a full sentence to introduce the list. For example, in the following section of an article on Dr. Frank Press' speech at MIT the student reporter might have written: *Dr. Press listed numerous actions to benefit the environment.* Custom, however, seems to favor using *the following* combined with a colon.

One obvious irregularity in the sample list is an item introduced by a verb: item six—*replace CFC by other chemicals.* All the other items are introduced by nouns or modified nouns. To bring this incongruent item into line with the other six items, you might edit it to read: *CFC replacement.* Another obvious departure is the lengthy item at the end of the list. To achieve consistency with the first six items, shorten the final item by omitting everything after the phrase *increased research in other forms of energy.*

Even after these two improvements, the list has a jagged quality. When you are creating your own lists, you can more readily determine what form of parallelism you want to use: long or short phrases, sentences, or even short paragraphs. When creating your own lists, you'll find it easier to control in advance the sort of introductory element you wish to use for each bulleted item. One of the most popular forms for corporate education brochures is the list that begins each item with an *ing* verbal, either a participle or a gerund. The *ing* verbal gives your list a sense of vitality and ongoing activity that's attractive for marketing purposes.

Although the following example of parallel listing doesn't use the *-ing* verbal, it's nevertheless a good example of a simple bulleted list. The example describes a seminar in information systems management. The seminar description includes information on the seminar format, its participants, seminar goals, and the planned methodology. With all this information to include, the writer had to devise a method for highlighting the material of greatest interest to the potential customers. That material is presented in the eye-catching vertical format. The author has combined both prose in horizontal format and prose in a vertical list. He has sorted out one kind of information from the other by using a visual device.

Good Parallelism

INFORMATION SYSTEM MODERNIZATION:
MANAGING EXPECTATIONS

This three-day seminar is tailored to the information system modernization needs of the client organization. Clients differ in the urgency of information system change, the understanding of the difficulty and cost of modernization, and the achievements already in place. Using interviews, group sessions, and joint problem-solving, participants will:

- learn to prioritize applications tied to business needs
- develop appreciation for management and user information need
- assess realistic costs and effort needed to satisfy information needs
- develop a plan for achieving useful systems

- produce foundation documents for post-seminar use
- establish future roles for themselves

Typical seminar groupings include top management, IS staff, and user department representatives, but other groupings are possible. An advance visit to the client site is required to assess the current expectations of management and the IS response to date.

Note that the writer has used both horizontal and vertical parallelism in this seminar description. In the second sentence of the introduction, which is written in normal horizontal prose, balance is maintained among the three items about which clients differ:

- the urgency of information system change
- the understanding of the difficulty and cost of modernization
- the achievements already in place

The writer realizes that too many blocks of bulleted listing within a brief segment of writing can diminish the impact of the list he intends to emphasize. Consequently, he saves his major emphasis for the results that seminar participants can expect to achieve. This caveat does not apply for briefing slides where almost all information is conveyed by way of bulleted lists.

As a rapid reference, here are a few shortcuts to using bullets and parallelism correctly. (Note that the list is introduced without resorting to *the following* plus a colon.)

TIP 1: Choose round bullets over square bullets in lists.
TIP 2: Use filled bullets rather than open bullets.
TIP 3: Use the combination keys that produce real bullets.
TIP 4: Sequence your bullets if you have sets in descending orders of importance; for example, first use a series of large bullets, then a series of long dashes, then a series of small bullets.
TIP 5: Omit conventional punctuation at the end of items.
TIP 6: Follow company standards for initial capital letters (caps/no caps) to begin list items.
TIP 7: Use parallel structure throughout bulleted lists.

It usually isn't necessary to make every list within a document follow the same pattern of parallelism. For example, you may introduce one set of items with nouns, another set of items with verbs, and another set with infinitives. Some lists may include items expressed in short phrases while other lists may be composed of full sentences. The rule is to maintain a consistent pattern within each list.

Acronyms and Initialisms

Engineers often say that working in high technology is like swimming in alphabet soup. Alphabet soup refers to the prevalence of acronyms in the high-tech workplace. The use of acronyms is one of the most characteristic features of technical communications, spoken or written. While numbers and symbols are the scientist's tools, acronyms and special terminology are the technical writer's stock-in-trade. When diagrams, tables, and charts are added to the equation, it's easy to see that technical writing incorporates a high degree of graphic material in addition to nontraditional treatment of prose elements. These items—equations, acronyms, bulleted lists, diagrams, charts—make it possible to identify a piece of technical or scientific writing without reading any of the text. Visually, written products from high-tech companies look different from documents published by nontechnical companies. Even memos written in a high-tech company have a distinctive look because they often include subheadings, acronyms, and bulleted lists.

DEFINITIONS

One edition of Webster's defines *acronym* as "a word formed from the first (or first few) letters of several words" while another edition defines it as "a word (as *radar* or *snafu*) formed from the initial letter or letters of each of the successive parts or major parts of a compound term." These dictionary definitions are far from adequate in describing all the kinds of acroynms used in technical communications. For example, alphanumeric combinations (C^3I for command, control, communications, and intelligence) are acronym-type forms that would not be covered by the preceding definitions. The heavy use of acronyms has outstripped their original definitions. As in the case of coined words, which will be discussed later in this chapter, the inventiveness and exuberance of engineers and scientists have resulted in forms that almost defy the efforts of those who codify language.

When the efforts of lexicographers fall behind the needs of technical communicators, it's necessary to turn to internal specialists for defining terms and for creating lists and glossaries of acroynms. Many scientific and technical companies throughout the United States, have developed their own directories of acronyms; one that comes to mind is AVCO, whose massive book contains almost 500 pages of AVCO work-related acronyms. Another valuable glossary of project-related acronyms and related forms was compiled by a technical communications specialist more than a decade ago as a working paper for public distribution. It includes definitions to clarify various types of abbreviations. These definitions go well beyond Webster because they take into account almost all the permutations of a classic acronym, beginning with the generic abbreviation.

Some Useful Definitions[1]

An *abbreviation* refers to a letter or short combination of letters having an alphabetical similarity to the parent word (MIL = military as in MIL standard).

An *acronym* is a pronounceable word formed by combining initial letters (AWACS = Airborne Warning and Control System).

An *initialism* is formed by combining initial letters, but is generally unpronounceable (DCTCC = Data Communications Technical Coordinating Committee).

A *contraction* is formed by omitting letters and bringing the elements together (COMAFFOR = Commander Air Force Forces).

A *code word* is a recognizable and pronounceable word or words usually assigned to represent or title a classified program (River Joint).

A *mnemonic* represents the coded parent word designed to be easily remembered (Mickey Swig = MCCISWG).

You'll note that alphanumeric is missing from this list, although it might be considered a variant of initialism because by its very nature it can't be pronounced as a word. For example, C^3I and more recently C^4I (command, control, communications, computers, and intelligence) can only be spoken as "C, cubed, I" or as "C, three, I." The B–2 Stealth Bomber has the privilege of having both an alphanumeric and a code word. Other commonplace alphanumerics are the countless security codes and computer passwords that combine letters (alpha) and numbers (numeric) along with punctuation and even symbols. An example of a seven-digit alphanumeric password that includes punctuation (period) and a symbol (pound sign) is j.4#b5c.

There are also curious creatures that can be classified as either acronyms or initialisms depending upon their conventional usage. Those who teach and study at MIT always refer to their school as *em-eye-tee* (M-I-T) and never as *mit*, although the letters of the school's abbreviation are certainly pronounceable as a single word. (Although the pronunciation of MIT is settled, no agreement has been reached as to how to write the abbreviation: MIT or M.I.T.)

Collections of acronyms usually don't provide definitions in the usual sense of a dictionary explanation. If you look up NATO in an acronym list, you will find what amounts to a translation of the acronym: North Atlantic Treaty Organization. The entry won't tell you what the North Atlantic Treaty Organi-

---

[1] A. E. Ward, *Acronyms, Abbreviations, and Code Words.* The MITRE Corporation, WP 22424, rev. 3, July 1983.

zation is, when and where it was founded, or how it's funded. What you have is a gloss of the word, and *gloss* here is Webster's third level of meaning: "a brief explanation of a difficult or obscure word or expression."

Thus, we have glossaries of acronyms rather than dictionaries of acronyms. At the same time that the literary meaning of the verb *to gloss* is fading out of use by the general populace, its existence is being secured in the realm of technical documentation.

GUIDELINES FOR USE

More vexing than the question of what are acronyms is the issue of how to use them. In their wisdom, compilers of acronym glossaries don't try to explain how to use acronyms. Merely collecting, classifying, and glossing them is problematic enough. The acronym lexicographers leave usage decisions to those who create standards for technical documentation: the style and format partners. There are three frequently asked questions regarding the use of acronyms.

How do I use the acronym with its glossed term?
When do I reintroduce a term and its acronym?
Are there occasions when I can omit using the term?

In addition, there are problems with format compatibility between the acronym and its term, as well as a question about the internationality of acronyms.

HOW DO I USE THE ACRONYM WITH ITS GLOSSED TERM? Your company style guide will doubtlessly address this question, so check there first. If, however, your company hasn't issued a style guide, you need to make your own decision.

If you are writing an article for a journal, check the style sheet of the journal for which you're writing. (Journal style sheets may or may not talk about acronyms.) Each journal has its own guidelines regarding acronyms, paragraphing, and many other publication details. If the journal doesn't provide advice on acronyms, again you must make your own decision.

Most important, for everyday use, you need to decide on a consistent way of handling acronyms. It may help you to know that the most widely used treatment is to follow the relevant term immediately with the acronym inside a pair of parentheses, like this:

automatic voice network (AUTOVON).

Make sure that you really need to use an acronym in your document. If, after your first reference to automatic voice network, you never again refer to it in your document, you don't need to introduce an acronym. Acronyms exist as shortened versions of a frequently repeated term. This shortened version saves space in documents and briefing charts. If the term is used only once in a document, the rationale for the acronym disappears. Unfortunately, the use of needless acronyms is the most frequent acronym error made in technical documentation.

WHEN DO I REINTRODUCE A TERM WITH ITS ACRONYM? This problem requires you to use your own good judgment. If your document is very long, with many chapters, you help your reader by reintroducing the full term with its acronym the first time you use it in each chapter. If you are submitting a technical report that has an abstract and an executive summary, you need to use the full combination in each major section. Because abstracts and executive summaries are often read as stand-alone documents, they must be independently complete. Finally, you should seriously consider creating a glossary of acronyms as an appendix to your document if you have more than a half dozen acronyms in your report. When a glossary exists at the back of your document, your reader can always use it to look up the translation for an acronym if he or she can't find its first use in a chapter.

ARE THERE OCCASIONS WHEN I CAN OMIT USING THE TERM? If your acronym is internationally known—NATO is an example—it's safe to introduce it without its associated term. Here again, a judgment call is needed. What you think is internationally known may not be what someone else thinks is. A similar question is what information is in the public domain. Some information is obviously general knowledge: Everyone knows that the sun rises every morning. More sophisticated information about the planets, stars, and constellations, even though not known by everyone, can be readily found in any encyclopedia; hence, it's in the public domain. But it's unclear at what point a journalist is expected to quote an authority on some more scientific aspect of astronomy or astrophysics. If the journalist can't decide, he or she will credit a source of information. Similarly, if you think it's questionable that an acronym may not be universally recognized (isn't in the common domain), then take the time to provide its term.

An associated problem is that of multiple terms for the same acronym. Surprisingly, many acronyms have multiple translations. You need only refer to an existing acronym glossary to see this illustrated. ATM may mean *automatic teller machine* to you but it may mean *airtask message* or *antitank missile* to your military colleague. Project-related acronym glossaries sometimes list three, four, or five glosses for one acronym. If one acronym can have that many translations within the workplace, think about what happens when you go beyond the workplace. That's another reason to think about the global picture. In this respect, you, as an ESL professional, have much greater sensitivity to the international use of acronyms than your English-only colleagues.

NASA may be a safe acronym to use without a gloss because like NATO, it has the rare privilege of no competition. An internationally recognized organization like the United Nations, whose acronym seems to have worldwide acceptance as UN, is another example of a "safe" acronym, especially if it's used in the context of international relations.

COMPATIBILITY. When you looked at the example of a term-acronym combination, probably the first thing you noticed was the difference in capitalization between the term and the acronym—automatic voice network (AUTOVON). Your acronym glossary won't help you here because the author usually decides on a capitalization (or no capitalization) system for his or her listings that ignores the case conventions of individual terms. For example, if he or she has decided to list all acronyms, initialisms, and abbreviations in caps and all terms in lowercase, you won't be able to tell which terms ordinarily use which form. As an example from the naming of computer languages, LISP is an acronym for *List Processing* that uses all caps, whereas Pascal uses initial caps, and AppleScript is mixed. Such format differences probably wouldn't show up in a glossary.

The rule, and it's one that some writers and editors don't like to accept, is that there doesn't have to be a correlation between the representation of a term and its acronym. If AUTOVON is the accepted form for the acronym, the term doesn't have to match with all caps. If your acronym is NASA, you know it's derived from a proper name (National Aeronautics and Space Administration) and you would initial cap each word of the term. On the other hand, some terms are not titles of organizations or government agencies. As common nouns they can remain in lowercase while you use an uppercase acronym.

INTERNATIONALITY. ESL writers will be alert to this issue. In the United States we confidently assume that our acronyms are everyone's acronyms. Recognizing that we probably lead the world in the number and complexity of acronyms, we forget that other countries sometimes do have their own acronyms. We write with confidence about the OECD (Organization for Economic Cooperation and Development) without realizing that this acronym is meaningless in France where OCDE (Organisation de Coopération et de Développement Économiques) is located. If you expect your document to have an international readership, you need to be even more careful than usual about glossing your terms and about deciding which acronyms can go unglossed. Some quick tips for acronym use follow.

TIP 1: First check your company style guide for advice on how to use acronyms.

TIP 2: Review a journal's style sheet before writing an article for submission.

TIP 3: Don't introduce an acronym if it won't be used again in the text.

TIP 4: Gloss your term with its acronym the first time you use it in the text.

TIP 5: Repeat the term-acronym combination at the beginning of each chapter.

TIP 6: Introduce an acronym without its term only if it's internationally recognized, or if it's universally understood by a specialized audience to which your document is restricted.

TIP 7: Don't expect perfect correlation between the format of the term and its acronym.

TIP 8: Be sensitive to other language variants of an English acronym.

Coined Words and Transferred Terms

Coined words and transferred terms are special style practices for communicating technical information that may confuse an employee who has recently acquired English as a second language. When acquiring a foreign language, the student has many complex tasks to accomplish. Although the acquisition of vocabulary is not one of the more difficult tasks, it's extremely upsetting to discover that sometimes words are used differently in actual speech from the way they are presented in the classroom. Classroom examples are always artificial, although new technologies are improving that situation.

The situation is compounded when an ESL employee is additionally confronted with specialized jargon in the laboratory or at the office. Professional vocabularies are usually acquired rapidly and with ease. Jargon, however, is different. Like slang, it may carry hidden allusions or subtle references known only to a special interest group. You'll find it harder to "crack the code" for slang and jargon than to simply adopt the specialized terminology of a craft or profession.

Engineers and computer scientists are noted for manipulating existing language to their own purposes. Nouns that do not have verb forms are turned into verbs by engineers. (*Priority* becomes *prioritize* and is used with such frequency that it spreads to other professions.) Secretaries find themselves puzzled about how to form past tenses for verbs that don't exist. Technical editors have to make arbitrary decisions about whether to fuse compound words that have just sprung into existence. Writing specialists are asked how to spell words that no one can find in an unabridged dictionary.

Software engineers and computer scientists entered the profession during a period of technological exuberance. After launching the software revolution, they looked around for ways to describe it. While writing software and rendering existing software obsolete as quickly as possible, software engineers also pushed beyond the restrictions of language. The rapidly evolving technology and its associated uses called for rapid decisions regarding nomenclature. If a name didn't exist, the developer invented one. If a word didn't exist to describe a function, the developer adapted an existing one or simply took a word from a different discipline and gave it a new application. Traditional labels exist for these practices. In the case of invented words or phrases, we refer to *coined words* (newly minted), and for the appropriation of words or phrases from different disciplines, we refer to *transferred terms*.

TRANSFERRED TERMS

The next few pages list some of the most commonly used transferred terms. The list is by no means comprehensive. Nevertheless, you will find it helpful for several reasons:

- First, it will make clear the concept of transferred terms.
- Second, it will explain the relationship between some of the original meanings and the new meanings.
- Third, it will define new meanings, some of which are not available in conventional dictionaries.

ABORT

Think about the different uses for the word *abort*. Even though aborting pregnancy is legal in the United States, the subject of abortion remains highly charged. If a computer-literate employee speaks of aborting programs, tasks, and processes, a worker who is not computer-literate might visualize aborting a human fetus. The first worker sees nothing but the abnormal termination of an event. If such a cultural difference exists among the speakers of the same first language, how difficult might it be for someone who has recently entered the culture and language of the United States to accommodate for these twists in vocabulary?

ADDRESS

Another transferred word is *address* used as a noun. Close to the original dictionary meaning is the computer-related definition of *address* as the location in computer storage of a piece of data, or perhaps an instruction in a stored program. Like *application*, it too has been invested with numerous modifiers to extend its usefulness: virtual address, indirect address, instruction address, and others.

APPLICATION

An example of an old word being transferred into computer terminology is *application*. Again, a lover of words can trace connections between the newly devised interpretation and the original word. Like *architecture, application(s)* in its new incarnation has been given both general and specific meanings. Generally, it means the productive use to which a computer system is put. There are payroll applications, inventory control applications, market forecasting applications, and so forth. More specifically, the term will refer to the software program written for a desired use. For the ESL professional, it's important to understand that applications are in contrast to other types of software such as operating systems or database management systems. All this is a heavy load for a newly incarnated word to carry.

ARCHITECTURE

Perhaps the most graphic example of a transferred term in computer vocabulary is *architecture*. While its new uses have affinity with its original meaning, they have infused the word with multiple possibilities. In fact, its new uses can verge into vagueness because the word is often used so loosely. In its most general sense it describes a structure, a scheme of interconnections, and the way things fit together. In addition to these generalized uses, the borrowed word has been endowed with greater specificity in terms like *computer architecture, software architecture,* and *network architecture.*

CHIP

Chip is one of the more famous transferred words. People used to think of diamond chips and potato chips; now the great issue is chip manufacture and marketing. Of course, these latter-day chips are made of neither potatoes nor diamonds, but of tiny pieces of semiconductor material. Used in manufacturing electronic components, these chips can contain the equivalent of hundreds of thousands of logic elements.

COMMENT

This is the portion of a computer program that the programmer inserts for documentary purposes. *Comments* haven't any effect on the machine program that performs the logic. They explain to readers of the program what the programmer intended the program to accomplish. Good programmers can be identified by well-commented programs.

COMPILE

This latest meaning of the verb *to compile* refers to translating a computer program expressed in a problem-oriented language like COBOL or FORTRAN into a computer-oriented language of machine instructions.

CONFIGURATION

Configuration has moved fairly gracefully from general usage into computer terminology. While it may refer to hardware or to software, *configuration* usually refers to the arrangement of a computer system or network. The arrangement elements vary greatly according to the nature, number, and chief characteristics of its functional units.

DEFAULT

Default is a word that had fairly infrequent use before it was embraced by the computer crowd. Its relationship to traditional usage is obvious, but it has grown into a multipurpose catchword. In the lexicon of computerese, *default* refers to options that a computer system will invoke if the user or programmer doesn't express choices. Having proven its usefulness in that context, *default* has become almost as popular an expression as "the bottom line."

EDITOR

Editor hardly refers to a living human being any more. While technical writers may be acutely aware of the existence of such human beings, their colleagues in the neighboring office are referring to a computer program that allows a user to modify, rearrange, or display textual material. The editor is an essential component of a word processing system.

GLOBAL

Global contrasts with *local* in the sense that it pertains to data defined in one subdivision of a computer program as well as in at least one other subdivision of the program. *Local*, on the other hand, refers to data defined in and referenced by only one program subdivision.

HARDWARE

This word has a new meaning. In addition to hammers, pliers, wrenches, and the like, *hardware* now means the physical equipment used in data processing.

HOST

If you think *host* is someone who gives a party or invites you to a weekend at his summer house, you are correct, but computer illiterate. The transfer from earlier meaning isn't strained because a host computer may provide services such as computation or database access. More recently, host computers would be contrasted with personal computers, which service only one user at a time.

INITIALIZE

A verb form transferred from a noun, *initialize* is most frequently used in personal computers to describe the initial recording of track and sector identifiers on a diskette prior to using it for storing actual data.

INTERACTIVE

In its new technical sense, *interactive* pertains to an application in which each entry calls forth a response from a system or program. Airline reservation systems and inquiry systems are examples of interactive systems.

LOOP

Closely related to its original definition, *loop* now means a series of computer instructions that may be executed repeatedly under certain conditions. Loops may fail to terminate as the result of programming errors. This creates the new dilemma of the *endless loop*.

MATRIX

Matrix has one meaning in geology and a very different meaning in technology. The technology usage is based on matrix algebra. It refers to a rectangular array of elements, arranged in rows and columns. This meaning, in turn, has been transferred to programs that store data in two-dimensional tables such as in a spreadsheet program.

MENU

Menu is one of those fantastical transfer terms that suggest their origin but give it entirely new meaning. Basically, a *menu* is a display of possible processing options available for selection by a program's operator. Some user interfaces are menu-driven and some are command-driven.

MONITOR

Rather than the teacher who watches over students during a test, today's monitor is the display screen of a computer. It is separate from the keyboard and from the electronics (see Figure 4.1).

NETWORK

A *network* is an interconnected group of nodes. In digital computers, a network consists of computers, terminals, and interconnecting communication media that permit the interchange of digital data.

PACKET

The new meaning of *packet* refers to a sequence of binary bits (ones and zeroes) that is transferred from one computer to another as a composite whole. The term is most often used in data communication technology.

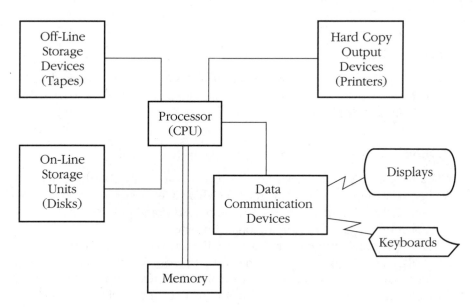

FIGURE 4.1   Schematic of a data processing or computer system.

PERIPHERAL

In any computer system, *peripherals* are the equipment that provides the processing unit with auxiliary storage or outside communications. Examples of peripheral devices are keyboards, printers, disk and tape storage units, plotters, and character readers.

PORT

Like the ports of call of ships, today's *ports* are access points or connectors for data entry or exit to a computer. The word is sometimes used as a shortened version of *telecommunication port* or *terminal port*.

PROTOCOL

Modern *protocols* are sets of rules that govern the operation of functional units of a communication system. They must be followed if communication is to be successful.

QUEUE

Similar to the queues outside elevators and at cash registers, *electronic queues* are lines or lists formed by items in a system waiting for service by some shared device. For example, lines of jobs waiting to be started, print files waiting to be printed, or user programs competing for the attention of a central processor are all modern queues.

SCROLL

Like their parchment counterparts, *electronic scrolls* can be moved up or down. Modern electronic scrolls appear on a video display tube and have only 24 to 27 lines of displayable space.

WINDOW

Window is an obvious transferred term. It's commonly used to refer to a defined segment of the display screen on which a user can view a portion of a document. Also, windows are used to help users communicate between several concurrent processes running on a computer.

These examples of transferred terms will alert you to new dimensions of vocabulary acquisition in the technical workplace. While commercial companies that deliver ESL coursework to visiting businesspeople from overseas provide specialized vocabulary lists for finance, for medical services, for transportation services, and for operations research, they are less likely to provide similar instruction in the specialized vocabulary of computer science. The reason is that those people who understand the new vocabulary are in the workplace where they are busily creating new software and even newer vocabulary to describe it.

As a result, you need to purchase a computer dictionary to help you in this area of vocabulary acquisition. A good one in print is Donald D. Spencer's *Computer Dictionary,* Fourth Edition, published by Camelot Publications and listed at $24.95. As ever, you also need to listen to your co-workers; and you may sometimes find it necessary to interrupt them and ask them to define a term. Because everyone uses the newly transferred terms with abandon, it does seem awkward to ask for a definition; however, it's only painful once or twice. You are, in fact, helping your colleagues. Faced with a need to define terms during conversation may cause them to use the new terminology with greater care.

COINED WORDS

Webster's isn't very helpful with defining *coin* in either its verb or adjective form with reference to the creation of new words. The closest the Collegiate comes is a very brief, secondary definition of the verb form: *create, invent.* There is no reference to the practice of creating or inventing words. More helpful is James Murray's magnificent *Oxford English Dictionary*: "To frame or invent a new word or phrase; usually implying deliberate purpose; and occasionally used depreciatively, as if the process were analogous to that of the counterfeiter."[2] The usage dates back to the late 1500s in England, and throughout that century and the following, the sense of deprecation persisted.

But now coining words is no longer looked upon as a form of counterfeiting even though language lovers outside science and technology look with dismay upon the seemingly irresponsible creation of new words. All judgment aside, you need to know about this new category of words. Coined words exist in other professions, but technology professionals have created their own assortment. Here are a few examples.

ADA

Ada or the *Ada language* is the name for the standard computer language for all programs written for the U.S. Department of Defense. It's named rather delightfully after Lady Augusta Ada Lovelace, the daughter of Lord Byron. Ada was a protege of Charles Babbage, the Englishman who might be thought of as the father of digital computing. Hardly anyone had heard of Lady

[2] *The Compact Edition of the Oxford English Dictionary.* Oxford University Press, 1971, p. 603.

Augusta Ada Lovelace until some enterprising computer scientist reinvented her.

ALPHANUMERIC

The word *alphanumeric* has been used several times in this book, and it serves as an example of a word that didn't exist before 1950. Obviously a fusion of *alphabetic* and *numerical*, it's the same sort of shorthand that you find in many of the acronyms that fuse two words to form a vendor term, like QuickMail.

BIT

Bit is so universally used as a standard word that few people remember that it's an acronym culled from binary digit. The sequence of binary digits (zeros and ones) are called *bits*.

BUG

Bug (and its close relation *debug*), to mean a mistake or malfunction in a computer program, is a brand new use of the insect word. It has become so popular that people now find bugs in everything: textbooks, recipes, plans. The exuberance of its use is only surpassed by the speed with which its applications are growing. Figurative and literal bugs surpass in numbers the earth's population of humans.

BYTE

Byte (easily confused with *bit*) is a perverted spelling of the standard word *bite*. A common definition is an 8-bit subdivision of a computer word, representing the storage of an alphanumeric character. You can see from this definition that these coined words feed upon one another. If you don't understand *alphanumeric*, you can't understand *byte*.

KLUDGE

Kludge is the most dramatic of all the computer technology coinages. The term was invented in 1962 to describe an ill-assorted collection of matched parts forming a poorly constructed entity. *Kludges* were most often seen in software programs that had been jammed together by inexperienced programmers. Whoever invented the term appears to have been an experienced practitioner of word creation. The joy with which this word is used causes it to be called into conversation far more frequently than necessary.

MOUSE

Mouse is a term that's quite distant from its rodential meaning. We are told that the pointing device to which mouse refers was so named because with its trailing wire, it resembles a mouse. There is considerable argument over how to form the plural of *mouse*. Some say *mouses* while others say it remains *mouse*. The experts are adamant that the plural form is not *mice*.

SPREADSHEET

Spreadsheet is a widely used term invented to name the computer-assisted worksheet that organizes data in a two-dimensional tabular format. These programs are very popular for use with personal computers, and no one remembers a time when the word simply did not exist.

THROUGHPUT

Throughput is an awkward word like many such compounds created in the highlife of the computer age. It might be defined as a measurement of the amount of work performed by a computer system over a given period of time. One suspects that it is sometimes used with less precision, much like the darling of engineering hyperbole: order of magnitude.

These examples of coined words with their associated definitions will give you a notion of the demands of your vocabulary acquisition task. Not only nonnative speakers of English have to cope with these terms; many who have spoken English from their earliest childhood have difficulty understanding them. Fortunately, there seems at present to be a slowing down of term coinage in computer technology. That is not to say that computer technicians are dead poets. More terms will be invented.

Helpful Tips

It's difficult to provide helpful tips for coping with transferred terms and coined words. Probably the best aid is a recent edition of a respectable computer dictionary. If your edition isn't recent, it will lack words that have just been invented. In addition to Donald Spencer's *Computer Dictionary*, you may find a library copy of Charles Sippl's *Computer Dictionary* from Howard W. Sams & Co. helpful.

Electronic bulletin boards and Internet newsgroups will provide you with a forum for puzzling issues. The Internet Archives is another electronic source of vocabulary information. And long-suffering secretaries who have had to struggle with these practices during the past three decades will be a good source of advice. If they can't advise you, they can at least sympathize with you. In addition to a computer dictionary, electronic communications, and long-suffering secretaries, the *IEEE Standard Dictionary of Electrical and Electronics Terms* is useful, although it isn't updated as often as some of the computer dictionaries.

Premodification

Extensive quantification and qualification have always been used by scientists to describe their subjects. Measurement can be stated with precision because numbers exist to account for sub-atomic particles. Qualification is more difficult. Multiple words exist to describe functions and qualities; qualities often need further specification. As the technical writer struggles to describe as completely, accurately, and graphically as possible, qualifier begins to modify qualifier. Out of such extreme conscientiousness grows what is known as *premodification*.

Premodification consists of long strings of modifiers in front of nouns. Heavy premodification is awkward, and it sometimes causes ambiguity. You'll recognize premodification when you meet it because you'll have to wait a long time before you encounter the subject or the object of a sentence. The writer has so conscientiously buttressed the noun with qualifiers (modifiers), that you may even have difficulty unwrapping it from its ornamentation. Here's an example of a sentence with heavy premodification.

The Sears catalogue advertised a mobile hopper fed compressed air operated grit blasting machine.

Reduced to its essentials, this sentence would read:

The Sears catalogue advertised a grit blasting machine.

Everything after the verb (advertised) and before the noun-object (machine) serves to qualify machine—to endow it with greater specificity. Because the technical writer has been taught to be as concise as possible, he or she has discovered that the most economical way to include all the additional information about the machine is to pile it up in front of the noun, hence premodification.

The best way to untangle the premodification maze is to break out some of the descriptive elements into phrases and to place them in various positions in the sentence. This, of course, means that you won't be as economical as you'd like to be. However, if there's ever a choice between economy and clarity, you are obliged to choose in favor of clarity. Here's one solution to the problem this sentence poses. There are other ways of solving it. You may be able to devise a better solution.

> The Sears catalogue advertised a grit blasting machine, which is fed from a hopper and operated by compressed air.

While the revised sentence is longer (17 words) than the original version (14 words), it's far easier to read and to understand.

Military training courses in effective writing call these collections of multiple modifiers with a noun "hut 2–3–4 phrases." This refers, of course, to the marching cadence that propels foot soldiers over long distances without having to think too much about where they're going. The U.S. Air Force Effective Writing Course advises its students, "Don't build hut 2–3–4 phrases, long trains of nouns and modifiers. Readers can't tell easily what modifies what or when such trains will end. You may have to use official hut 2–3–4 phrases like *Air Traffic Control Radar Beacon System*, but you can avoid creating unofficial ones like *increased high-cost-area allowances*. Adding one small word will make it more readable: *increased allowances for high-cost areas.*"[3] To illustrate the absurd lengths to which premodification in technical writing can be carried AF Pamphlet 13–5 offers the following sentence that includes the world's longest hut 2–3–4 phrase.

> Orderly time-phased priority-based civil engineering work planning and design budgeting supply and procurement center support was not maintained.

Here are three sentences with heavily premodified nouns. They're not as absurd as the previous example, and you can practice improving them by sorting out the qualifiers.

Heavy Premodification

Follow procedure twelve in the user's manual to maintain the system's low current measurement capability.

It is critical to remember that the circuit must have a balanced ring trip detector input device.

Finish the prototype by using a pressure sensitive low temperature glass-cloth coating varnish.

Suggested improvements follow. There may be several ways of improving each sentence. Your way may be different but equally effective.

[3] Superintendent of Documents, *U.S. Air Force Effective Writing Course* (AF Pamphlet 13–5). Washington, DC: U.S. Government Printing Office, 1980, p. 31.

Improved Modification

Follow procedure twelve in the user's manual to maintain the system's ability to measure low currents.

It is critical to remember that the circuit must have a balanced input device for the ring trip detector.

Finish the prototype by using a grasscloth coating varnish that is sensitive to pressure and cures at low temperature.

or

Finish the prototype by using a pressure-sensitive, low-temperature varnish for coating glasscloth.

The alternative solution to the third sentence employs two strategies for improving heavy premodification: redistribution of elements and the use of hyphens to identify unit modifiers. Often, technical writing depends too heavily on the hyphenation of unit modifiers to improve premodification. If used alone, hyphenation will not be an adequate solution.

UNIT MODIFIERS

Unit modifiers are used in both general and technical prose, but they tend to surface more frequently in technical writing. They are an important tool in sorting out premodifiers, but they must be used correctly or else they add to the confusion. In brief, unit modifiers, sometimes called hyphenated adjectives, consist of a series of words acting as a unit. These units are hyphenated when they come before the noun. The following sentence contains three unit modifiers suitably hyphenated.

In the begin-block declarations, several word-block declarations may refer to single-block identifiers.

If you had used unit modifiers to help clarify the earlier Sears sentence, it would have looked like this:

The Sears catalogue advertised a mobile hopper-fed compressed-air-operated grit-blasting machine.

While the hyphens help greatly in clarifying meaning, they often need to be augmented by moving some elements into different positions. In the following short sentences, practice by inserting hyphens to show clearly which words are intended to serve as unit modifiers.

This module drives a single decade tube.

Purchase a hot wire cutter.

The following diagram identifies the terminal classes with two character terminal class identifiers.

Select stable transformants in a methotrexate containing culture medium.

Generally, unit modifiers are not used after the noun in technical writing. Scott Rice[4] provides a colorful example from creative writing of before and after unit modifiers. The rule is simply to hyphenate when using such adjectives before a noun but not after a noun.

Bright-feathered birds screech, snakeskins glitter, as the jungle peels away.   Bharati Mukherjee, *The Middleman*

Rice demonstrates using hyphens following the noun: *The screeching birds were bright feathered.*

Long strings of modifiers in front of nouns are peculiar to technical writing, and you aren't likely to find them in general prose. Perhaps this practice is a vestige of the German language that so strongly influenced early scientific writing in English. Premodification is one of the special style features of technical writing. It can influence your general writing in a negative fashion if you find yourself transferring it from technical reports to, say, social correspondence. The best policy is to avoid it in general prose, and reduce it as much as possible in technical prose.

Compound Nouns

Technical documentation in the United States is also characterized by a high incidence of compound nouns. Compounding is not limited to technical prose in English; it also occurs in European scientific writing. However, your task is to learn the conventions of compounding in American English.

The *U. S. Government Printing Office Style Manual* (GPO Style Manual) defines a compound word as "a union of two or more words, either with or without a hyphen. It conveys a unit idea that is not clearly or quickly conveyed by the component words in unconnected succession."[5] To avoid confusion,

[4] Scott Rice. *Right Words Right Places*. Belmont, California: Wadsworth Publishing Co., 1993, p. 128.

[5] Superintendent of Documents. *U.S. Government Printing Office Style Manual*. Washington, DC: U.S. Government Printing Office, 1984, p. 73.

although this definition refers to a *unit idea*, it is not referring specifically to a unit modifier. Compound words most frequently used in technical writing are nouns serving as subjects or objects in sentences.

Compound nouns and their forms are the most dramatic prose expressions of technology's dynamic nature. Their formats are fluid, and it isn't possible to memorize whether a compound is one word, two words, or a hyphenated word. The compound may be two words in 1990 and one word in 1991. That's the best argument for having a latest-edition dictionary.

COMPOUND PATTERNS

In the normal world of language change, compounds follow an evolution:

- When the idea they express is still unfamiliar, they exist as separate words.
- When the idea becomes more familiar, they become linked by a hyphen.
- When the idea is totally familiar, they are fused into one word.

rain forest
rain-forest
rainforest

This evolution usually takes a number of years; however, technology and its vocabulary are both in a hurry. Sometimes they don't take the time to go through the three evolutionary stages. They may enter at the hyphenated stage or they may skip a stage, as with this compound:

data base
database

In the third edition of the *IEEE Standard Dictionary of Electrical and Electronics Terms*, *data base* was two words without a hyphen. In the fourth edition of the same dictionary, *database* was fused. And a new compound may enter the language with such a flurry of use that it will enter immediately as a fused compound.

RESOURCES AND REFERENCES

The lesson learned is that despite any collection of rules for compounding, technical writing often makes its own rules. You need the latest edition of the *IEEE*, a recent computer dictionary, dictionaries for special sciences (chemistry, physics, biology), and an up-to-date general dictionary to cope with compound nouns used in technical and scientific writing. Here's a case when asking your co-worker for a correct form is very dangerous.

In addition to these resources, the *GPO Style Manual* used to be the very best source for determining if a compound noun was separate, hyphenated, or one word. It contains an entire chapter (35 pages) listing compounds and their forms. For that reason, it was an invaluable reference. However, the latest edition of the *GPO* was published in 1984. The edition before that was published in the 1970s. It just isn't updated frequently enough to be definitive for fast-moving technologies like computer science.

Here's another instance where companies producing style manuals need to establish their own authority. They must standardize the use of compounds. Documents from overseas branches of a corporation should look like documents from mainland branches or from corporate headquarters. If company standards seem arbitrary, that's the nature of standards. When standards change every few years, no one has any confidence in them.

Here are some compounds that you might submit for your company style manual. You can think of many others depending upon the fields in which your company works.

Separate	*Hyphenated*	*Solid*	
air base	anti-satellite	antijam	nonoperational
crew member	cost-effective	antimissile	nontechnical
database	hands-on	bandwidth	nonvolatile
data processing	letter-quality	baselined	overstaffed
decision maker	long-range	buzzword	pretest
gray scale	off-line	checkpoint	redline (verb)
narrow band	on-line	counterproductive	sidelobe
order wire	quasi-(anything)	download	spreadsheet
policy maker	self-test	mainframe	subset
spread spectrum	short-range	microcomputer	subsystem
test bed	stand-alone	microprocessor	timeframe
wide band	start-up	milestone	workplace
		multichannel	workstation

These choices are not random. They're based on a tallysheet of compounds used frequently in a research and development center. The compound form for each was decided with reference to authoritative guidebooks, but they may not conform to the *GPO* listing. This company's resident authority decided that in observance of language movement toward simplification, hyphens would not be used following the suffixes *micro* and *non*. No such blanket decision could be made with respect to the suffix *anti*, although the *GPO* was deferred to for all *quasi* suffixes as hyphenated forms.

Latin

Despite all the exhortations of the Modern Language Association (the arbiters of language use in America), scientists and engineers still insist on sprinkling their texts with Latin. This scientific practice dates from Victorian times when educated people differentiated themselves from the uneducated masses by displaying their knowledge of classical languages. The practice has been passed down in the classroom, and scientists who attended secondary school decades ago still believe that Latin is superior to English.

Overall, simplification is today's preference: lighter punctuation, lighter capitalization, and English instead of Latin. Here's a selection of Latin terms that have been used widely until recently. Some of them have been used in their abbreviated forms, which adds to the confusion. Whenever they occur in your writing, replace them with the English equivalent. Too few people today know the difference between i.e. (id est) and e.g. (exempli gratia), so if you use these and similar terms you may be introducing obscurity or confusion into your text.

Latin	Abbreviation	English Translation
ad hoc		for this particular purpose
confer	c.f.	compare
et cetera	etc.	and so forth
et alii (masc.) or et aliae (fem.) or et alia (neut.)	et al.	and others
exempli gratia	e.g.	for example
id est	i.e.	that is
loco citato	loc. cit.	in the place cited
opere citato	op. cit.	in the work cited
via		by way of
vice versa		conversely
videlicet	viz.	namely

You probably won't be able to overcome the widespread use of *ad hoc*, as in *ad hoc committee*, although there are lots of people out in the workplace who really don't know what an ad hoc committee is. Neither are you likely to prevail against *etc.* which seems to be used whenever the writer doesn't know what else to say. For starters:

- Eliminate the pretentious *viz.* and *c.f.*
- Replace *e.g.* and *i.e.* with their English equivalents.

- Replace the lazy *etc.* with the missing information.
- Substitute *through* or *by way of* whenever you see *via*.

The bibliographical references *ibid., loc. cit.,* and *op. cit.* are simply no longer in use.

Summary Tips

Premodification, unit modification, compounding, and use of Latin terminology are practices endemic to technical writing. You can control them by observing these tips.

TIP 1: Break up strings of modifiers.
TIP 2: Place some modification before a noun and some after.
TIP 3: Sacrifice economy to clarity.
TIP 4: Redistribute modifiers and hyphenate unit modifiers to improve premodification.
TIP 5: Hyphenate potential unit modifiers with great care.
TIP 6: Avoid premodification in general prose and limit it in technical writing.
TIP 7: Use dictionaries and glossaries to find correct formats for compounded words.
TIP 8: Learn the general rules for compounding (see the *GPO Style Manual*).
TIP 9: Recognize that company style manuals may cite arbitrary rules forcompounding.
TIP 10: Order new editions of dictionaries as they are published.
TIP 11: Steer away from collegial advice for compounding decisions.
TIP 12: Substitute English for Latin whenever possible.

5

ESL

TROUBLESPOTS

Style and Grammar

The definitive difference between style and grammar is choice. In style, a range of choices is available. The manner in which a veterinarian, a chemist, an engineer, a computer scientist, a botanist, a mathematician, and an astrophysicist express themselves will certainly vary as a result of the writer's scientific discipline, cultural background, and individual personality. Some kinds of style are more appropriate than others for technical presentations. Some kinds of style are unsuited for business writing. Other styles seem to fit the needs of social correspondence. In any event, you have a choice of styles for expressing your message. Even with the high degree of standardization in technical writing, under the same circumstances two or three engineers will express themselves differently about the same topic.

With grammar, on the other hand, the range of choice narrows so much that you can't really talk about choice. Grammar is rule-based, and a discussion of choice in rules is limited to how the rules are formulated: through prescription or through description. Older grammarians functioned as prescribers of rules. They believed that they created the rules of use for a language, and that all the practitioners of that language had to follow the grammarians' rules. In such an authoritarian environment, students were expected to memorize and obey the rules of grammar without quibble.

Today, prescriptive grammar is being replaced by the philosophy and practice of descriptive grammar. The new grammarians believe that language has patterns that have grown over decades or even centuries of use. These patterns are the bases for any rules that become established. This rather organic view of grammar reverses the direction of prescriptive grammar. Rather than believing themselves the creators of rules, the descriptive grammarians believe themselves to be the recorders of rules. In other words, rules evolve as certain language practices develop distinctive patterns. By observing and recording these patterns, the new grammarians describe the language, thereupon formulating rules of acceptable use This nonauthoritarian approach to grammar is valuable for looking at certain grammar items that are particularly troublesome to nonnative speakers of a language. One such item is that of the article system in English.

The Article Issue

From a book of prescriptive grammar, you learn that there are three articles in English: *a, an,* and *the*. You learn that *a* and *an* modify in an indefinite sense, and you simply determine whether the noun they modify begins in a vowel or in a consonant. *The*, you learn, modifies in a definite sense without reference to the beginning letter of the noun it modifies. As an ESL writer, however, you've discovered that there isn't any rule that tells you when to use an article and when not. And you've also discovered that this is a very important piece of information to have because there are many instances when articles are not used in English. For someone coming to English from a language that doesn't include articles, that is, someone with absolutely no experience in dealing with articles, it's impossible to know when to use articles in front of nouns or when not to use them.

LANGUAGES WITHOUT ARTICLES

Many of the world's languages don't include articles. Oriental languages, most Slavic languages, and many African languages are among these. Reviewers familiar only with English cannot be aware of the difficulty articles present to someone grounded in a nonarticle language. For example, a mathematician from India may know the grammar of English better than his or her American co-workers. But behind his or her British English (which is behind the American English) is the writer's mother language, which perhaps is Hindi, a language with a different article system. Someone reading the mathematician's draft document will sense some vaguely unusual aspect of the writing. Only a close analysis reveals that articles are missing from where they obviously belong, or are inserted where they're not really needed, or convey an air of awkwardness in some (but not all) spots.

Here's an example of a paragraph written by a freshman college student from Japan. Yuji has been in the United States for six years and has gone through high school on the East Coast. He's certainly an advanced student of English, and his article errors are not so conspicuous as they would be during an earlier stage of acquiring English. Nevertheless, they persist.

The Manhattan Project

In the early 1940s, scientists started building atomic bombs, using two radioactive isotopes, Uranium–235 and Plutonium–239. They applied the principle of chain reaction of radioactive isotopes to make a powerful weapon, which was suggested by Albert Einstein. They used a method called implosion to exceed the critical mass of plutonium for one type of bomb, and used "gun barrel" method to exceed the critical mass of uranium for another type of bomb. Both types of bomb yielded tremendous amount of energy, including radiation energy, which resulted in an unexpected long-term harm on people in Hiroshima and Nagasaki.

Because these are subtle errors, you may have difficulty finding them. In the third sentence, an article is missing before *method*, which is modified by "gun barrel," and the article *a* is missing before *tremendous amount of energy* in the fourth sentence. In addition, the article *an* is used before *unexpected long-term harm* where an article is not required.

If a writer recognizes an article problem—and many do—he or she will ask for help: "What is the rule of grammar that governs the use of articles in English?" Anxious to help, an officemate or secretary checks in a reliable book, possibly Sabin's *The Gregg Reference Manual,* and finds the rule that the definite article is *the* and the indefinite article is *a* or *an*.[1] That, of course, is correct, but it is the only grammar help that either writer or officemate will find other than the instruction to use *a* before consonant sounds and *an* before vowel sounds, except . . . . However, this prescriptive rule doesn't take into account when not to use an article because the grammar books were written when everyone in their audience spoke English as a first language. And an English-only audience learns by imitation from childhood when not to use an article. The traditional grammar book does nothing to foster understanding of the more basic issue: when or even why do native writers of English use or not use an article.

As a result of these two factors—the influence of languages without articles and the failure of traditional grammars to probe the article system—a serious writing problem is emerging in the United States. R. Covitt in a graduate thesis at UCLA found that ESL teachers working in the Los Angeles area reported article usage as their number one teaching problem.[2] So neither editor nor technical writer need feel uncomfortable about difficulty in explaining the awkwardness of a sentence like, "The science promises to give us many answers and informations."

In fact, there are not three limiting articles, there are four: *a, an, the,* and *ø* (or no article). The recognition that there is a pattern for deleted articles is an extremely important insight. Further, the article system goes well beyond the definite/indefinite, consonant/vowel system. It's fortunate that descriptive grammar emerged just in time to provide help to ESL writers and speakers. This more sophisticated and less doctrinaire approach to grammar has led to a new kind of analysis of articles in English, one based on patterns of use that are quite different from the categories of definite and indefinite modification.

[1] William A. Sabin. *The Gregg Reference Manual,* Seventh Edition. McGraw-Hill Book Company, 1994.

[2] R. Covitt, "Some Problematic Grammar Areas for ESL Teachers," M.A. thesis in TESL, UCLA, 1976.

COUNT AND MASS NOUNS

Basically, the article system in English is more genuinely responsive to the concepts of mass and count. Mass (or noncount) nouns usually refer to whole groups of items that may have many individual parts or pieces within them. (This is not unlike the concept of collective nouns.) Mass nouns rarely have a plural form, and they are not preceded by *a, an,* or *one.* Some commonplace mass nouns that answer this description are *postage, mail, physics, homework, jewelry, clothing.* You wouldn't write about *a physics, *a mail, or *a homework.

In Yuji's paragraph, *harm,* an abstract quality like *evil* or *good,* is a mass (noncount) noun that doesn't take an article.

> Both types of bomb yielded [a] tremendous amount of energy . . . which resulted in *an* unexpected long-term harm . . . .

Count nouns are simply what the name says: items that can be easily counted. These nouns have both singular and plural forms, and they are modified by *a, an,* and *one* in the singular. There are many more of these nouns than there are noncount nouns. Examples are abundant: *apple/apples, missile/missiles, computer/computers, test/tests, figure/figures, office/offices.* Pause here to list other count nouns.

In Yuji's paragraph, *method* is a noun that can have a plural form (*methods*) and is thus a count noun; consequently, it requires an article. His use of *amount of energy* requires an article for an entirely different reason. Measure words can make mass nouns countable; in this case *energy,* which ordinarily would be a mass noun without an article, becomes quantifiable with the addition of a phrase of measurement: *[an] amount of.* This is a slightly unusual measurement phrase, but it is legitimate. More commonplace measure words are container-based (a can, a bottle, a carton), or portion-based (a unit, a piece, a bit, a pair).

An and its shorter form *a* are descendants of the number word *one.* (It's easy to see the historic relationship between *an* and *one.*) Once you start thinking of one and two and three, you are starting to think of counting. If you accept the idea that all common nouns are either nouns of mass or nouns of count, you'll be able to decode the article system. A count noun will usually take an article and a mass noun usually not.

SOME SIMPLE GUIDELINES

A descriptive grammar looks at groups of words and finds patterns. You can call these patterns generalizations if you like. Here are some patterns of mass derived from such generalizations. Because nouns of mass are noncount, you will know not to use counting articles with them.

- Natural phenomena are often mass.
    Example: I'm afraid of *storms* at sea.
    Example: Will there be *thunder* and *lightning*?
    Example: How much *rain* has fallen this month?

- Many foods in growth are mass.
    Example: Our plane flew over fields of *corn* and acres of *wheat*.
    Example: *Barley* will replace *oats* in next year's crops.
    Example: Please cut *hay* for the horses.

- Most abstract qualities are mass.
    Example: The President must have *courage* when dealing with the enemy.
    Example: Our candidates have not permitted *truth* to stand in their way.
    Example: *Wealth* doesn't equate *happiness*.

- Periods of life are mass.
    Example: *Youth* is always a time of learning.
    Example: *Maturity* is the mark of a successful businessman.
    Example: I'm unable to do in *old age* what I used to do in *middle age*.

- Fields of study are always mass.
    Example: My student's program of study includes *music* and *literature*.
    Example: *History* will prove him right.
    Example: *Geometry* is a core requirement at our university.

- Names of languages are always mass.
    Example: You must write the documentation in *English*.
    Example: Can you speak *Chinese,* either Mandarin or Cantonese?
    Example: *Arabic* is the language of at least 20 nations.

- Some unclear ideas are mass.
    Example: Seek *advice* whenever you need it.
    Example: *Homework* will be required every day of the course
    Example: Our husbands need to find *work* to help pay the bills.

- Liquids are mass.
    Example: We drank *water, milk*, and *juice* during the bicycle race.
    Example: After the race we celebrated with *beer* and *wine*.
    Example: Do you drink *cream* in your *coffee*?

- Gases are mass.
    Example: Everyone needs fresh *air*.
    Example: *Oxygen* will be provided as needed during the flight.
    Example: Mexico City now suffers from *smog*.

A WORD OF WARNING

The idea of mass (noncount) nouns versus count nouns is widespread throughout many languages. This fact can create an additional problem for you as an ESL writer, because what's considered count and what's considered mass varies from language to language. You can't simply transfer your idea of count (or mass) in your first language over to English. For example, while *information* and *furniture* are mass nouns in English, they're countable in French and Spanish. There are similar differences between English and Japanese nouns, and even between British English and American English.

TWO-WAY NOUNS

Granting that some nouns in English are basically countable while others are basically mass (or uncountable), it's also important to realize that what may be count in one instance (taking a limiting article) may be mass in another (taking no article at all). For example, "Hugo Landiver has brown *hair*" is different from "Hugo has *a hair* on his jacket." In this case, the meaning of *hair* changes from a mass of hairs to one strand of hair, a countable object. Huckin and Olsen call nouns that can be used in more than one way "two-way nouns."[3]

Another opportunity for confusion results from marking a countable noun with the wrong article. For example, a sentence from a technical on-site inspection (TOSI) report reads:

The technical on-site inspection team observed that the Siberian factory stored *the* inaccurately marked missiles.

The is used here as a pointer suggesting that a specific type of missile (inaccurately marked) was identified earlier in the report. This means that the Siberian factory stored certain missiles that were inaccurately marked. Actually, the writer intended to generalize the situation, meaning that all the missiles stored in the factory were marked inaccurately. In that case the writer should have omitted the article modifying *missiles. Missile* is clearly a count noun, but the writer intended to shift the sense from count to mass. As is often the case when dealing with rules of grammar, mistakes are made when rules are applied to words without respect for context. The context of a word's use in a technical document is more important than the rule of grammar.

Regardless how authoritative the grammar rule may be, how experienced your technical editor may be, and how authoritarian your peer reviewer may be, you as author are the person who alone knows exactly what you intend to express. Before an editor or reviewer changes any word in your document—

---

[3] Thomas N. Huckin and Leslie A. Olsen. *Technical Writing and Professional Communication*, McGraw-Hill, 1983, p. 510.

no matter how small the word may be—you should be consulted. In the previous example, the inclusion or the omission of the article *the* influences meaning. Sometimes editors and reviewers believe themselves to be mind readers. Like all mind readers, sometimes they're right and sometimes they're wrong.

THE MASS/COUNT SYSTEM

Figure 5.1 is a chart illustrating the mass/count article system. Various such charts exist, but this chart is widely used in ESL studies and is less complex than others.

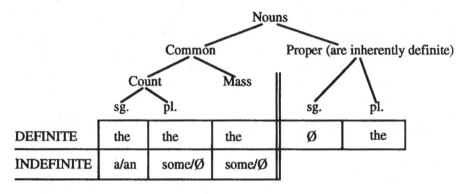

FIGURE 5.1   MASS/COUNT Article system.

RESOURCE TIP

The use of mass and count nouns becomes slightly more complicated if you need to modify them with expressions of quantity (*most, some, a lot*), or if you replace them with pronouns of quantity such as *some, any, many*. An excellent grammar book by Betty Azar deals with these additional aspects of the count/noncount issue.[4] Written especially for midlevel students of English as a second language, Azar's book also contains useful practice exercises.

The Tense System

English verb tenses are taught in primary school where the simple and compound tenses are learned, and the paradigms for singular and plural forms for the first, second, and third person are memorized. If grammar school children

---

[4] Betty Schrampfer Azar. *Fundamentals of English Grammar.* Second Edition. Englewood Cliffs, NJ: Prentice Hall Regents, 1992.

can learn tense formation, why does verb tense present difficulty for ESL scientists? One reason may be that the English verb tense system is the most complicated of any language in the world. English provides the ability to express extraordinary refinements of time reference. Think, for example, of the time nuances expressed by, say, past perfect progressive where a sentence describes an action taking place over a period of time in the past, prior to some other past event. Even a native speaker of English has to pause a second before writing, "The reconnaissance plane had been flying before the navigational plan was changed."

TRADITIONAL TENSES

Traditional grammarians list 12 tenses, which are listed here. Sometimes they are listed in a different order: present, past, future, present perfect, past perfect, future perfect, present progressive, past progressive, future progressive, and so forth, but the following order makes sense from the point of view of tense as time.

The Traditional Tenses

simple present
present progressive
simple past
past progressive
simple future
future progressive
present perfect
present perfect progressive
past perfect
past perfect progressive
future perfect
future perfect progressive

If the *be going to* form (future of the present) is also included as a tense along with its progressive form, future of the present progressive, you have a choice of 14 tenses. Fourteen tenses are certainly more than anyone needs to write an ordinary technical report. This great range of tenses represents a significant challenge in acquiring English.

A COPING STRATEGY

To help you associate meanings with the various tense forms, the Appendix offers some tables relating tenses to uses. After scanning these tables, select the tenses you use most frequently in technical writing. You might wish to review some documents you've already had approved to see which tenses you used. You'll discover that some tenses seem more appropriate than others for technical writing, just as some styles and some tones are more suitable. After looking over the tables, you may also mark some tenses that you're unlikely to use in a technical document. Probably the conversational tenses like the future of the present (we *are going to visit* the site next week) will not be used in place of the more concise simple future (we *will visit* the site next week). In your self-help program, don't try to master all 14 tenses at the same time. You have a good precedent for this strategy: If you listen to President Clinton's speeches, you'll notice that he uses a fairly limited range of tenses.

It's more important for you to understand the meanings of the tenses than it is for you to simply memorize the forms. Again, listen to and mimic good practitioners of the target language. Studies in second language acquisition repeatedly support the observation that although acquisition by study is effective, it's acquisition by immersion that's more durable.

In passing, remember that a nonnative speaker of any language brings a fresh perspective to the target language, just as the visitor from overseas has a fresh eye for the incongruities of a culture. This "view from abroad" has been used in literature for centuries by creative writers employing the character of a naive visitor to comment on cultural absurdities. A similar perspective on grammar can sometimes have useful results.

A New Paradigm

Take the case of the traditional paradigm for tenses. Does the classical paradigm represent the nature of an English verb? Contemporary linguists claim that it does not. They believe it represents a paradigm for Latin conjugations that has been superimposed on English verbs. Grammar books, like etiquette books, suddenly became popular following the industrial revolution in England. A newly monied class needed to know how to speak correctly as well as how to act properly in polite society. Because the university graduates who were called upon to supply the need for grammar books were familiar with Greek and Latin, they turned to Latin to illustrate their own language. Rather than accept existing paradigms, contemporary grammarians have a new (and simpler) way of portraying tense in English. The simpler paradigms have been enthusiastically adopted for teaching English as a second language.

If you learned British English before American English, or if you learned American English in U.S. schools a few decades ago, you learned how to conjugate verb tenses according to a Latin-like format. Here's what the present tense of the verb to go looks like in the traditional paradigm:

	Singular	*Plural*
First Person	I go	We go
Second Person	You go	You go
Third Person	He goes She goes It goes	They go

A grammar revolutionary—perhaps someone with the "view from abroad"—would look at this paradigm and see how repetitive it is. By eliminating excess verbiage (something you do all the time in technical writing), you devise a new paradigm that's simpler, shorter, and easier to remember. Still offering grammatically correct information, this simplified paradigm is more concise for everyone and easier for you as an ESL communicator to understand.

Uninflected: I, you, we, they go
Inflected: He, she, it goes

A Word of Comfort

The process of simplification continues in English. Simpler paradigms, plainer style, lighter punctuation and capitalization, and less Latin are signposts of this process. Unfortunately, you'll find yourself working with colleagues who have assigned themselves the mission of safeguarding the language, by which they mean safeguarding the language as they know it: Latin phrases, heavy punctuation and frequent capitalization, and copious qualification. As a result, you may have difficulty getting acceptance from the guardians of the past for your correctly streamlined English. Take comfort from the fact that even native speakers of English who teach technical English in the corporate classroom have difficulty in convincing seasoned writers to simplify their prose. They are repeatedly interrupted by comments like, "But I was taught in school that it's never correct to use the first person singular"; or, "Contrary to what you just said, I learned that you should never repeat the same noun in the same paragraph." These comments are intended to put the instructor on the defensive; they generally don't display any attempt on the part of the challenger to better understand modern principles of style or new perspectives on grammar.

The Modal Maze

Other techniques are used to express other dimensions of the verb. The decision to use active or passive voice is one such technique. You'll find help with the voice decision in Chapter 7, "Grammar Troublespots," because voice is a problem for technical and scientific writers generally, not just ESL writers. More subtle than voice are the verb shadings that express conditionality or perhaps demand. These shadings are made possible by verb helpers or auxiliaries that can be added before the main verb. The verb helpers or auxiliaries are called modals, and undertaking a self-help program to understand them may seem to you like entering the labyrinth of the Minotaur at Crete.

The name modal is best explained by Scott Rice as expressing "the kind of ideas once expressed more commonly by the subjunctive mood—*mode* and *mood* mean almost the same thing."[5] Modals are especially valuable in spoken communications, but they can also be useful in technical writing. In the technical workplace they might occur in a trip report, a letter of commendation, a technical exchange note, a memo to employees, or a report containing recommendations.

The primary modals or modal auxiliaries, as they are sometimes called, are given in the following list. They express a wide range of meanings, and many

[5] Scott Rice. *Right Words Right Places*. Belmont, California: Wadsworth Publishing Company, 1993, p. 143.

of them have more than one meaning. They can be used in forming questions and sometimes in negative constructions. Because of their many meanings, their various uses, and the subtlety of their shadings, they constitute a difficult area of ESL grammar.

Modal Auxiliaries

can
could
(had better)
may
might
should
must
will
would

have to
(have got to)
ought to

In the list, modal forms that are more applicable to conversational usage are enclosed by parentheses. The list also separates the modals that are used directly with the verb (top group), and the modals that are used with *to* in addition to the verb (bottom group). In the first group, it would be incorrect to add *to* before the verb. In both groups, it would be incorrect to inflect the verb by adding *s* to agree with the subject.

Here are some examples of verb modals in sentences or questions. Note that these sentences use the simple form of a verb, not progressive or perfect forms.

Auxiliary Modal Plus Simple Form of a Verb

can	We can install the LAN whenever you wish.
	Incorrect: We can *to install* the LAN.
could	He could install the LAN tomorrow.
	Incorrect: He could *to install* the LAN.
	Incorrect: He could *installs* the LAN.
may	Our experiment may succeed this time.
might	It might snow and prevent the landing.
should	You should report for duty immediately.
must	Their report must arrive this afternoon.
will	Will you be there on time?
would	Would you bring the X2 file to our meeting?

Auxiliary Modal Plus to Plus Simple Form of a Verb

have to   Do I have to report your unsatisfactory performance?

ought to   I ought to report your lack of cooperation, but won't do so this
time.

Many grammar books oversimplify the meaning of modal forms, stating that *could* is the past tense of *can*. In fact, modals go beyond the common notions of time as expressed through tense. Pastness in modals might be viewed more as an expression of remoteness than it is of measured time. While modals evolved from tensed forms, they no longer really express time.

FORM

Before exploring the categories of meaning that modals convey, it's useful to look at some characteristics of their form. There are some factors of a modal's form that are entirely predictable. Modal problems occur more frequently in speaking, which rarely offers an opportunity for revision. Since technical writing goes through many reviews, modal irregularities tend to disappear.

TIPS FOR USING MODALS

Here are some useful facts about modal form. Sentences marked with an asterisk (*) are incorrect. They show frequently occurring mistakes in modal use that you need to avoid.

Modals are always the first element of a verb phrase.
Example: He *might have flown* the plane.

A simple form of the verb always follows the modal.
Example: She will *fly* the plane.

The simple form of the verb following a modal is not inflected.
Example: He could *help* them.
Example: *He could *helps* them.

A participle or infinitive following a modal violates the impulse for a simple verb form.
Example: *He might *to fly* the plane.

Modals act as the operators or action agents in a verb phrase; they are the elements of the verb phrase that invest it with significance.
Example: We *shall* implement the plan.

Modals can carry markings that indicate negation or interrogation.
Example: The team *may not* abort the launch.
Example: *Will* the project cover expenses?

Modals never carry the -ing ending nor do they carry the usual third person singular ending.
Example: *The scientist can *speaking* English.
Example: He walks on the moon.
Example: *He *wills* walk on the moon.

Modals incorporate past and nonpast forms. The past forms convey a sense of remoteness more than of measureable past time. Modern modals are untensed.
Example: Ventana's Group Systems V *would* be an example of successful groupware.

MEANING

From the viewpoint of use, modals offer a range of expression that includes the following:

statements of ability
statements of permission
statements of possibility and expectation
statements of advisability and obligation
statements of necessity or inferred certainty

Different linguists apply different labels to these meaning groups, but similarities exist among the different interpretations. Here are illustrations of these meanings, including some positive and negative versions. Some typical ESL errors are also illustrated.

Meaning	Example	Typical Error
Ability— *can* and *could*	I *can* solve the problem.	I *can to* solve the problem.
The modal of ability for a one-time event is *able to*.	Our leader was *able to* get to the meeting by 8 a.m.	*Cannot* the engineer redesign the circuit?
	Can't the engineer redesign the circuit?	

Meaning	Example	Typical Error
Permission—*can, may, could, might* The negative of *may* does not contract. While *can* and *may* are interchanged in speaking, don't interchange them in writing.	*May* my assistant attend the meeting? Yes, he *may*. No, he *may not*. *Might* the scientist offer a solution to the problem?	*Can* my assistant attend the meeting? Yes, he *can*. No, *he mayn't*.
Possibility—*can, may, could, might* *Can* is more likely to express theoretical possibility, while *may* appears in expressions of factual possibility.	Our next step *could* be into the fourth dimension. We *might* meet our project milestone tomorrow.	
Range from Required to Advised—*must, have to, should, ought to*. There are additional modal forms that express obligation, especially in spoken English: *had better, have got to, should have*	You *should* ask your manager to review your proposal. We *have to* ask the general's permission to videotape his speech.	
Necessity or Inferred Certainty—Same forms as Obligation This meaning introduces the question of *must* versus *should*. *Must*, when used to mean necessity, is usually stronger than *should*.	My exams are over, so I *should* have time to visit you. Summer is here, so the results *should* be ready soon.	My exams are over, so I *must* have time to see you. Summer is here, so the results *must* be ready soon. He *should* think the conference is informative because he attends every year.

Another way of thinking about modals is to identify their relative degree of strength. In general, it's safe to assume that *can* or *may*, *might* and *could* express less urgency than *should*, which yields to *must*, which, in turn, yields to *will* or *shall* in situations of authority or urgency. Here's a list of the relative strengths of these modals, moving from weakness to strength.

can, may
might, could
should
must
will, shall

THE PHRASAL FACTOR

Another variant of the verb system is the phrasal verb. A phrasal verb can be defined as a verb followed by a particle. Particles are newly defined parts of speech in English that can be described as, "A word that combines with a verb to create an expression with an idiomatic meaning."[6] Particles exist in other languages such as Japanese, but there they have a different form and a different function. In English, particles are derived from prepositions or adverbs. Regardless of the combination, however, phrasal verbs act as single verbs. Phrasal verbs are problematic for ESL communicators for several reasons.

- As used in English, they don't exist outside the Germanic languages: English, German, Dutch, and the Scandinavian languages. Consequently, they're unfamiliar to a large proportion of scientists and engineers from overseas.
- They have multiple parts like a two- or three-word verb in a compound or progressive tense (examples: *have gone, have been going, will be instructed*). But the multiple parts of phrasal verbs are not tense indicators. Further, because they aren't explained in traditional grammar books, it's hard to find information about them.
- They have an inexplicable format peculiarity: Some can be separated and some cannot.

SPECIAL MEANINGS

When a verb and a preposition are used together in such a way as to have a special meaning, then you are dealing with the phrasal verb. The same combination of words can be used to express a conventional meaning. For example, in a user manual you might read:

[6] Adrian Akmajian, Richard A. Demers, Robert M. Harnish. *Linguistics: An Introduction to Language and Communication*, Second Edition. Cambridge, Massachusetts: The MIT Press, 1988, p. 526.

Turn off the main switch in case of a lightning storm.

In this sentence, *turn off* means *disengage*. This is a special meaning for the verb *to turn*. In conventional usage, *turn* with the preposition *off* means to move in a different direction. For example:

To go to New York, turn off the Massachusetts turnpike at exit 10.

Here you have a simple present verb followed by a preposition that introduces the prepositional phrase "turn off the highway."

CONVERSATIONAL QUALITY

Phrasal verbs tend to have a conversational quality. You may find yourself using them frequently in oral communication. Technical briefings, scientific forums, business meetings, and collegial conversations are all replete with discourse using phrasal verbs. Moreover, with the growing emphasis on user-friendly documentation, you'll see phrasal verbs used frequently in handbooks and manuals. User documentation prose often includes sentences like:

Make do with a simple editor.
Come up with a new format.
Get off the system promptly.

These sentences are all introduced by phrasal verbs. Phrasal verbs are translatable into more conventional verbs that are often shorter and usually more formal. In the preceding three sentences, *make do* can be replaced by *manage*; *come up with* can be replaced by *create* or *present*; and *get off* can be replaced by *leave*. By practicing substitutions, you'll learn that some phrasal verbs are more readily translated than others. Keep in mind, however, that there is nothing incorrect about using phrasals verbs. Deciding to use them is a style choice; using them as separated or unseparated units is a point of grammar.

Computer manuals often present instructions in phrasal verbs. In the following list of instructions, the verbal phrases are italicized. How would you convert the six phrasal verbs into more formal verbs?

As a new user of the Macintosh IIsi, you should follow these simple instructions:

1. *Take off* the keyboard and monitor covers.
2. *Turn on* your computer by pressing the ◁ key.
3. *Check out* the icons on your display.

4. *Look up* the meaning of unfamiliar icons in Appendix A.
5. *Cut out* text loss by frequent saves.
6. *Turn off* your computer at the end of the day.

> **Answers**: 1-Remove, 2-Start, 3-Examine, 4-Research, 5-Eliminate, 6-Stop. You may have come up with additional alternatives.

THREE-WORD PHRASAL VERBS

There are two-word phrasal verbs and three-word phrasals. The three-word phrasal usually take a required preposition—one that can't be changed without changing—the special meaning. Here are a few example of intact phrasal verbs used in sentences.

Some Intact Three-Word Phrasal Verbs

Do you *get along with* your co-workers?
Our client will *end up with* a better product.
Illustrators must *keep up with* the latest software.
Please *get back to* the original argument.
Come up with a new design by January 30.
Read the RFP to *catch up with* our plans.
He'll *get back from* temporary duty next week.
Watch out for security checks at the gate.
Let's *get through with* this report today.
Please don't *drop out of* the candidate pool.

TWO-WORD PHRASAL VERBS

More phrasal verbs have two-word units than three-word units. The following list of two-word phrasals is not intended to be comprehensive; it serves merely as a ready reference for your use. Many phrasals aren't appropriate for use in technical or scientific communication, either written or spoken. Consequently, this list represents the author's selection, and is shorter than a list you would find in a general ESL grammar book.

Common Two-Word Phrasal Verbs

Phrasal Verb	*Meaning*
break down	to take apart
break up	to decompose
call back	to return a telephone call
call off	to cancel

Phrasal Verb	Meaning
call on†	to request an answer
call up	to make a telephone call
catch on	to understand
come across†	to find by accident
come back	to return
come over	to visit
cross out	to draw a line through
cut off	to disconnect
do over	to repeat
figure out	to find a solution
fill in	to supply information
fill out	to complete a form
fill up	to fill completely
find out	to discover
get away	to manage to leave
get back	to return
get in†	to arrive
get off†	to leave a plane, bus, streetcar, or train
get over†	to recover from
get up	to arise
give back	to return
give up	to surrender
go back	to return
go over	to review
hand in	to submit homework, reports
hand out	to distribute
hang up	to complete a telephone call
keep up	to continue
leave out	to omit
look into†	to investigate
look over	to review
look up	to search for information
make up	to invent
pass out	to distribute
pay back	to return money or service
pick up	to lift
pick out	to select
prop up	to support
pull down	to demolish
pull in	to stop at a destination
put down	to stop holding
put off	to postpone

Phrasal Verb	Meaning
put out	to extinguish
run into†	to meet by chance
shut off	to disconnect
stand up	to remain intact
start over	to start again
take back	to withdraw or to return
take up	to discuss
throw away	to discard
throw out	to discard
turn off	to stop
turn out	to extinguish
turn on	to start
wear out	to exhaust
wind up	to finish
write down	to make a note

†Phrasal verbs that cannot be separated.

To Separate or Not to Separate

In addition to learning the special meanings of verb phrasals, you must address one important point of grammar. Earlier, you were advised not to separate the parts of three-word verb phrasals. Many two-word verbal phrasals can be separated but some cannot. There is no general principle to help you determine which are separable and which are not. This peculiarity of verb phrasals will cause you trouble if you don't study the two groupings. If you don't recognize them from speech, then you simply have to memorize them until they become second nature to you. The number of two-word verb phrasals that are nonseparable is small. In the previous list of two-word verb phrasals, those preceded by the dagger symbol cannot be separated. Nonseparable verbal phrasals can never be divided; separable phrasals, on the other hand, must be separated if the direct object of a sentence is a pronoun. Here are examples of some erroneously unseparated separables.

Separable Phrasal Verbs	Incorrectly Unseparated Phrasal Verbs Having Pronoun Objects
Our chief of staff *threw away* the report.	
Our chief of staff threw the report away.	*Our chief of staff threw away it.
The head engineer *left out* critical data.	
The head engineer left critical data out.	*The head engineer left out it.

Separable Phrasal Verbs	Incorrectly Unseparated Phrasal Verbs Having Pronoun Objects
Please *pass out* the seminar description. Please pass the seminar description out.	*Please pass out it.
Leave out the chemical additive. Leave the chemical additive out.	*Leave out it.
We need to *take up* item two in the agenda. We need to take item two up in the agenda.	*We need to take up it.
Look up our most recent price quotation. Look our most recent price quotation up.	*Look up it.
Give up item 34C to cut costs. Give item 34C up to cut costs.	*Give up it to cut costs.

The Inflection Enigma

How does inflection in English affect you as an ESL professional? And what is it? Inflection in the linguistic sense does not refer to the lilt of spoken language. It refers to syntax or sentence structure whereby words change their forms to reflect their role in the sentence. Words can also be influenced by other words in the sentence.

If the words in a sentence change to show case, gender, number, tense, person, mood, voice, and comparison, there are quite a lot of factors influencing the variability of words in sentences. This observation alone answers the question of how inflection in English affects you as an ESL professional. For the adult learner of a new language, inflection can represent an enigmatic area of grammar.

RELEVANCE IN ACQUIRED LANGUAGES

If all languages were inflected for the same reasons and at the same rate, it would be a purely mechanical exercise for those acquiring a target language to reapply known conjugations and declensions. But this isn't the case.

Some languages are not inflected. For example, in some character-based languages, one word has one symbol, a pluralization of a word has a different symbol, a different meaning of the word has a different symbol, and so on. Some languages—of which English is an example—are moderately inflected. In English there are, for example, rather predictable positions in the sentence for major parts of speech, and there are several parts of speech (largely the function words like prepositions and conjunctions) that never change their form in relation to surrounding influences.

And there are languages that are highly inflected. Latin belongs to this group. If you studied Latin, you remember memorizing numerous paradigms so you could apply correctly the many forms of a noun or a verb. You may also remember that the position of a part of speech in a Latin sentence is not terribly important because its suffix is a signal or marker. The mark or suffix endings indicate how the word functions in the sentence and provide the key to additional aspects like number or possession. Examples are the *s* plural marker in English or the *d* and *ed* past tense markers.

A Moderately Inflected Language

As a moderately inflected Language, English spares us the necessity of memorizing as many charts as Latin. Also, English, although having a large vocabulary, does not contain the seemingly infinite number of symbols as do some uninflected Asian languages. Learning noninflected parts of speech is fairly easy (although the meanings of prepositions sometimes causes trouble). By identifying which parts of speech are inflected and which are not, you can master the matter of inflection more readily.

INFLECTION AND PARTS OF SPEECH

Words in English serve certain functions in sentences. Based on their function, they're labeled as *parts of speech*. Traditional grammarians identify nine parts of speech, which are arranged alphabetically in the following box, but not according to their frequency of use or the importance of their functions. Of these nine, interjections (*oh*, *ah*, *alas*, and similar exclamations) wouldn't be appropriate for use in a technical document, so you won't find them discussed here.

Parts of Speech

adjectives
adverbs
articles
conjunctions
interjections
nouns
prepositions
pronouns
verbs

A CLASSIFICATION

There are numerous ways of classifying parts of speech; for example, linguists often classify them either as content words or function words. From the viewpoint of inflection, they can be classified as noninflected (those that don't change their form), and inflected (those having a greater or lesser tendency to change). The parts of speech having a capacity for inflection require special attention from nonnative speakers of English. You can set aside the non-inflected parts of speech as less troublesome. Conjunctions and prepositions are stable. And although adverbs change for comparison, their changes are so much less extensive than other parts of speech that you can treat them as noninflected.

Noninflected

adverbs
conjunctions
prepositions

The inflected parts of speech are more numerous. Articles have already been discussed; the declensions of nouns and pronouns and the conjugations of verbs can be found in any conventional grammar book; adjectives respond to the nouns and pronouns they modify.

Inflected

adjectives
articles
nouns
pronouns
verbs

These categories of inflected and noninflected words are reasonably but not perfectly dependable. A case in point is that of the preposition.

PREPOSITIONAL INFLECTION

Prepositions don't change their forms so we can consider them uninflected. *Of* is *of*, regardless of where it occurs in a sentence. However, while prepositions don't change their own form, they do wield influence over some words within their domain. Every student of English is aware of the grammar rule stating, "all prepositions require an object," and the grammar principle that, "objects are in the objective case." As soon as you encounter the word *case* (changes to reflect nominative, objective, possessive roles) you're dealing with inflection. So while prepositions don't respond to case, pronoun objects over which they have dominion do. This relatively simple situation traps both native and nonnative speakers.

The next list includes the most commonly used prepositions in English. A few prepositions not appropriate for technical documentation have been excluded. For example, the list excludes *save*, meaning *except*, because it can be ambiguous. It also excludes *ere* meaning *before,* because it's too archaic for scientific or technical writing. *Per* and *via* do not appear because they're Latin. You may think of a few more prepositions to add to your list.

Commonly Used Prepositions in English

about	before	down	of	till*
above	behind	during	off	to
across	below	except	on	toward**
after	beneath	excepting	onto	under
against	beside	for	out	underneath
along	besides	from	outside	until
alongside	between	in	over	unto
amid	beyond	inside	regarding	up
among	by	into	since	upon
around	concerning	like	through	with
at	despite	near	throughout	within
				without

till is a short form of *until* and is probably not as appropriate for technical writing as the longer form.

**toward, towards: *toward* is the primary and preferred spelling in American English.

In addition, there are some prepositions used in British English that never occur in American English. Here's an example of a professor of science speaking in a British spy novel.

> We're talking about the combined and simultaneous effect of a massive thermo-nuclear detonation, a volcanic eruption and an earthquake. This lies *outwith* the experience of mankind so we can't visualize those things except to guess, and it's a safe guess, that the reality will be worse than any nightmare.
>
> Alistair MacLean, *Santorini*

Outwith (and its antonym *inwith*) can be found in the Oxford English Dictionary (OED), but not in Webster's, and it certainly isn't familiar to American writers.

The danger of prepositional inflection occurs when the preposition is followed by a pronoun (which responds to case), and when the preposition and its pronoun-object become too widely separated.[7] Pronouns in English are

[7] *American Scientist* published an excellent essay that discusses problems caused by great separations between important elements within a sentence. See George D. Gopen and Judith A. Swan. *American Scientist.* "The Science of Scientific Writing," vol. 78, no. 6, November-December 1990, p. 550 ff.

inflected in response to number, gender, and case, and it's especially important to watch out for the case. Number and gender are self-evident. The classic problem for both native and nonnative speakers looks like this:

*The off-site meeting was attended *by* Judy, Susan, Mike, Dave and *I.*

Two things have influenced the error here. First, the number of proper nouns following the preposition makes the speaker search for a more "elevated" pronoun: *I.* This is known as hypercorrection, or the urge to dignify the prose to the extent that it becomes ungrammatical. Second, the distance factor occurs. The separation between the preposition *by* and the pronoun is too great. A safer approach is to keep the pronoun close to the preposition as follows:

The off-site meeting was attended *by me*, Judy, Susan, Mike, and Dave.

Relative Pronouns

The relative pronouns in English are *who, whom, whose, which,* and *that.* Relative pronouns sometimes present difficulty to ESL professionals because not all languages possess the capability to relativize. Further, many languages that do provide for the creation of relative clauses have different ways of accommodating for them. For example, in Asian languages like Japanese and Chinese, the relative clause is placed in front of the noun to which it refers. And Semitic languages have a way of handling relative clauses that will cause errors if transferred directly into English.

So, while the "tucking in" of a relative phrase is second nature to a native speaker of English, ESL writers may create erroneous sentences based on first language experience. Someone whose first language is Arabic, for example, may provide a noun with two pronouns—a relative pronoun and a personal pronoun—instead of one.

Our group leader appointed a Member of the Technical Staff *who* she know *him* to be a good analyst.

At best, an ESL writer is likely to create less efficient syntax. For example:

Jim, *who* had been in the National Guard, acts like a top sergeant.

is more likely to be written as:

Jim acted like a top sergeant. He had been in the National Guard.

by those for whom creating relative clauses or phrases is a recent skill. Lack of relativization in technical writing doesn't represent ungrammatical prose. It's simply more wordy, and it provides the technical editor with another opportunity to correct your document.

WHICH RELATIVE PRONOUN TO USE?

Quite a bit of discussion surrounds the issue of which pronoun to choose. While you may find the following explanations familiar, they will nevertheless be helpful to both native English and ESL speakers.

- *Who, whom,* and *whose* always relate to human or animate beings. *Whom* carries the special marker *m* , indicating that it's to be used in the object case—either the object of a verb or the object of a preposition.
- *Which* can relate to either animate beings or inanimate objects. It is very popular in general writing, but more judicious choice considers restrictive or nonrestrictive use in a sentence. (Restrictive and nonrestrictive clauses are covered in Chapter, "General Grammar Troublespots.")
- *That* usually refers to inanimate objects. Consequently, it will be used more frequently in technical writing than in general writing. It will also be used in nonrestrictive clauses instead of *which*.
- *Whose* is a rather special relative pronoun. It almost always refers to human or animate beings, but once in a while it can refer to an inanimate object, as in:

The blueprints were of an old wing design whose aerodynamics have been greatly improved.

It also indicates possession.

A REMINDER

Because *whose* shows possession, although it functions primarily as a relative pronoun, you might become confused about which noun replacements (pronouns) are primarily possessive pronouns. The following list should help to clarify these possessives. They are sometimes called *genitives*, a word that derives from Latin nomenclature for the possessive case.

Possessive Pronouns

Singular	*Plural*
my	our
mine	ours
your	your
yours	yours
his	their
her	theirs
hers	
its	

DELETION OF RELATIVE PRONOUNS

After practicing when and how to write relative clauses, you might then think about when you can delete the relative pronoun. In formal English the pronoun is generally expressed, whereas in informal English it can sometimes be omitted. An example of the expressed relative pronoun in a formal document or conversation might be:

The mathematician *to whom* I talked was helpful in explaining the algorithm.

In a less formal situation, the sentence might read:

The mathematician I talked to was helpful in explaining the algorithm.

This alternative is especially useful when dealing with the relative pronoun *which*. Editors are known for the glee with which they go "which" hunting. In so doing, they sometimes erase the distinction between formal and informal prose. Here are examples of the same sentence. The first version expresses the relative pronoun and the second version implies it.

Expressed pronoun: The plane in which we flew to Diego Garcia had elaborate radar equipment.
Implied pronoun: The plane we flew in to Diego Garcia had elaborate radar equipment.

Because *whose* carries the double burden of relation and possession, it can't be deleted. It's more deeply embedded into a sentence than the other relative pronouns.

A Resource Tip

What was referred to earlier as the "tucking in" of a relative pronoun and its clause would be called *embedding* by linguists. Embedding can be illustrated graphically by several types of diagrams. Although the older line diagrams have been supplanted by tree diagrams, both line and tree diagrams can be very helpful for understanding sentence structure. Engineers and scientists are adept at reading diagrams, and you might be interested in seeing tree diagrams used to illustrate relative clauses. The topic of sentence diagramming lies beyond the boundaries of the *ESL Resource Book*, but if sentence diagramming interests you, you can look at an interlibrary loan copy of *The Grammar Book: An ESL/EFL Teacher's Course*[8] for an idea of how *whose* differs from the other relative pronouns.

Tips for ESL Troublespots

TIP 1: Distinguish between count and noncount (mass) nouns before applying articles.

TIP 2: Recognize Ø (no article) as an article choice.

TIP 3: Don't create plurals for mass nouns.

TIP 4: Remember that measure words or phrases before nouns can change your article decision.

TIP 5: Watch for meaning shifts from mass to count or from count to mass.

TIP 6: Simplify your tense choices for technical documentation.

TIP 7: Emphasize tense meaning before tense form when studying verb tenses.

TIP 8: Persist in using streamlined English.

TIP 9: Learn the verb modals.

TIP 10: Don't inflect main verbs that have modals.

TIP 11: Don't assign tense to verb modals.

TIP 12: Use phrasal verbs to relax your style.

TIP 13: Keep together the units of three-word phrasal verbs.

TIP 14: Memorize two-word phrasal verbs that cannot be separated. (There aren't many.)

TIP 15: Divide the units of separable two-word phrasal verbs that have pronouns as direct objects.

---

[8] Marianne Celce-Murcia and Diane Larsen-Freeman. *The Grammar Book: An ESL/EFL Teacher's Course*. Cambridge: Newbury House Publishers, 1983. While Celce-Murcia and Larsen-Freeman use tree diagrams throughout their book, the diagrams on p. 363 and p. 370 are of special interest. Two diagrams on p. 363 show relativization of *who* clauses, and a diagram on p. 370 shows how *whose* affects a sentence.

TIP 16: Keep pronoun objects close to their prepositions.

TIP 17: Use relative clauses to decrease verbiage.

TIP 18: Use *that* to refer to inanimate objects.

TIP 19: Consider deleting relative pronouns. Use good judgment.

TIP 20: Don't delete *whose* in relative clauses.

AN EXTRA TIP

Congratulate yourself because you've now completed reading the most difficult part of the *ESL Resource Book.*

6

MORE ESL

TROUBLESPOTS

Less Difficult Troublespots

Technical prose by writers from overseas often reflects style features of home cultures. With so many cultures represented in the United States, departures from mainstream technical style can be numerous and difficult to predict. In contrast, multiple samples of ESL prose indicate that grammar problems, unlike style problems, are relatively predictable. The same grammar problems appear repeatedly regardless of the author's first language.

It is a curious fact that the most frequent areas of difficulty are not restricted to major points of grammar. The article, as an example, is not a major part of speech. However, it's so frequently problematic that it's predictably troublesome for nonnative communicators.

Chapter 5 covered the most frequently occurring ESL grammar troublespots, some of which are highly visible and others less so. Chapter 6 will cover less frequently occurring ESL grammar problems. It's encouraging to believe that they rank among the troublespots that are easier to overcome. Here are areas where you can improve the quality of your documents quickly, easily, and in a very visible manner.

Other: Another, the Other, Others, the Others

While not a critical issue, confusion among *other, another, others, the other, the others* occurs often enough to merit attention. If you find it confusing to use these terms, you can tackle the problem from several approaches:

- Study the meanings of each term.
- Identify the parts of speech for each term and consider how these parts work.
- Practice using the terms.

Set your own pace in working through this issue. If the distinctions remain unclear, discuss the five terms with ESL friends. Many of them will have already sorted out the distinctions of meaning, and you can benefit from their experience. To assist you further, a short practice exercise follows the discussion.

The root word is *other* and the other four terms are its extensions. The dictionary meanings of *other* ("one that remains of two or more" or "a different or additional one") are extended by placing articles (*an* or *the*) before the word, or by adding the plural marker *s* at the end.

ANOTHER

The article *an* is joined to *other* to make one word that is used to express additional but singular references. The new word, *another*, means "one more out of a group that's been previously mentioned." If you write the sentence:

Please hand me another test tube.

you imply that the subject of test tubes has already been raised. In this instance, someone has already provided a first test tube. Here, the number of test tubes you may request is limited only by the number of test tubes available (see Figure 6.1). You can go on to say:

Please hand me another test tube. (test tube #3)

I need yet another test tube. (test tube #4)

Please give me another test tube. (test tube #5)

And so forth . . . .

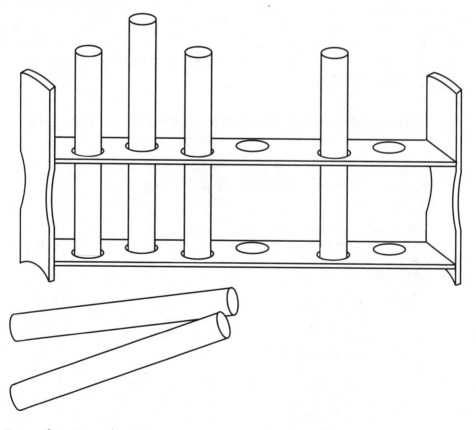

FIGURE 6.1   Test-tube rack.

THE OTHER

Unlike *another*, which fuses the limiting article *an* with the root *other*, *the other* remains two separate words. Also, a significant change in meaning takes place when you move from *(an)other* to *the other*. *The* is a pointing word that designates a specific or definite item. It is also singular by nature. *The other* is more restricted than *another*. It means the remaining one. Here, you are talking about two test tubes, one of which has already been used.

I've used one test tube; please hand me the other one.

Jinzy used one test tube; Shida will use the other one.

Cho gave me the large test tube; Aaron has the other.

Without changing meaning, these terms can change their function in a sentence. For example, *another* can function as an adjective modifying a noun (please hand me *another test tube*) or it can function as a pronoun replacing a noun (please hand me *another*). It's been argued that this pronominal use is still essentially adjectival, with the noun understood rather than expressed. (Please hand me *another* [*test tube*]). In the first two sentences in the previous example, *other* modifies the word *one* (a substitution for *test tube*). It is clearly an adjective. In the third sentence—Cho gave me the large test tube; Aaron has *the other*—*the other* replaces the noun *test tube*. In the act of replacement, it functions as a pronoun. This flexibility makes for additional usefulness, and shouldn't cause undue confusion.

OTHERS

Adding the *s* plural marker to *other* enables you to talk about "the ones remaining in a specific group." Again, there is the implication that the topic discussed has already been raised. A typical situation might read:

Rebecca will use some test tubes; Sabrina may use some *others*.

A WORD OF CAUTION REGARDING OTHERS

Others has a limitation unlike any of the related forms of *other*. *Others* cannot function as an adjective; it can only function as a pronoun. This peculiarity creates a possible ESL error. Incorrect examples are starred.

There are *others* in the cabinet.
* Please give me *others* test tubes.
* Please give me *others* ones.

THE OTHERS

Also having the plural meaning of "the ones remaining in a specific group," *the others* can be used as either an adjective or a pronoun. It's important to stress the meaning of remainders. "The remains from a given number of similar items" might be another way of defining this plural, specific form of *other*. The idea that the discussed topic has already been introduced also applies. In the following sentences, the previous reference is supplied.

> We have six test tubes. Cho gave me the large one; Aaron has *the others*.

> The laboratory's stock of test tubes is down to a half dozen. I've used four; please give me *the others*.

> Jinzy used one of our six test tubes. Shida will use *the others*.

Tabular Summary

Here is a tabular summary of *other* and its variants.

OTHER, OTHERS, ANOTHER, THE OTHER, THE OTHERS

	Adjective	*Pronoun*
Singular	*another* test tube	*another*
Plural	*other* test tubes	*others*†
Singular	*the other* test tube	*the other*
Plural	*the other* test tubes	*the others*

†cannot be used as an adjective

APPLICATION

To practice using these terms, fill in the blanks in the following 10 sentences. If you can fill them in correctly by ear, you won't have to return to the discussion for review.

1. The Priestley Chemistry Prize and the Hodgkin Physics Prize were awarded yesterday in Switzerland. Dr. Malinda Lutz won the Priestley Prize, and Dr. Alberto Diaz won _____.
2. Dr. Diaz won _____ prize last week.

3. _____ prizes will be awarded in January.
4. And _____ are planned for next June.
5. The electron microscope and the transistor are recent inventions.
   _____ are radar, the integrated circuit, and the laser gyro.
6. The laser x-ray was one post-World War II discovery. Superconductivity
   was _____. Can you name _____?
7. Some supercomputers are used for constructing human genomes.
   _____ are used for processing seismic data.
8. Our nuclear engineering department is in the General Groves Building.
   There are also two laboratories there: one is the isotope separation lab;
   is the high-temperature fusion laboratory.
9. Professors Alan MacLeod and Pierrette Frickey are Principal Investigators for the project. _____ is Professor Robert Hamner.
10. Our corporation has bought a Cray supercomputer. In five years we
    hope to purchase _____ one.

Answers: 1-the other, 2-another, 3-Other, 4-others, 5-Others, 6-another
one, another, 7-Others, 8-the other, 9-The other, 10-another

Say and Tell

Fairly new speakers of English as a second language sometimes confuse the
two verbs *to say* and *to tell*. It's likely that you've passed well beyond the stage
of early acquisition, and can ignore this section. However, a brief review is
offered here for the benefit of technical professionals who may still have some
difficulty deciding which of these two verbs to use.

When you use *say* and *tell*, you are reporting the speech of others. For this
reason, you are more likely to be using these two verbs in speaking than in
writing. There are, however, certain writing situations in which you would
need to allude to the speech of others. For example, in a trip report you might
have occasion to record what transpired during a conversation with colleagues
in a competing company or at an affiliated laboratory. Whether producing a
written document or presenting an oral report, your credibility is in some
measure judged by your choice of words.

In reported speech you are providing an approximate version of what someone said. This differs from quoted speech in which you provide an exact word-
for-word reproduction of what someone said, using quotation marks to show
where the exact words begin and end. Reported speech does not use quotation
marks; it's sometimes referred to as indirect quotation or indirect speech.

In technical situations, word choice is often a matter of finding the very best
word to describe an idea or object. You search for concrete words rather than

abstract words, and you seek the most specific word you can find. The choice of *say* versus *tell*, unfortunately, is not this sort of good, better, best choice. Because the weight of usage has resulted in such a consistent pattern, rules indicate a right or wrong choice. The correctness of your choice is determined by how you construct your sentence. Here's a case where you should focus on format because the meaning remains constant for both *say* and *tell*.

To Say

Both words convey the sense of one person speaking to another or others. If you are using a direct quotation, use *to say*.

> Dr. Mandel said, "The growth of tumors is dependent on the growth of blood vessels."

You can also use *to say* in reporting an indirect quotation.

> Dr. Mandel said that the growth of tumors depends on the growth of blood vessels.

If you look at the structure of the last sentence you will see the grammar rule that governs *to say* in indirect (reported) speech: Say is followed immediately by a noun clause. Here are some examples. Watch for the word *that*. It introduces the noun clauses, the entire clause serving as the object of the verb *said*. Note too that the relative pronoun *that* can be either expressed or implied.

> Vidia said *that MIT's Lego Robot Competition needed additional funding.*

> Bill Baker said *that sponsors for the competition can supply both money and parts.*

> What did Carlos say? He said *[that] Motorola supplies their 6811 mini-controller for robot control.*

To Tell

To tell is always used to report speech, not to quote it. Instead of being followed by a noun clause, *tell* is followed immediately by a noun or personal pronoun that serves as an object.

> Trang *told me* that he had been assigned to the Lego Robot Competition Team A.

> Let me *tell you* that we're very happy to have you join our team.

> Jennifer will *tell Ali* how to get to the Computer Museum.

Some incorrect examples follow. As usual, they are marked with an asterisk.

Dr. Rushdie *told that* the competition educates students about real engineering challenges.

I *told that* it provides a sophisticated programming environment.

QUICK TIPS

TIP   1: Many ESL grammar problems are simple and easy to overcome.
TIP   2: Small grammar corrections yield big prose improvements.
TIP   3: *Others* (note the *s*) cannot be used as an adjective.
TIP   4: *Another* and *the other* modify singular nouns.
TIP   5: *Another* can refer to an extended number of singular nouns of the same category.
TIP   6: *The other* can only refer to one singular noun of the same category.
TIP   7: *The others* refers to a group of nouns of the same category.
TIP   8: All these terms—*other, others, another, the other, the others*—require some former reference to the category being discussed.
TIP   9: *To say* is used in quoted speech.
TIP 10: In reported speech (rather than quoted speech), *say* is followed by a noun clause.
TIP 11: *To tell* is used in reported speech.
TIP 12: *To tell* is followed immediately by a noun or a personal pronoun.
TIP 13: The important difference between *say* and *tell* is how they are used in a sentence.

The Quantification Thermometer

In technology and the sciences, qualification and quantification are extremely important. Chemists need to express just how much or how little of a specific liquid should be added to a solution; engineers must state exactly how much or how little stress a girder or a wing component can tolerate; veterinarians must tell a client how large or how small a dosage should be given to a certain breed of dog of a certain weight. As long as you can express quantities in exact numbers, you have no communication problem. Problems can arise, however, when the communication context requires a nonnumber expression of quantity or of frequency. Sometimes the subtle differences among words or phrases of quantity and frequency are unclear. Because lack of clarity is unacceptable to scientists, quantification needs to be mastered.

It's useful to break quantifiers into two groups: numberlike quantifiers and adverbs of frequency. You can interpret quantifiers as modifiers—indications of the amount, number, or proportion of a noun that follows. In other words, quantifiers (like qualifiers) come before a noun, investing it with increased precision.

Adverbs of frequency also indicate amount, number, or proportion, but they modify the verb of a sentence. Their position is less predictable than that of the numberlike quantifiers. Many adverbs of frequency are preverbal (they come before the verb), but some can come at the end of the sentence while others may begin a sentence. Enough adverbs of frequency come in the middle of a sentence to form a group called midsentence adverbs. You'll read more about sentence position of adverbs of frequency later in this discussion.

NUMBERLIKE QUANTIFIERS

Both the prenominal quantifiers and the adverbs of frequency include words that range through a scale of positive and negative meanings. The highest point of the scale of quantifiers is occupied by the word *all* and the lowest point is occupied by *no, none* and *not any*. The scale, from all (100 percent) to none (0 percent), may contain several words or phrases at any one level. No such scale is exhaustive. You can doubtlessly add words and phrases to this scale of noun modifiers indicating amount.

Some Positive and Negative Modifiers

all
all
most
much, many, a great deal of, a lot of, lots of
some, several, a few, a little, a couple of

---

not all
few, little, hardly any, scarcely any, not much, not many
no, none, not any

You can see that some of these words and phrases have a positive-negative relationship to one another: *all* and *not all, much* and *not much, many* and *not many*. Some of the words and phrases are opposites: *all* and *none, most* and *hardly any, a lot of* and *few*. There are also words and phrases that don't have pairs in the positive or negative field. Your first task in selecting a numberlike quantifier is to understand where the words fall in the scale of meaning.

How to Use Them

Having chosen a range of meaning and thereby understanding the positive or negative value of your proposed modifier, you'll want to make sure that it fits properly with the noun it will modify. You'll discover that not all quantifiers fit with all nouns. This is a problem of syntax. Careful examination of prenominal quantifiers shows that some fit well with count nouns, some with mass nouns, and some with both. Assuming that you'll be talking about the plural of count nouns when you're dealing with quantity, here's a table showing how the modifiers in the previous table align themselves.

Some Positive and Negative Quantifiers

Count	*Mass*	*Both*
many	much	all
several	a great deal of	most
a few	a little	a lot of
a couple of		lots of
		some
few	little	not all
not many	not much	hardly any
		scarcely any
		no
		none
		not any

There are more quantifiers than the ones listed in the tables, and they all involve decisions of both meaning and syntax. You also need to realize that native speakers of English often prefer one or another of the quantifiers in the same range of meaning. Some preferences do not appear to follow any particular rule of logic; other preferences respond to what the writer believes to be formal or informal levels of diction. For example, in a formal context, the writer might select *a great deal of* over *a lot of. A lot of* is a very popular quantifier, and its popularity seems to detract from its formality. *Much*, on the other hand, is less frequently used as a quantifier. As a result it assumes an air of formality that is not inherent in the word itself. (Remember that *much* is limited to use with a mass noun.) The three following sentences are all correct. They reflect perceptions of different levels of formality among the quantifiers.

I recommend Mary because she has acquired *a lot of* experience in my laboratory.

I recommend Mary because she has acquired *much* experience in my laboratory.

I recommend Mary because she has acquired *a great deal of* experience in my laboratory.

A range of meanings, rule-bound features of fit, and author preferences combine to make your job of selecting correct modifiers difficult. However, you'll discover that the closer you come to full fluency in English, the more successful you'll become in making correct selections. You'll see in the following error analysis exercise how well you've already mastered these selections. In each sentence, the quantifier has been underlined. Correct the error. Also explain to yourself why the sentence is ungrammatical.

ERROR ANALYSIS

1. *Scientific American* has published *a great deal* of interesting articles about chemistry, biology, and physics.
2. *Few* information arrives by way of the local area network.
3. *American Scientist* contains *lots* drawings and photographs.
4. *Professor Wu assigns too *many* homeworks.
5. *Kendall Square Center's R&D department completed *a great deal of* experiments using liquid nitrogen.
6. *Why does your laboratory use so *much* thermometers?
7. *Not *many* equipment passed durability testing for exposure to extreme temperatures.
8. *Do you have *a lot* positive results to report this week?
9. *A couple of* lightning struck our research facility.
10. *A few* chalk were left in the auditorium.
11. *We need *some* advices regarding energy loss when temperature remains constant.
12. *There are *much* differences between centigrade and kelvin temperature scales.

A WORD OF CAUTION

Some languages have only one word that does the work of both English words *much* (for mass nouns) and *many* (for count nouns). If you have this first language experience, be careful not to use *much* for both these quantifiers. Here are some examples of this not infrequent ESL error.

*Do you need *much* books on materials science from the library?

Much items are too expensive for our department to purchase.

*Do you still have *much* problems learning Japanese?

ADVERBS OF FREQUENCY

Like the modifiers that express quantity, the adverbs that express frequency
fall into a range of positive and negative meanings. At the top of the positive
scale is *always* (100 percent) and at the bottom of the negative scale is *never*
(0 percent). This scale can also contain either one or several words at the same
level. The following scale is neither exhaustive nor exact. You can doubtlessly
think of additional adverbs of frequency.

Some Positive and Negative Adverbs of Quantity

always
usually, generally, regularly
often, frequently, ever
sometimes, occasionally

---

not always
not usually, not generally
rarely, seldom, hardly ever, not often
never, not ever

Like the numberlike quantifiers, some of these adverbs have positive-
negative relationships to one another: *usually* and *not usually, generally* and
not generally, often and *not often*. Others are opposites: *always* and *never,
often* and *seldom, frequently* and *rarely*. And you will encounter words and
phrases that don't have pairs in the positive or negative field. Your first task in
selecting an adverb of frequency is to understand where it falls in the scale of
meaning.

THE THERMOMETER EXERCISE

Engineers and scientists are more comfortable if they can assign number
values to expressions of quantity and frequency. The thermometer exercise is
an entertaining way of satisfying this urge to quantify. In the exercise, please
assign a percentage value to each adverb in a graduated list. These values can't
be truly exact; you might think of them as numerical metaphors for vague
words and phrases. Remember, the number values you choose to assign to the
adverbs provided are merely meant to help you visualize more meaningful
placement in a scale. First assign a percentage value to each adverb. Then
place each adverb at an appropriate position on the thermometer. The adverbs
are already arranged in descending order of strength.

Adverbs of Frequency

Use percentages to indicate the meanings of the
adverbs of frequency in the following chart.

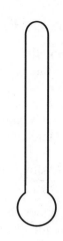

100%	always
_____%	usually
_____%	often
_____%	sometimes
_____%	rarely
_____%	hardly ever
_____%	never

Place each adverb of frequency at an appropriate
position on the thermometer.

PLACEMENT IN SENTENCE

Some adverbs of frequency can occur at the beginning or end of a sentence,
but most of them usually occur in the middle of a sentence. Here is an
alphabetized list of some positive and negative adverbs of frequency, indicating both usual and possible placements.

Placement of Some Common Frequency Adverbs

Adverb	*Placement*
almost always	midsentence
almost never	midsentence
always	midsentence
ever	midsentence
frequently	midsentence, beginning, end
generally	midsentence, beginning, end
hardly ever	midsentence
never	midsentence
not ever	midsentence
occasionally	midsentence, beginning, end
often	midsentence, beginng, end
rarely	midsentence
seldom	midsentence
sometimes	midsentence, beginning, end
usually	midsentence, beginning, end

The following examples show that some adverbs of frequency are flexible in
their sentence position but some are not. The previous list will serve as a useful
reference when you are writing your own sentences.

Flexible Position

Staff meetings are *occasionally* held at noon.
Occasionally staff meetings are held at noon.
Staff meetings are held at noon *occasionally*.

You can *sometimes* turn in your monthly report after the first week.
Sometimes you can turn in your monthly report after the first week.
You can turn in your monthly report after the first week *sometimes*.

Inflexible Position Errors

Staff meetings are held at noon *seldom*.
Never staff meetings are held at noon.
Staff meetings are held at noon *not ever*.

PLACEMENT IN RELATION TO THE VERB

You might also find the following rules for exact placement helpful.

1. After a *to be* verb, the adverb follows present and past verbs.

   Mary Margaret is *always* punctual for her briefings.
   David was *never* on time for his meetings.

2. In a statement, the adverb comes in front of present and past verbs.

   Mary Margaret *always* comes to briefings on time.
   David *never* comes on time to his meetings.

3. Midsentence adverbs come between a helping verb and a main verb.

   Mary Margaret is *usually* finished on time.
   David has *never* completed his monthly report on time.

4. In a question, midsentence adverbs come directly after the subject.

   Does Mary Margaret *often* leave briefings early?
   Did David *never* give you his monthly report?

5. In a negative sentence, most adverbs (except *always* and *ever*) come in front of the negative verb. *Always* and *ever* follow the negative.

   Mary Margaret *usually* doesn't come to briefings late.
   David doesn't *ever* arrive on time.

A FINAL NOTE ON PLACEMENT

Since some adverbs of frequency are negative, you must remember not to use them with a negative verb. This is the old problem of double negation. Double negation is both ungrammatical and self-canceling. Decide in advance if you are going to express your negation in the adverb or in the verb. It's usually a matter of where you wish to place the negative emphasis. Here are some incorrect double negatives involving adverbs of frequency.

Mary Margaret doesn't never present a poor briefing.

David rarely didn't turn in a trip report.

Interestingly, writers have favorite adverbs of frequency. Because there are often several from which to choose, preference is a factor. What are some of your preferred adverbs of frequency?

ADVERBS OF INTENSITY

Other useful adverbs that invest a sentence with increased precision are the intensifiers or emphasizers. These adverbs are used to increase or decrease the strength of an element in the sentence. Essentially, they specify the degree to which an adverb applies. Because the notion of degree operates like the adverbs of frequency, you can also envision these adverbs according to a scale of strength. Unlike adverbs of frequency, however, adverbs of intensity are easy to place. Intensifiers always come before the element they modify. Some examples of intensifiers in action follow.

A Lot

Commercial off-the-shelf (COTS) software is *increasingly* useful for military systems.

It's *definitely* fashionable these days to use COTS instead of customized software.

COTS is *extremely* useful for building office automation suites.

A Little

In comparison to customized software, COTS can be *somewhat* limiting.

It's become *rather* difficult to coordinate all the office communication options available.

It was *barely* possible to keep up with telephone messages and electronic mail; now we have fax messages and voice mail too.

Here's a table of some adverbs of intensity divided according to the notions of a lot or a little. The adverbs are arranged alphabetically within each category. Can you arrange them along a thermometer?

Some Adverbs of Intensity

A Lot	*A Little*
absolutely	barely
definitely	comparatively
even	hardly
extremely	not enough
increasingly	rather
quite	relatively
really	scarcely
very	somewhat

Where would you place *entirely, completely, perfectly, almost, nearly, especially, certainly, surely, fairly, just about, virtually, practically*?

TWO CURIOUS FEATURES

One curious feature of intensifiers is that a few of them can be repeated. In linguistic terminology this repetition is called *reduplication*. The most frequently reduplicated intensifier is *very*. In these examples, it's grammatically correct to repeat the adverb of intensity.

The software code for this project must be *very, very* quickly written.

It's *really, really* important to make the software as transparent as possible.

But such extreme emphasis is hardly appropriate for technical documentation.
Another curious feature of adverbs of intensity is that they can be modified by other intensifiers. Grammatically acceptable examples follow.

The software code for this project must be written *really very* quickly.

User-unfriendly software is *rarely very* effective.

In both examples, the effect is that of strengthening the intensifier. In technical documentation, you need to pause before you elect to intensify an intensifier. It can be tantamount to using an exclamation point—a mark of punctuation rarely used in technical writing where sobriety is the norm.
The use of adverbs of intensity is a low-frequency ESL problem. You probably shouldn't double or modify an adverb if you feel that the result is awkward (rather than incorrect), as in these examples.

Corporate downsizing is *increasingly really* frequent across the United States.

Unemployment is *surely, surely* the result of corporate downsizing, re-gardless of what the President claims.

Repetition of intensifiers and modification of an intensifier by another inten-sifier are commonplace in Anglophone Caribbean islands where these Shake-spearean modes of emphasis are still practiced. The effect is delightful, but a technical editor may not be sympathetic.

The Partitive Puzzle

Logically related to quantification are the English language *partitives*. Partitives are measure words that denote what part or segment of the whole is being specified. Partitives aren't independent parts of speech any more than idioms, modals, or verbals are parts of speech. (See Chapter 5 for a discussion of modals and Chapter 7 for verbals.) Nevertheless, they constitute a fascinating subset of English that causes difficulty for nonnative speakers of English for the simple reason that many of the partititives are deeply rooted in the history and culture of English.

Partitives help us measure material expressed through nouns of mass. They also help to describe quantities encompassed by plural nouns. Because parti-tives promote increased precision, they are important to engineers and scien-tists. They are modest in their syntactic nature (syntax refers to structure: form and order), and are quickly assimilated by speakers of other languages. Be-yond the satisfaction of mastering another subset of grammar, you will derive added delight in your new language from understanding the varied forms and curious origins of partitives.

To facilitate discussion, partitives can be broken into three groups: container-based, portion-based, and quantity-based. There are also some par-titives that are idiomatic; that is, they don't belong to any of these three groups. Often they reflect some physical reality associated with the object measured. And these idiomatic partitives frequently transmit vestiges of ideas inherited from the past. After considering the container-, portion-, and quantity-based partitives and the idiomatic partitives, you'll be able to generalize their basic syntactic pattern. From that information, you'll be qualified to recognize ESL departures from the pattern.

CONTAINER-BASED PARTITIVES

Conventional grammar books usually cite examples of container-based parti-tives from items on the shelves of food stores and supermarkets because these examples are so readily accessible. They are used in everyday life regardless of your occupation or profession.

Some Container-Based Partitives

a bottle of ketchup	a box of crackers
a jar of jelly	a bag of sugar
a carton of juice	a can of peas
a tube of tomato paste	a basket of fruit
a keg of beer	a jug of wine

Without the count word of the partitive phrase, it would be difficult to quantify such mass nouns as *jelly, juice, cereal, sugar,* and *tea.* Commonplace as the foods and beverages in the previous list may be, you would have difficulty telling your spouse what to buy on the way home from work if you didn't have the partitives as tools.

PORTION-BASED PARTITIVES

Similar to the container-based partitives are those that employ notions of portion. These may be somewhat more abstract because there is certainly nothing more concrete than a jar or a can or a box. While you may have no trouble with *a loaf of bread* or *a slice of cake* (both portions) you may have some trouble with *a pinch of salt* or *a bit of trouble.*

Some Portion-Based Partitives

a loaf of bread	a piece of candy
a pinch of salt	a mound of grits
a bit of seasoning	a shot of whiskey
a slug of gin	a serving of pie
a slice of cake	a dose of medicine
a drop of vanilla	a dollop of gravy

QUANTITY-BASED PARTITIVES

The quantity-based partitives rely on measures of weight, length, or size. These are not only easier to understand, but they are also more likely to occur in technical or scientific descriptions.

Some Quantity-Based Partitives

a quart of milk	a pound of rice
a bushel of corn	a gallon of cider
an ounce of salt	a yard of fabric
a pint of cream	a peck of berries
a bale of hay	a cord of wood
a pound of pressure	a ton of steel
a foot of cable	an inch of fiber
a byte of memory	a bit of RAM

Partitives also include some curious count or measure words. They may reflect some physical feature of a fruit, vegetable, or other natural material.

Some Idiomatic Partitives

a head of lettuce	an ear of corn
a stalk of celery	a stick of cinnamon
a head of cabbage	a bunch of grapes
a hand of bananas	a clove of garlic
a clump of grass	a bunch of flowers
a hank of wool	a cake of soap

GENERALIZED PATTERN

From all these examples of various types of partitives, you can easily generalize a rule for their formation:

a (or number) + partitive + of + noun.

With this formula, you can now designate exact quantities for mass nouns. The mass nouns are italicized in the following sentences. They have become countable by the addition of the partitive phrase.

We added six bytes of *memory* to my computer.

Junko placed two drops of *serum* onto the petri dish.

Our supervisor bought six gallons of *punch* for the party.

The force was increased by three orders of *magnitude*.

EXCEPTIONS TO THE PATTERN

When the partitive is a number word, the inclusion of the preposition *of* becomes ungrammatical. This exception to the pattern produces the major ESL partitive error. Because the formation rule is so widely applied, nonnative speakers will apply it universally. This is known as the ESL error of overgeneralization.

A *thousand* people watched the experiment.
*A *thousand* of people watched the experiment.

A *hundred* samples supported the conclusion.
*A *hundred* of samples supported the conclusion.

A *dozen* tests produced the same results.
*A *dozen* of tests produced the same results.

A *million* votes in his favor will not convince me.
*A *million of* votes in his favor will not convince me.
*Incorrect sentences.

When the partitive is a number word, it remains singular even though it may be modified by a number greater than one. This constitutes the second most frequent ESL partitive error. It's tempting to inflect the partitive in response to its modifier, but you must resist this temptation when the partitive is a number word.

Two thousand people watched the experiment.
**Two thousands* people watched the experiment.

Three hundred samples supported the conclusion.
**Three hundreds* samples supported the conclusion.

Four dozen tests produced the same results.
**Four dozens* tests produced the same results.

Five million votes in his favor will not convince me.
**Five millions* votes in his favor will not convince me.
*Incorrect sentences.

As a subset of these exceptions, the preposition *of* is reintroduced but the article (or number) is dropped when the partitive is general rather than specific.

Hundreds of samples supported the conclusion.
**Hundreds samples* supported the conclusion.

Dozens of tests produced the same results.
**Dozens tests* produced the same results.

Hosts of employees were forced into early retirement.
**Hosts employees* were forced into early retirement.

Waves of refugees left when the border was opened.
**Waves refugees* left when the border was opened.
*Incorrect sentences.

Application Exercise I

In Figure 6.2, you'll find an internal order form used at a large corporation. The form is to be sent to the corporation's stationery supply department. Note that a number of different designators are used to indicate the size of your order for

QUANTITY					QUANTITY			
CODE	NO.OF UNITS	UNIT PACK	DESCRIPTION	CODE	NO.OF UNITS	UNIT PACK	DESCRIPTION	
BINDERS, LOOSELEAF SUPPLIES, AND REPORT COVERS				**DESK ACCESSORIES**				
1005		Ea	Accopress-11 x 8-1/2, Dk Blue					
1010		Ea	Cover—Amberg 11 x 8-1/2, Blue	1405		Pr	Bookends—Black Steel	
1015		Ea .	Date Binder—14-7/8 x 11, Lt. Green	1410		Ea	Calendar Base—Standard, Brown	
1020		Ea	Date Binder—11 x 14-7/8, Dk. Blue	1415		Ea	Calendar Refill—Standard	
1025		Pkg/C	Filler Sheets—11 x 8-1/2—3HP, Ruled	1420		Ea	Copyholder—Metal, Tan	
1030		Pkg/C	Filler Sheets—8-1/2 x 5-1/2—3HP, Ruled	1425		Ea	Desk Blotter—Green	
1035		Pkg/25 tabs	Indexes—Blue, 1/5 Cut, 11 x 8-1/2, 3HP	1430		Ea	Desk Blotter Cover—Acetate	
1040		Set	Indexes A-Z, 3HP, 8-1/2 x 5-1/2	1435		Ea	Desk Pad—with Blotter	
1045		Set	Indexes—A-Z, 3HP, 11 x 8-1/2	1440		Ea	Knife—Xacto	
1050		Set	Indexes—Data Binder, 11 x 14-7/8	1445		Ea	Letter Opener	
1055		Set	Indexes—Data Binder, 14-7/8 x 11	1450		Ea	Memo Holder—for #1180 4 x 6 loose sheets	
1060		Box	Reinforcements, Gummed	1460		Ea	Paper Clip Bowl	
1065		Ea	Ring Binder—11 x 8-1/2, Blk., 1" Capacity	1465		Ea	Pencil Sharpener—Wall Mount	
1070		Ea	Ring Binder—11 x 8-1/2, Blk., 2" Capacity	1470		Ea	Punch—Paper, 3 Hole	
1075		Ea	Ring Binder—8-1/2 x 5-1/2, Blk., 1" Capacity	1475		Ea	Rack—Eldon Add-A-File, Plastic, Beige	
1080		Box/50	Sheet Protector—Acetate, 11 x 8-1/2, 3HP, for ring bndr.	1480		Ea	Ruler—Wood with metal edge, 15"	
				1485		Pr	Scissors—7"	
				1490		Ea	Stapler—Desk Model	
BOOKS, PADS, AND PAPER SUPPLIES				1495		Ea	Staple Remover	
1100		Ea	Add Rolls—2-1/4" wide	1500		Ea	Stationery Rack—Desk Drawer type (holds letterhead & envelopes)	
1105		Pkg/10	Carbon Paper—8-1/2 x 11, Solvent					
1110		Pad	Columnar Pad—11 x 8-1/2, 6 col.	1505		Ea	Telephone List Finder—Complete	
1115		Pad	Columnar Pad—11 x 16-3/8, 13 col.	1510		Ea	Telephone List Finder—Refill	
1120		Ea	Notebook—Spiral Bound, 3 x 5	1515		Ea	Tray—Eldon Stackable, Letter, Plastic, Beige	
1125		Ea	Notebook—Spiral Bound, 11 x 8-1/2	1520		Ea	Typewriter Pad	
1130		Ea	Notebook—6 x 9, Steno					
1135		Pad	Pad—Scratch, 8-1/2 x 11, White, 1/4" Ruled (Narrow)					
1140		Pad	Pad—Scratch, 8-1/2 x 11, White, 3/8" Ruled (Wide)	**ENVELOPES**				
1145		Pad	Pad—Scratch, 8-1/2 x 11, Canary, 3/8" Ruled	1600		Ea	Clasp—7 x 10	
1155		Pad	Pad—Graph, 8-1/2 x 11, 1/4" Squares	1605		Ea	Gummed—9-1/2 x 12-1/2	
1160		Pad	Pad—Graph, 17 x 11, 1/4" Squares	1610		Ea	Clasp—11-1/2 x 14-1/2	
1165		Pad	Pad—Graph, 17 x 22, 1/4" Squares	1615		Ea	Clasp—12 x 15-1/2	
1175		Pad	Pad—Plain White, 34 x 22	1620		Ea	Classified—11-1/2 x 14-1/2	
1180		Pkg/200	Refill—4 x 6 White, Loose, for #1450 memo holder	1625		Ea	Expanding—10 x 15	
1182		Ream	Paper—Letterhead	1630		Pkg/25	Inter-Office—4-1/8 x 9-1/2 Buff, no holes	
1184		Ream	Paper—Plain, Use With 1182	1635		Bx/C	Inter-Office—10 x 13, with holes	
1186		Ream	Paper—Memorandum	1645		Pkg/C	Inter-Office—4-1/2 x 10-3/8 with holes #11	
1188		Ream	Paper—Plain Use With 1186	1650		Pkg/25	White—4-1/8 x 9-1/2, with Bedford return address	
1190		Pad	While You Were Out					
1194		Pad	Memo, Mitre 5-1/2 x 8-1/2	**FILING SUPPLIES**				
1195		Pad	Post-It-Notes, 3 x 5	1700		Pkg/100	Cards 3 x 5 Ruled White	
1197		Pad/25	Requisition for Stationery Products	1705		Pkg/100	Cards 4 x 6 Ruled White	
1198		Pad/25	Requisition for MCF Forms	1710		Pkg/100	Cards 5 x 8 Ruled White	
				1715		Set	Card Guides 3 x 5 Buff, A-Z	
CLIPS, CLAMPS, FASTENERS				1720		Set	Card Guides 4 x 6 Buff, A-Z	
1200		Bx/50	Accopress Fastener—2-3/4" C to C	1725		Set	Card Guides 5 x 8 Buff, A-Z	
1205		Bx/50	Accopress Fastener—8-1/2" C to C	1730		Ea	"Out" File Guides, letter size	
1210		Bx/12	Binder Clips—3/4" wide, #20—3/8" CAP	1735		Ea	"Open/Closed" Guides for File cabinet	
1215		Bx/12	Binder Clips—1-1/4" wide, #50—5/8" CAP	1740		Ea	File Box—3 x 5 x 3	
1220		Bx/12	Binder Clips—2" wide, #100—1" CAP	1745		Ea	File Box—4 x 6 x 4	
1225		Bx/12	Paper Clamp—X-type, Large	1750		Ea	File Box—5 x 8 x 6	
1230		Bx/50	Paper Clamp—X-type, Medium	1755		Bx/25	Folder—Hanging, letter, 1/3	
1235		Bx/100	Paper Clips—#1, Standard Size	1760		Bx/25	Folder—Hanging, letter-2" Box Bottom	
1240		Bx/C	Paper Fastener—Round Head, 2"	1765		Bx/C	Folder—Manila, letter-1/3	
1245		Bx/C	Paper Fastener—Round Head, 1-1/4"	1770		Set	Frames—Hanging, letter size	
				1780		Ea	Magazine File, 11-3/4 x 9	
CORRECTION SUPPLIES				1785		Pkg/100	Blank Inserts for Tabs, White	
1300		Ea	Correction Fluid—White					
1303		Ea	Correction Fluid for Photo Copies	**LABELS—PRESS-A-PLY**				
1305		Ea	Correction Fluid Thinner	1800		Roll/250	File Folder Label—White	
1310		Roll	Tape—One typewriter line wide-1/6"	1805		Roll/250	File Foler Label—Yellow	
1315		Roll	Tape—Two typewriter lines wide-2/6"	1810		Roll/250	File Folder Label—Red	
1320		Roll	Tape—Five typewriter lines wide-5/6"					

FIGURE 6.2 Stationery store order form.

CODE	NO.OF UNITS	UNIT PACK	DESCRIPTION	CODE	NO.OF UNITS	UNIT PACK	DESCRIPTION
			LABELS—PRESS-A-PLY (cont'd)				**MISCELLANEOUS OFFICE SUPPLIES**
1815		Roll/250	File Folder Label—Green	2320		Can	Cleaner—Desk Spray
1820		Roll/250	File Folder Label—Dark Blue	2325		Ea	Cleaner—Hand for grease, ink, dirt
1825		Pkg/120	Plain—4 x 2 White	2330		Ea	Clipboard—Letter size
1830		Box/1000	Labels, Plain, 5/16" x 1/2"	2335		Ea	Eraser—Pink Pearl
				2340		Ea	Eraser—Pencil, Stick Style
			RIBBONS	2345		Ea	Eraser—Typewriter, Pencil type with brush
1900		Ea	IBM—Selectric 71	2350		Ea	Eraser—Art Gum, 1 x 1 x 1
1925		Ea	IBM, Correctable, Orange Code for SEL II & III	2355		Ea	Eraser—Chalkboard, Felt
1930		Ea	IBM, Lift-Off Tape, Orange Code, Use w/1925	2360		Ea	Hangers—Coat, Wooden
1940		Ea	Calculator Ribbon B/R	2365		Ea	Ink, Black, 2 oz. for Stamp Pad
				2370		Ea	Ink, Red, 2 oz., for Stamp Pad
				2373		Pk/10	Magnets
			TAPES AND TAPE DISPENSERS	2375		Ea	Protector—Acetate folder for Multilith Masters
2000		Ea	Dispenser—Hand, Plastic, 3/4"	2377		Pkg	Paper Towels
2005		Ea	Dispenser—Desk, 3" Core	2380		Bx/1/4 lb.	Rubber Bands—1/4 lb. 16 (small)
2010		Roll	Tape (for VuGraphs) 3/4" x 60 yds. 3" Core	2385		Bx/1/4 lb.	Rubber Bands—1/4 to 33 (medium)
2015		Roll	Tape—Double Coated, 1" x 36 yds.	2390		Ea	Glue Stick
2020		Roll	Tape—Masking, 1" x 60 yds.	2395		Ea	Rubber Finger Tips—Size 11-1/2
2025		Roll	Tape—Masking, 2" x 60 yds.	2400		Ea	Rubber Finger Tips—Size 12
2030		Roll	Tape—Transparent, 1" Core, 3/4" x 1296"	2405		Ea	Stamp Pad—Felt, Size #1, Black
2035		Roll	Tape—Transparent, 3" Core, 3/4" x 2592"	2410		Ea	Stamp Pad—Felt, Size #1, Red
				2415		Bx/5M	Staples—Standard (to fit desk stapler #1490)
				2420		Ball	String, White
			WRITING INSTRUMENTS	2425		Bx/50	Tabs—White Plain
2100		Pkg/12	Chalk White—Dustless	2430		Bx/5	Tabs—Mark-Ur-Own, 1/2" Clear (5-6" strips/bx)
2105		Pkg/12	Chalk—Assorted Colors	2435		Pk/50	Tay—Key, White, 1-3/4" Diam.
2110		Ea	China Marker (Grease Pencil), Red	2440		Bx/C	Thumb Tacks—3/8"
2115		Ea	China Marker (Grease Pencil), Green				
2120		Ea	China Marker (Grease Pencil), Black				**RUBBER STAMPS**
2122		Ea	Highlighter, Green	2500		Ea	Date
2123		Ea	Highlighter, Yellow	2505		Ea	Unclassified
2125		Ea	Marker—Felt Tip, Broad Point, Blue	2510		Ea	Secret
2130		Ea	Marker—Felt Tip, Broad Point, Black	2515		Ea	Confidential
2135		Ea	Marker—Felt Tip, Broad Point, Red	2520		Ea	Privileged
2163		Ea	Pen—Ball Point, Fine Black	2525		Ea	Open By Addressee Only
2165		Ea	Pen—Ball Point, Med. Black	2530		Ea	Personal
2170		Set	Pen Set—Desk, Pen and Base, Med. Point, Black	2535		Ea	Corporation Use Only
2175		Ea	Pen—Replacement for Desk Set, includes refill	2540		Ea	Proprietary Info.
2180		Ea	Refill—to fit Desk Pen Set, Med. Pt., Blue	2545		Ea	Controlled Distribution
2185		Ea	Refill—to fit Desk Pen Set, Med. Pt., Black	2550		Ea	When Separated from ... Page is Unclassified
2190		Bx/12	Pencil—Writing #1	2555		Ea	Draft
2195		Bx/12	Pencil—Writing #2	2560		Ea	Original Signed By
2200		Ea	Pencil—Non-Reproducing, Sky BLue	2565		Ea	Block Unclassified (Downgrading Stamp)
2205		Ea	Pencil—Non-Reproducing, Non Photo Blue	2570		Ea	Block, Confidential (Downgrading Stamp)
2210		Ea	Pencil—Colored, White	2575		Ea	Source Selection Sensitive
2215		Ea	Pencil—Colored, Purple				
2220		Ea	Pencil—Colored, Black				
2225		Ea	Pencil—Colored, Orange				**TRANSFER SHEETS**
2230		Ea	Pencil—Colored, Brown	2600		Sheet	Arrows and Diamonds (Large)
2235		Ea	Pencil—Colored, Blue	2605		Sheet	Arrows and Diamonds (small) 17134
2240		Ea	Pencil—Colored, Red	2610		Sheet	Mathematical Symbols 9872
2245		Ea	Pencil—Colored, Yellow	2615		Sheet	Dots (large) 9874
2250		Ea	Pencil—Colored, Green	2620		Sheet	Greek and Mathematical Symbols 10108
2255		Ea	Pencil—for VuGraphs #1550, Blue	2625		Sheet	Brackets 9879
2260		Ea	Pencil—for Vu Graphs #1550, Yellow	2630		Sheet	Dots (small) 10356
2265		Ea	Pencil—for VuGraphs #1550, Black				**VELLUM PAPER**
2270		Ea	Pencil—for VuGraphs #1550, Orange	2700		Sheet	Vellum Plain 8-1/2 x 11
2275		Ea	Pencil—for Vu Graphs #1550, Violet	2705		Sheet	Vellum Grid 4 x 4-8-1/2 x 11
2280		Ea	Pencil—for Vu Graphs #1550, Brown	2710		Sheet	Vellum Grid 4 x 4-11 x 17
2285		Ea	Pencil—for Vu Graphs, #1550, White	2715		Sheet	Vellum Grid 4 x 4-17 x 22
2290		Ea	Pencil—for VuGraphs, #1550, Red	2720		Sheet	Vellum Grid 8 x 8-8-1/2 x 11
			MISCELLANEOUS OFFICE SUPPLIES	2725		Sheet	Vellum 8 x 8-11 x 17
2300		Ea	Acetate—Clear, 8-1/2 x 11	2730		Sheet	Vellum Grid 10 x 10-8-1/2 x 11
2305		Pkg/15	Blades—Xacto, Rounded #10	2735		Sheet	Vellum Grid 10 x 10-11 x 17
2310		Pkg/15	Blades—Xacto, Pointed #11				
2315		Ea	Cassette—Dictating, 60 min.				

DELIVER TO STATIONERY STORES—E060

BX = Box   C = Hundred   M = Thousand   Dz = Dozen   Ea = Each   Pk = Pack   Pr = Pair   Rl = Roll each item. Some of the designators are container-based and some are portion-based; many are quantity-based.

A shortened version of the order form will enable you to work more quickly. All the supplies on the shortened form are available from the stationery supply department. First fill in the appropriate partitive for each item you wish to order. Then indicate whether it's container-based, portion-based, or quantity-based. Are there any items that don't fit into the three categories? Here's an alphabetized list of the applicable partitives.

a ball of	a pair of
a box of	a ream of
a can of	a roll of
a jar of	a set of
a package of	a sheet of
a pad of	

Stationery Store Order Form Short Version

Quantity	Unit	Item
6		filler sheets
1		card guides
2		reinforcements
1		graph paper
1		letter paper
1		paper fasteners
2		scotch tape
1		scissors
1		envelopes
1		string
2		math symbols
1		desk cleaner
2		glue

APPLICATION EXERCISE II

What are some plural or mass nouns that the following partitives could describe?

liters of	ounces of
grams of	molecules of
amperes of	particles of
watts of	degrees of
units of	rods of
reels of	pixels of

The Idiom Conundrum

Idiomatic expressions are conundrums. (Webster's calls a conundrum "an intricate and difficult problem," among other definitions.) The difficulty lies in the fact that there is no grammatical explanation for an idiom. For this reason, ESL grammar texts don't even talk about idioms. There's nothing to talk about.

From a linguistic viewpoint, idioms are expressions with meanings that are *noncompositional*. That is to say, these often complex expressions can't be understood by adding together the meanings of their constituents. Further, they are peculiar to a language or to some level of usage within a language. Consequently, there's no transfer of idioms from one language to another. That's probably the first lesson to learn: An idiom in one language isn't an idiom in another. Having learned that first lesson, however, you're spared all the errors that result from trying to apply to your target language what you know from your first language. In sum, there's no way to learn idioms other than to memorize them and use them.

Can you translate these ten idiomatic expressions that you might encounter in the workplace? The idioms in the statements or questions are italicized. Note that some idioms can be used only in the positive sense while others can be used in both positive and negative sentences.

Don't *make a big issue over* our failure to deliver on time.

She *can't help talking about* her daughter's new patent.

We'll have to *cut down on* our expenses by introducing an early retire-ment program.

They're *grasping at straws* by submitting this proposal.

This new initiative won't *make or break* our department.

Now that the initiative has failed, our supervisor will have to *take his medicine like a man*.

I *have half a mind* to turn in my resignation.

Will the CEO *lay it on the line* at next week's forum?

Fractal creators with his talent are *few and far between*.

Our design was accepted so we don't have to *go back to square one*.

EACH A LAW UNTO ITSELF

Not only is there no grammar to explain idioms, there's no grammar that binds them. An idiomatic expression may violate grammar, and it often violates logic.

Nevertheless, it will be acceptable. It's acceptable because it's widely used and widely understood. In this respect it differs from slang which is never widely understood and may or may not be widely used. Of course, saying that an idiom is widely understood means that it's widely understood by native speakers of a language. For a nonnative speaker, it can be unintelligible. If you had just arrived in the United States, would you be able to interpret these idiomatic expressions if you overheard them in a public place?

My old man just *kicked the bucket.*

Poor Sarah *wears her heart on her sleeve.*

He *made a pass at* me last night.

She won the lottery; *eat your heart out!*

Keep a stiff upper lip during the company reorganization.

He keeps his windows open during the coldest weather. I think he *has bats in his belfry.*

His accusation is *the pot calling the kettle black.*

The issue was *a tempest in a teapot.*

I believe the new consultant is *a flash in the pan.*

My boss told me to go through the files *with a fine tooth comb.*

Never Literal

Part of the unintelligibility of idioms derives from the fact that the combination of words doesn't mean what the words say. The combination creates an entirely new meaning, the source of which is quickly forgotten. The speed of forgetting suggests that idioms are more informal than formal: that they have their origins in conversation. That doesn't mean that they won't be used in the technical or scientific workplace.

Shifting Terms

You've already learned that an idiom can't be interpreted through semantics (meaning of the words) and that it can't be generalized through structure (syntax). Beyond all that, a single idiom may have close variants with slightly shifting terms. Idiomatic expressions frequently contain adverbs or prepositions plus other parts of speech. With a change of preposition, either the meaning or the use of the idiom may change. As a result, you may select the "wrong" preposition for your idiomatic expression and be considered ignorant at worse or be judged incorrect at best.

A commonplace example of this situation involves the verb *to differ* plus a preposition. The idiomatic bundle requires that you say *differ with* when you're talking about your position relative to another person's, and that you say *differ from* when you're talking about a contrast between two objects.

With a Person

Professor Baldwin *differs with* Professor Goodwin on the limitations of superconductivity.

About an Object

The Celsius scale *differs from* the Farenheit scale on the location of its zero point.

About a Question

You and I *differ over* the practicality and costs of super-conducting technology.

No Quick Tips

In London some decades ago, people realized that idioms were becoming a big problem. People in England became aware of this earlier than people in the United States because immigrants from all over the former empire were coming to live in London. British English is every bit as idiomatic as American English, and people coming from Pakistan and India, as examples, could not understand the idiomatic expressions that were bandied about every day. Even though many people from the former empire had studied English in school, their schoolroom English was too formal to include commonplace idioms.

Very quickly most bookstores in London and in the large cities of England began to carry little dictionaries of English idioms. Some of the dictionaries weren't so little. One, *A Learner's Dictionary of English Idioms*, contains over 5,500 entries.[1] Another, *Test Yourself on English Idioms*, recommends that the reader pick it up at odd moments "in a bus, in a train, or sitting under a coconut tree."[2] Even though this book is small, it contains 95 pages of self-tests. Little and not-so-little books of idiomatic expressions are now turning up in bookstores in the United States. If idioms interest you, you might visit your local bookshop to see what's available.

[1] Isabel McCaig and Martin H. Manser. *A Learner's Dictionary of English Idioms*. Oxford: Oxford University Press, 1986.

[2] M. J. Murphy. *Test Yourself on English Idioms*. London: Hodder and Stoughton, 1987.

British English and American English

A vast majority of idioms are interchangeable between British English and American English. It's always surprising to hear the same idiomatic expressions being used on both sides of the Atlantic Ocean. You should not be surprised, however, to learn that there are some idioms in one dialect (calling both American English and British English dialects begs the question of which is superior) that don't exist in the other. For example, in the United States it's not unusual to say, "That doesn't *amount to a hill of beans*," an idiomatic expression that isn't used in England. In England you might hear someone say, "Jeremy talks to shopkeepers *with a plum in his mouth*" or "The time has come for us *to grasp the nettle*," two idioms that don't exist in the United States.

It's important to talk about differences between the two dialects because so many nonnative speakers of English in the United States studied English in countries where British English is the standard. If that describes your personal situation, you may be unprepared for differences between the two dialects in areas such as idioms, spelling, word choice, grammar, intonation, pronunciation, and even measurement systems. The point to remember is that once you are living and working in the United States, you are expected to use American English. A doctoral candidate in a North American university serves as an example of someone who failed to learn that lesson. She had to revise (and retype) her 500-page doctoral dissertation because it was written in British English. Her committee chairman told her that she was now in America, and if she expected to graduate from an American university, she had to revise her dissertation to reflect that fact. The unexpected revision added a year to her program. To protect yourself from such dire consequences, you need to know the differences between the two dialects.

Another reason for understanding these differences relates to publication and research in your discipline. As a professional in the United States, you'll read books and articles published overseas. Invariably, overseas publishers favor British English over American English. You will, as a consequence, find elements of style and grammar that clash with what you've learned in the United States. You'll be less confused if you realize that you are encountering the rules of a different dialect, and you won't feel compelled to adapt your own writing to conform to a new model. Further, as a professional from the United States you may submit articles for publication overseas. Which English should you use? Write in American English and let the editors in England or Denmark change your punctuation to suit themselves. Don't take offense because they don't accept American English.

Some of the differences of intonation and pronunciation will be discussed in the chapter on spoken English. This chapter will describe differences in word choice, spelling, punctuation, grammar, and measurement systems.

WORD CHOICE

Word choice is called *diction* by language experts. Diction in the linguistic sense does not refer to clear speech as taught years ago in elocution lessons. It refers to the effectiveness, correctness, and appropriateness of each word you select. Because the selection of exact words is one of your top priorities as a technical writer, you doubtlessly realize that shades of meaning and peculiarities of usage are matters of vital concern.

As a scientific or technical writer you have an enormous advantage over writers from other trades or professions. You have a large built-in vocabulary that is understood internationally. Technical terminology is not jargon. It's the hallmark of a discipline. It not only conveys specific meaning, it acts as a code that informs readers everywhere, that you belong to a society of brothers and sisters.

While technical vocabulary communicates around the world, general vocabulary can be problematic. The function words like prepositions and conjunctions are fairly safe territory. However, nouns and verbs are more dangerous. Some nouns have very different overseas cousins. *Truck* and *lorry* don't share any similarities, and such dissonance can have real repercussions. For example, during a recent visit to London, a close friend ended up in the hospital because as a pedestrian she first looked in the wrong direction to check for oncoming traffic, and then turned to ask a passerby what he meant when he said, "Look out for the lorry." Most of the differences listed here will be familiar to you, and it's very likely that you can contribute additions to the list.

Some Differences in Word Choice

American	*British*
truck	lorry
car trunk	boot
gasoline	petrol
battery	accumulator
rotary	roundabout
underpass	subway
wrench	spanner
antenna	aerial
lawyer	barrister, solicitor
taxes	rates
elevator	lift

Expressions that are peculiar to British English are called *Briticisms.* Using Briticisms in the United States can cause confusion or even lack of comprehension. What might be the effect of using the following Briticisms in an American office?

1. "Ms. Myers, please add this item to my *docket*."

   Answer: Ms. Myers doesn't know whether to add an appointment to her boss's calendar or to file the paper in his personal folder.

2. "Nick, send me a *chit* to use for Friday's meeting in Washington."

   Answer: Unsure of what *chit* means, Nick doesn't know if his colleague wants a travel expense voucher or a brief note about a point of discussion.

3. "Patrick, I'd really appreciate it if you would use the *tram* to take our visitor sightseeing in Boston."

   Answer: The only tram Patrick knows is the one that goes up to the top of Mt. Washington in New Hampshire. He doesn't recognize this word for *streetcar*, and he fails to understand that his supervisor wants him to save money by not using a taxi.

4. "Judy, let's take the *underground* to go to lunch at the Chowder House."

   Answer: Judy would prefer to go to the restaurant by way of the street rather than through a tunnel somewhere.

5. "Elaine, please *post* this announcement before Senor Alvarez arrives at ten o'clock."

   Answer: Elaine doesn't know if she should tack the announcement onto the office bulletin board, or mail it immediately. She'll probably tack it up rather than ask her boss for a mailing address. This is the wrong decision.

An Exercise in Realia

While the previous examples of Briticism usage are creations for the *ESL Resource Book*, here are some samples of realia—examples from real documentation. These examples are from a British brochure about information systems management. The sentences are entirely understandable but they contain expressions that simply aren't used in the United States. See if you can detect the Briticisms.

1. "An invitation to tender will be sent to a short list of possible suppliers."

   Comment: In the United States, an *invitation to tender* would be an RFP—a request for proposal.

2. "For some, outsourcing is a portmanteau word that embraces the supply of anything from office cleaning to software packages."

Comment: In the United States, *portmanteau word* probably wouldn't be used. The sentence might read, "outsourcing is a collection of services including anything from. . . ."

3. "A U.S.-based manufacturer of lighting equipment has developed technical standards that enable the systems to interwork with independent field agents."

   Comment: To *interwork* is never used in the United States. Like *outwith* and *inwith, interwork* might be expressed by a phrase, *work in cooperation with*. Alternatively, it might be expressed by a word frequently used when talking about systems engineering: *interconnectivity—the systems would have interconnectivity with field agents.*

4. "Decentralising IS may get it closer to the customer, but it can also result in a rag bag of incompatible equipment and software."

   Comment: There are two items of note in this sentence. First, *decentralising* is spelled differently. Second, *rag bag* seems an old-fashioned concept that wouldn't appear in an American technical or business brochure. Perhaps an American brochure would use the expression *mixed bag*.

5. "A checklist of items that should be considered is shown overleaf."

   Comment: *Overleaf* is not a familiar word in the United States. The sentence would read, "A checklist of items that should be considered is shown on the next page."

Although the United States and the United Kingdom share a common language, it is used differently in London, England, from the way it is used in Washington, D.C.

All the preceding sample words and sentences show that using Briticisms in the American workplace results in a lack of clarity that ranges from incomprehension or misunderstanding to a sense of uncomfortable unfamiliarity. A few people from the United Kingdom or from countries where schooling follows the British system may preserve their Briticisms in an effort to distinguish themselves. It's understandable that men and women like to be a bit different from their associates, but to establish such a difference by using incompatible language is frivolous, especially in the worlds of science and technology.

SPELLING AND PUNCTUATION

Spelling differs between British and American English in seven areas. You may be able to enrich this discussion by adding other areas of difference.

Some Areas of Spelling Difference

Difference	British	American	Comment
preservation of -*our* spelling: -our/-or	honour, valour, color, splendor	honor, valor, color, splendor	American spelling is simplified; British displays Norman (French) influence.
inversion of final -re/-er	theatre, centre, litre	theater, center, liter	American spelling is modernized; British exhibits Middle English -re.
American substitution of z for middle s	centralisation, civilisation, customisation	centralization, civilization, customization	American spelling more closely approximates pronunciation.
British double letters	programme aerogramme (but) cardiogram (but) halogram (but) telegram	program air letter hologram cardiogram telegram	American spelling is simplified; British displays Norman (French) influence; Briitish begins to display American influence.
some past tense formations	dreamt, burnt smelt, spelt, spoilt	dreamed, burned smelled, spelled spoiled	Spellings approximate pronunciation differences between dialects.

Difference	British	American	Comment
American substitution of end z for s	realise, analyse, apologise, customise	realize, analyze, apologize, customize	American spelling more closely approximates pronunciation.
end c and end s	defence, offence, licence	defense, offense, license	British closer to spelling of Latin roots.
miscellany	gaol, gaoler tyre kerb story specialty cheque	jail, jailer tire curb storey specialty check	Various explanations; British usually exhibits an older form or a closer reflection of Norman influence.

It's sufficient to note that spelling differences exist in some areas between the two dialects. The reasons are of no consequence. It does appear that American spelling in general has moved toward simplification and away from middle English or Normanized English. However, there doesn't seem to be any reliable rule to enable you to generalize in which cases simplification has taken place, or where simplification might take place in the future.

PUNCTUATION

American English punctuation has also departed from that of British English. The differences do not affect every mark of punctuation. They are confined to punctuation with quotations. The underlying difference is that the British English system is entirely logical whereas American English punctuation has changed in response to an arbitrary system devised by typesetters and proof-readers in the U.S.

The American system was devised to save time. If compositors who set lead type had to stop to figure out the internal logic of each quotation in text they were typesetting, their jobs would have taken much longer. Accordingly, a standard was devised whereby the two most frequently used marks of punctuation (comma and period) would arbitrarily always fall inside a closing quotation mark. Less frequently used end stops (question mark and exclamation point) were left to follow the British system. In these cases, compositors did have to stop to figure out where to set the marks with relation to the closing quotation mark. Similarly, the proofreaders had to stop to check if the compositors had worked out correctly the internal logic of each sentence that included a quotation. These vestiges of the British system were more time-consuming, but they didn't occur anywhere near as often as the comma and period. The result was a composite system that looks like this.

American Punctuation with Quotation Marks

Punctuation Mark	Relation to Closing Quotation Mark	Example
comma and period	always inside	"Scientists launched ozone-mapping balloons and rockets yesterday," said a NASA spokesman.
semicolon and colon	always outside	We looked up the following in Spencer's article entitled "Some Everyday Acronyms": WYSIWYG, COTS, MIS, and LAN.
question mark and exclamation point	outside quotation mark unless it's part of the quotation	Did she say, "my computer has enough memory"?
		"Has my computer enough memory?" she asked.

For unexplainable reasons (one would not wish to cite ignorance as a reason), some American copyeditors, proofreaders, and even consultants in technical documentation have ignored this standard. Either because they're enamored of British standards or because they have personal views on the subject, they resist the rules regarding the comma, period, and the two colons.

At first a feeble explanation was offered to the effect that the advent of word processing required a change in the rules. The reasoning was that if commas and periods were placed inside the closing quotation mark, computer commands will be garbled. The example provided was something like this:

Input the command "LOGON."

True. If you type LOGON. (with a period included in the command), you will have a computer reaction that differs from the reaction produced by typing LOGON (without a mark of punctuation). Of course, this argument became invalid as soon as word processors progressed to the point where they were typesetters instead of typewriters. Everyone who operates a computer has become a compositor of sorts.

Typewriters $\Rightarrow$ Word Processors $\Rightarrow$ Computers

Not as knowledgeable as professional typesetters about producing kerning, inserting rules, bleeding pages, and recognizing point differences, we can nevertheless recognize when it's not necessary to overturn a rule of grammar.

With the ability to use italics, you no longer need to type quotation marks to indicate a special word. Now special words are italicized and no additional marks are required to set them off. However, despite the fact that the original rationale for ignoring the American standard for punctuation has disappeared, would-be experts continue to support the changed standard, thereby confusing the issue. As a technical writer, you are encouraged to follow the American punctuation system illustrated in this discussion. It will enable you to write more quickly, more easily, and more correctly.

COLLECTIVE NOUNS

Collective nouns are an element of grammar that elicits different responses from the two dialects. A collective noun describes a group of persons or items considered to be one unit. All the members of the group share similar characteristics. Collective nouns are not unlike mass nouns in this respect. Here are some examples of collective nouns.

Some Collective Nouns

army	group
assembly	herd
clergy	jury
committee	mob
company	multitude
couple	orchestra
crew	pair
crowd	personnel
family	squad
flock	team

Both British and American English require verbs to agree with subject nouns or pronouns. This agreement is largely a matter of number: A singular subject takes a singular verb and a plural subject takes a plural verb. In American English, collectives are considered singular in number. This rule is excepted only when the writer wishes to signal that the constituents of the group are to be considered as individuals. Most frequently, however, in American English the collective is treated as singular and the verb is also singular.

> The U.S. Army *grows* smaller every month as the current administration cuts the budget for military spending.

> NASA *has* launched 17 weather balloons and 19 small rockets from Wallops Island, Virginia, in support of the ozone-mapping survey.

> The crew of space shuttle Atlantis *plans* to make its own survey of the Earth's ozone layer.

British English observes the opposite rule. It considers collective nouns as plurals; verbs agree accordingly.

> The jury *have* requested pizzas to be sent to the jury room.

> Throughout the year, the government *have* progressively cut the budget for military spending.

> The shuttle crew *were* pleased with the survey results.

MEASUREMENT SYSTEMS

At first, the United Kingdom and the United States used the same system of measurement: the English system. Europe and the rest of the world adopted the metric system that was introduced in France early in the eighteenth century.

THE METRIC SYSTEM

The metric system covers weights, measures of capacity, measures of length, and measures of surface area. All the measures are related by decimal multipliers, unlike the English system in which these measures were independently defined. (The two systems use the same measurement of time.)

Basic Components of the Metric System

The gram is the basis for weights.
The liter is the basis for capacity or volume.
The meter is the basis for length.
The are is the basis for surface, although the term is rarely used in that form.
The second is the basis for time.

To avoid measurements taking on inconveniently large or small numeric values, larger units of measurement are commonly used which are multiples of the basic units. The multipliers are powers of 10. For example, distances on the earth are usually given in kilometers (*kilo* means 1,000 in Greek). Here are some equivalencies in the metric system. They all use powers of 10.

1 decameter is 10 meters.
1 hectare is 100 ares.
1 milliliter is 1/1,000 liter.
1 kilometer is 1,000 meters.
1 micosecond is 1/1,000,000 second.

- Volume and weight are defined by a factor of 10: The liter is the volume of 1,000 grams of water.
- Volume and length are defined by a factor of 10: A liter is 1,000 cubic centimeters.
- Area and length are defined by a factor of 10: A hectare is 10,000 square meters.

THE ENGLISH SYSTEM

In contrast to all this, the English system interrelates the basic measures by factors that are not powers of 10. Several different units of volume are used, and they are not related by powers of 10.

A fluid ounce is about 29 cubic centimeters.
A gallon is four quarts.
A quart is 32 ounces.

Various measures of length are used that are not related by powers of 10.

A foot is 12 inches.
A yard is 3 feet.
A mile is 5,280 feet.
An acre is 4,840 square yards.

Numerous interesting stories circulate regarding the probable origins of these old English measurements. For example, a foot was the length of some noteworthy person's foot, and an inch was the measurement of some person's toe.

Remembering these relationships is much more difficult than remembering the metric counterparts. As an example, the hectare is 10,000 square meters—a number far more easily remembered than the square mile at 4,840 square yards or 43,560 square feet!

Realizing the relative difficulty of the English system, the United Kingdom recently decided to convert to the metric system. The United States, however, elected to retain the measurement system with which it was familiar—the English system. So when engineers come to visit the United States, they find that "the tail wags the dog." In other words, even though the rest of the world now uses the metric system, the United States doesn't. Consequently, engineers lecturing or writing in the United States need to convert their numbers in order to be understood in the United States. This situation affects engineers more than scientists, because scientists are more internationalized with respect to measurements. What if you are writing for a British or European journal? As with the punctuation puzzle, when writing from the United States, you can use U.S. measurements and let European editors make the changes. If, however, the journal style sheet specifies metric measurements, then follow the journal requirements.

Every dictionary has an extended conversion chart for comparison of the two systems. The following comparison includes only measurements of length. You can check for area, volume, capacity, and weight under *metric system* in your dictionary. This example serves not so much as a ready reference as to illustrate the incompatibility of the two systems.

British (Metric) and American (English) Measurements of Length

British (Metric System) Number of Meters		American (English) System Approximate U.S. Equivalent	
1,000	meters	0.62	mile
100	meters	109.36	yards
10	meters	32.81	feet
1	meter	39.37	inches
0.1	meter	3.94	inches
0.01	meter	0.39	inch
0.001	meter	0.039	inch

Having reviewed the British measurement system which is now the British metric system and the American measurement system which is actually the English system, you can appreciate how Alice in Wonderland felt.

Here the Red Queen began again. "Can you answer useful questions? She said, "How is bread made?"
    "I know that," Alice cried eagerly. "You take some flour—"
    "Where do you pick the flower?" the White Queen asked.
    "In a garden or in the hedges?"
    "Well, it isn't picked at all," Alice explained. "It's ground—"
    "How many acres of ground?" said the White Queen. "You mustn't leave out so many things."
    "Fan her head," the Red Queen anxiously interrupted.

"She'll be feverish after so much thinking."

So they set to work and fanned her with bunches of leaves, till she had to beg them to leave off, it blew her hair about so.

"She's all right again now," said the Red Queen. "Do you know languages? What's the French for fiddle-de-dee?"

"Fiddle-de-dee's not English," Alice replied gravely.

"Whoever said it was," said the Red Queen.

Alice thought she saw a way out of the difficulty this time.

"If you'll tell me what language fiddle-de-dee is, I'll tell you the French for it," she explained triumphantly.

But the Red Queen drew herself up rather stiffly and said, "Queens never make bargains."

"I wish Queens never asked questions," Alice thought to herself.

"Don't let's quarrel," the White Queen said in an anxious tone.

7

GRAMMAR

TROUBLESPOTS

Thus far, the focus of the *ESL Resource Book* has been on issues of style and grammar that affect the ESL writer. Topics covered in Chapters 5 and 6—partitive patterns, phrasal verbs, and the article system—don't appear in conventional grammar books or in the growing stack of technical writing texts. In Chapters 7 and 8, you'll find a focus on grammar issues that affect all technical writers. Native speakers of English have just as much difficulty with the agreement of various parts of speech within a sentence as do ESL writers. And technical writers for whom English is a first language struggle daily over the decision to use active or passive verbs. While Chapter 7 covers topics that you'll find in many books and articles about technical writing, the *ESL Resource Book* treats these topics for a dual readership: ESL and English-only. Consequently, some explanations may be longer or a bit different from those in general texts on technical writing.

Subject-Verb Agreement

In theory, the agreement of verbs with their subjects doesn't constitute a grammar troublespot. The rule of subject-verb agreement, either descriptively or prescriptively derived, is universally accepted. There are no conflicting arguments surrounding it. In practice, for the most part, writers successfully achieve agreement between subjects and verbs. It's only when the structure of a sentence (syntax) displays complications that confusion ensues. Some of these complications are quite minor. But they can be just distracting enough to muddy the waters of syntax clarity.

The fundamental sentence form in English is subject⟹verb⟹object.

Intel designed the Pentium processor chip.
  S   V   O

Over the centuries, English has become a sophisticated language that permits many variations on the fundamental sentence. Inversion is one such variation. In inversion, the subject and verb switch places: verb⟹subject. In another form of inversion, the object is placed at the beginning of the sentence: object⟹verb. This happens most frequently in a passive sentence. Inversion usually creates the effect of artificial or mannered prose. Consequently, it isn't used very often in technical documentation. Here are two examples of inversion.

Verb⟹Subject
Designed by Intel is the Pentium chip for higher speed and greater memory.

Object⇒Verb
The Pentium chip was designed by Intel.

Inversion also characterizes questions where part of the verb is placed before the subject:

Was the Pentium chip designed by Intel?

English also permits the inclusion of phrases to explain more fully the information conveyed by the three basic elements.

Intel, an American company, designed and also markets the Pentium processor chip.

All these variations on the fundamental sentence structure, plus many others, can confuse you when the time comes to make agreement decisions. Remember that the basic rule is: A verb must agree with its subject in number. Sometimes, however, it's difficult to identify the real subject of a sentence. There are numerous situations where sentence structure can cause subject-verb agreement problems. Keeping the basic rule in mind, for each sentence in the following exercise select the correct verb to agree with the subject provided. (There are no missing subjects in the sentences.) Before making your selection, analyze the structure of each sentence so that you can explain your choice.

Intervening modifiers
1. General Creech, a member of the USAF Thunderbirds, (were) (was) our March Distinguished Lecturer.
2. The medals, one of which belonged to Colonel Henry, (are) (is) in excellent condition.

Inverted order of subject and verb
1. In the afternoon (come) (comes) the advanced briefings.
2. (Have) (Has) any one of you seen the briefing charts?

Subject and subject complement with different numbers
1. Security leaks (represent) (represents) a problem at some sites.
2. A major problem at headquarters (is) (are) security leaks.

Collective nouns
1. The red team (have completed) (has completed) a successful review.
2. The committee of grey beards (have) (has) completed all aspects of the project review.

Subject nouns that appear to be plural

1. The news (is) (are) not favorable.
2. Both journal articles state that AIDS (was) (were) fatal in 98.7 percent of the recorded cases.

Words that are always plural

1. Sanitary clothes (is) (are) required in the chip production line.
2. Cattle (is) (are) creating an ozone problem by releasing gas into the air.

Words as words (words used merely as words rather than the idea they represent)

1. *Memoranda* (is) (are) our corporation's approved plural form of *memorandum*.
2. *Liaison* (is) (are) the word my administrative assistant misspelled.

Title of book, article, or lecture, or quotation as subject

1. "Characterization of the Iron Active Site of Phenylalanine Hydroxylase" (is) (are) the title of Dr. Glasfeld's lecture.
2. "Protein Engineering to Exploit and Explore Bovine Secretary Ribonuncleases" (are) (is) Dr. Kim's topic for Monday's lecture.

The word *number* as a subject

1. The number of proposals (was) (were) impressive.
2. A number of the best papers (was) (were) given honorable mention.

Expressions of quantity

(Subtraction and division take a singular verb.)
1. Six minus three (is) (are) three.
2. Six divided by three (is) (are) two.
(Addition and multiplication take either a singular or a plural verb.)
1. Four and six (is) (are) ten.
2. Four times six (is) (are) twenty-four.

Compound subjects

1. Completing the project and gaining a promotion (is) (are) his goals.
2. My colleague and a friend (has) (have) agreed to join our group.
3. My colleague and friend (has) (have) agreed to join our group.

Subjects connected with correlative conjunctions

The correlative conjunctions are either/or, neither/nor, not only/but also; in either/or correlatives, the verb agrees with the unit closest to itself.)
1. Either Colonel Abraham or his deputies (plan) (plans) to attend.
2. Either three deputies or Colonel Abraham (plan) (plans) to attend.

These pronoun subjects are singular: either, neither, each, one, and those ending in -one, -body, -thing.

1. Each of the prototypes (were) (was) made in our own shop.
2. Everybody in this department (has) (have) a Sun workstation.

What would you do about noun-pronoun agreement in a similar sentence?

> Everybody in this department has (their) (his) (his or her) Sun workstation.

What would you do about the sentence as a question?

> Does everybody in this department (have) (has) a Sun workstation?

Phrases as subjects

1. Attending a lecture (makes) (make) me drowsy.
2. Eating a big lunch and attending a lecture (makes) (make) me drowsy.

Not any of the preceding sentences are long or unduly complex. Nevertheless, quite a few of them require a second thought before you choose the correct verb. In speaking, grammar errors can't really be called back, and self-correction calls attention to the errors. So everyone is tolerant of occasional slips. But in technical writing, you have time to proofread your text and to ask editors for help with grammar.

A WORD TO THE WISE

If you decide to purchase a grammar book for personal use, stay away from college texts. The authors of these books incorrectly assume that college undergraduates don't need a review of basic grammar. As a result, college writing texts talk a lot about rhetoric (the art of persuasive writing) and only a little about grammar. For a comprehensive grammar book, you might ask the local high school what English book it's using in class. If you discover that the high school English department only offers courses like "The Literature of the Absurd," you might have to check with your local primary school to see if it is using a grammar book in English courses.

Active and Passive Voice

Engineers and scientists first learn to write in passive voice in undergraduate science courses. Models for laboratory reports are presented in the passive voice, and science faculty are comfortable with the models. It is the tradition of science for experimenters to distance themselves from their experiments in order to safeguard objectivity. In the workplace, engineers and scientists reinforce the models learned in science courses. It's impossible for writing consultants and editors, almost all of whom are former English majors or graduates of other liberal arts programs, to understand how pervasively passive voice reflects the culture of science. On a superficial level, the issue of active and passive voice may more effectively demonstrate the divide between C. P. Snow's two cultures of literary intellectuals and physical scientists than any other phenomenon.[1]

Writing problems involving the choice of active voice or passive voice aren't really matters of correct or incorrect grammar. The element of choice implies style rather than grammar. Despite what you may be led to believe, using passive voice is not grammatically incorrect. Using passive voice may be stylistically inappropriate if you choose it thoughtlessly and without justification.

The purpose of the active voice is to indicate the performer of the verb's action, whereas the purpose of the passive voice is to deflect the action away from the performer. To achieve passive voice, some form of the auxiliary verb *to be* is used with the past participle of the verb. From this piece of data, you learn that passive voice requires the addition of an auxiliary word. Here is the first indication of a wordier construction.

Active Voice

A team of experts *wrote* the guidelines for Division 6.

We *invited* our client to review the proposal.

The corporate controller *created* a new job title for me.

Passive Voice

The guidelines for Division 6 *were written* by a team of experts.

Our client *was invited* to review the proposal.

A new job title *was created* for me by the corporate controller.

If you decide that it's important to name the actor even though you wish to use passive voice to deemphasize his or her role, you have to create a prepositional phrase. The first and third sentences in the preceding examples of passive voice contain such phrases: *by a team of experts* and *by the corporate controller*. On the other hand, if you decide to economize and omit the prepositional phrase, the actor's identity remains a mystery as in the passive version of the second sentence. The reader cannot know who invited the client to review the proposal.

The prepositional phrase adds even more words to the sentence. With an

[1] C. P. Snow. "The Two Cultures and the Scientific Revolution," *New Statesman*, October 6, 1956.

auxiliary verb and a prepositional phrase, the sentence grows substantially. But it is not commensurately clearer. In fact, it's usually less clear. This is one reason why writing consultants so energetically support the use of active voice in technical writing.

ACTIVE IS VIGOROUS

Without question, active voice adds vigor to your prose. It's the primary means of protecting your reader from boredom with what could be a tedious text. (What might be a tedious text to an English major could be rather exciting to an engineer.) Consider the relative vigor of these two versions of the same information.

Passive Verb

The development and management of the Flight Data File *are governed* by the Crew Procedures Management Plan.

Active Verb

The Crew Procedures Management Plan *governs* Flight Data File development and management.

The first sentence is from an actual document; the second is the technical editor's revision. If that example doesn't convince you that active is more vigorous, this one might.

Passive Voice

The verification and validation tests *will be conducted* after the terabyte of Landsat data *is loaded* into the database.

Active Voice

I will *conduct* verification and validation tests after I *load* the terabyte of Landsat data into the database.

Transform the passive verbs in the following paragraph into active verbs. Does your transformation produce more vigorous prose? Does it produce more economical prose? The passive voice verbs are italicized.

The faults discussed in this paper *are limited* to STS Orbiter hardware faults (those most likely to be similar to the faults associated with the Space Station). Ground Support Equipment (GSE) faults and software faults *were not considered* in this study due to resource limitations, although much of this document's contents may also apply to software and

GSE fault management. However, it *should be noted* that Orbiter faults *are detected* during ground processing (routine maintenance, checkout, and testing), as well as during mission operations; therefore, both of these aspects *will be addressed.*

In revising the paragraph, you may have used these active constructions:

are limited	This paper *limits* the discussion of faults to STS Orbiter hardware faults.
were not considered	This study *does not consider* Ground Support Equipment (GSE) faults and software faults.
should be noted	Please *note* that . . . , or the reader *should note.* . . .
are detected	. . . technicians *detect* Orbiter faults during ground processing.
will be addressed	. . . the study *addresses* both these aspects.

The passive version of the first sentence contains 13 words before the parenthetic phrase, and the active version contains 12. Similar small reductions occur throughout the sentences. While the individual reductions aren't dramatic, you'll find that the economies are incremental throughout a long paper. Most important, the economies are not achieved at the expense of clarity.

ACTIVE IS CLEAR

More important than vigor is the clarity with which active voice endows a sentence. Not only is the mysteriously missing actor of passive verb sentences likely to elicit some questions from your reader, but the general fuzziness of many passive sentences also compromises clarity. While technical universities and science departments in liberal arts colleges remain bastions of passive verb usage, training departments in businesses and research centers wage warfare against it. Their foremost argument is that passive voice diminishes clarity. Even the U.S. military has joined the battle. "Sentences written passively are wordy and roundabout. They reverse the natural, active order of English sentences. Besides lengthening and twisting sentences, passive verbs often muddy them."[2]

The major clarity problem of passive voice is the lack of a doer in the sentence. Passive sentences readily elicit the colloquial reaction: "says who?" The following statements from the Air Force writing course show that passive sentences can be grammatically correct without a doer. The examples also indicate that despite grammatical correctness, passive sentences without doers call forth reader irritation and displeasure.

[2] Superintendent of Documents. *U.S. Air Force Effective Writing Course.* Washington, DC: U.S. Government Printing Office, 1973. p. 49.

Nominations must be approved beforehand. By whom?

Plans are being made. By whom?

Your proposal has been changed. By whom?

You will be notified. By whom?

The Air Force summary is especially apt: "Because passive verbs look back to whatever receives the action, reading passive sentences is like driving in reverse."

The vagueness created by passive voice verbs goes well beyond the lack of a doer in the sentence. The distancing effect promoted by passive voice tends to expand beyond your choice of a verb form. If you write passively, your prose will start to sound like one of President Clinton's addresses that always refer to "this administration" when an unpopular action needs to be defended. *I* gets lost in a retreat from responsibility while *you* becomes *The American People*. Be wary. If your writing begins to sound bureaucratic, you're probably writing passively. Of course, if you become very important, you might have to learn how to write bureaucratically.

A DEFENSE OF PASSIVE VOICE

Bureaucratic situations often do require passive writing, as do scientific reports and technical papers. This may be the crux of the passive problem. Principal investigators are not trying to render anonymous the leaders of an experiment. Rather, they are placing the emphasis on the results (object of the sentence) of the experiment. Scientific results, in the mind of any true scientist, is where the emphasis belongs. Movie stars can demand top billing, but not electrical engineers. Here are the four situations in which passive voice is preferable to active.

- **When the results of the action are clearly more important than the doer.**

The specifications for our project will be completed next week.

Laboratory supplies are being ordered today.

Hard copies of the briefing were handed out after Rashid completed his presentation.

Coffee and juice will be served twice during the seminar.

The completion date of the specifications is more important to your reader than the names of the people writing the specs. The name of the clerical worker who is ordering the lab supplies isn't very significant. Anyone can hand out the briefing notes; people want to know when they'll receive them. It doesn't matter who will serve beverages during the seminar; the attendees want to know when they can expect to have their coffee.

- **When the person or persons who performed the action are unknown.**

Sheila's office was cleared out while she was on vacation.

My unabridged dictionary was stolen while I was away.

Our telephone lines were cut and our electricity disconnected.

- **When identifying the performer of the action would be inappropriate, dangerous, or embarrassing.**

Your book was credited to the wrong author.

Incorrect data was included in the summary of the monthly progress report.

An improper comment was made about the President's wife.

During the Watergate scandal, former U.S. President Richard Nixon said, "The tapes were erased."

- **When the performer is understood and his or her actions are less important than the results.** This is a less clearly defined situation, but one that probably applies to many technical reports in the workplace. The team, group, or department might be well understood by readers of a specialized report. Furthermore, the readers are more interested in knowing what happened.

The data was collected quickly and interpreted rapidly.

Results will be compiled and mailed to division heads and section chiefs.

The survey conclusions were predicted correctly.

The preceding sentences presume that the participants of a survey know what organization was responsible for conducting it.

Candidates are requested to submit their applications immediately.

Participants will be required to pay their deposits before the opening session.

Students in this course are expected to arrive on time and to remain until the end of the class.

Volunteers are needed to collect equipment and return it to the supply closet.

In these sentences, various responsible agents are implied. Candidates for a posting know who is requesting applications; participants of a seminar know the company sponsoring it; students know their teacher; volunteers know the name of the agency requesting help.

FOUR QUICK TIPS

- Identify passive voice by looking for *to be* verbs that are auxiliaries to the main verb.
- Use editing programs like Writer's Workbench to identify possible passives, or use the grammar checker built into your word processor.
- Make an informed decision about choosing active voice or passive voice, depending on what's appropriate for your situation.
- If in doubt, use active voice.

Misplaced, Two-Way, and Dangling Modifiers

Because it's the nature of modifiers to expand on the meaning of the words they modify, they should be placed close to those words. Adjectives need to be near the noun or pronoun they modify, and adverbs should be before, after, or between verb elements. A high regard for precise quantification and quantification make it unlikely that engineers or scientists will misplace single-word modifiers. Two examples should show the need for care when placing single-word modifiers.

Misplaced Modifiers
Which Position Did You Intend?

Desmond *almost* completed 200 pages of his annual report.

Desmond completed *almost* 200 pages of his annual report.

Position of Modifiers—Double Meaning
What Did You Mean?

Denis was confident *on Monday* he would be named "Outstanding Young Scientist of the Year."

Employees who complain *often* get results.

In the first box, did Desmond almost complete his report, or did he complete somewhat less than 200 pages of his report? In the second box, was Denis confident on Monday, or did he believe he would receive his award on Monday? And do employees who complain frequently obtain results, or do employees who complain obtain results frequently? A reader must guess at the intended meaning. An editor can point out the problem, but an editor can't provide the answer. Only the author knows what he or she meant to write.

Placement is critical to the correct intended meaning. You've doubtlessly had to juggle which phrase to put where. Sometimes two phrases seem to compete for the same position in the sentence. In such a case you must practice triage like the orderly in a hospital emergency unit.

More frequent than the misplaced and two-way modifiers are the dangling modifiers. Rather than single words, dangling modifiers are usually entire phrases that hang loosely in the sentence and produce confusion. They don't attach to a word in the sentence, and sometimes they produce absurd results. They can drift to unlikely positions in a sentence, particularly if the sentence is long and complex. However, you'll typically find them at the beginning of a sentence. Good writers carefully edit their writing to see if modifying phrases are as close as possible to the sentence element they describe.

A dangling introductory phrase can produce absurd results by modifying a noun that appears to be the subject when the real subject is missing. For example:

While briefing the group, a fly flew onto the vugraph.

Less amusing sentences with introductory dangling modifiers can be harder to detect. If you do detect them, you can correct them by supplying the missing subject or by moving the real subject to the beginning of the main clause of the sentence. Try correcting the following sentences, all of which include dangling modifiers.

1. Before going into the complex, a pass must be shown.
2. Standing near the launch pad, a flare ignited.
3. Looking to the left and right, engineers everywhere were busy.
4. Stretching across the field, I saw a fiber optic cable.
5. Opening a valve, a jet of fuel struck the technician.
6. Stepping outside the hanger, a crew car arrived.
7. Having considered all the variables, a successful launch is certain.
8. To change launch procedures, mission headquarters must be notified.
9. To write a useful operations manual, the astronauts must be considered.
10. Being† a large classified facility, security guards are posted at the entrances.

　　†Warning: Watch out for sentences beginning with *being*. Keep out of trouble by not writing sentences that begin with *being*.

Here are the simplest corrections. There may be others.

1. Before going into the complex, you must show a pass.
2. Standing near the launch pad, I saw a flare ignite.
3. Looking to the left and right, I saw engineers busy everywhere.
4. I saw a fiber optic cable stretching across the field.
5. Opening a valve, the technician was struck by a jet of fuel.
6. Stepping outside the hanger, I was picked up by a crew car.
7. Having considered all the variables, we are certain of a successful launch.
8. To change launch procedures, you must notify mission headquarters.
9. To write a useful operations manual, you must consider the astronauts.
10. Security guards are posted at the entrances because our large facility is classified.

A Review of Verbals

Because the sentences in the preceding exercise all contain introductory dangling phrases, this is a good spot to go over the grammar of such phrases. The uncorrected versions of all 10 sentences are introduced by verbal phrases. The fact that the verbal phrases are dangling is coincident upon poor writing skills. Verbal phrases are not dangling by nature even though many of them feature *ing* forms of the verb.

Verbals are words that partake of the nature of a verb but function in some other way. In other words, they look like verbs but don't act like verbs. Conventional English grammar books pay little attention to verbals. Some grammar books completely ignore verbals. Because they are "little verbs" or "verbettes," their importance is underestimated. If native speakers of English understood verbals better, they would produce fewer grammar errors because almost all of the dangling constructions and many of the misplacement problems result from ignorance about verbals. The sentence fragment fault is almost always caused by a writer who mistakes a verbal for a verb.

Fragmentary Sentence

Nonnative speakers of English in Asia, Africa, and Europe *coming* to outnumber those who claim English as their mother tongue.

Full Sentence

Nonnative speakers of English in Asia, Africa, and Europe *are coming* to outnumber those who claim English as their mother tongue.

Fragmentary Sentence

Using English as a second, third, or fourth language, four nonnative speakers for every native speaker of English.

Full Sentence

For every native speaker of English there are at least four nonnative speakers who *use* English as a second, third, or fourth language.

Fragmentary Sentence

Being bilingual in English and Spanish, an increasingly useful skill in the U.S. business world today.

Full Sentence

Being bilingual in English and Spanish *is* an increasingly useful skill in the U.S. business world today.

Verbals are a subclass of *verbs*. They are classified as participles, gerunds, and infinitives. No one of these three forms has the strength to serve as a verb. A full-strength verb is required in any sentence that includes a verbal. The functions that verbals do serve are varied. While looking like verbs, they actually function as other parts of speech: nouns, adjectives, or adverbs.

INFINITIVE

Infinitives are the easiest verbals to recognize because they combine the word *to* with a verb. When you learned to conjugate verbs, you recited the infinitive form; for example, *to go, to read, to learn, to speak, to write, to communicate,* and so forth. The infinitive form of a verb isn't used in a sentence as a verb; it merely uses the verb word. Easy to recognize, the infinitive form of the verb is less easy to identify for function because it can have various functions. Infinitives can be used as nouns, adjectives, or adverbs. Here are some sample sentences.

Infinitive Verbals

The mission commander's greatest fear is *to abort* the launch. (noun—the infinitive phrase complements the subject noun, *fear*)

Lestat had three weeks *to spend* on perfecting his new technique. (adjective—The infinitive phrase modifies the noun *weeks*)

Jose was pleased *to earn* a gold seal certificate. (adverb—The infinitive phrase modifies the verb *was pleased*.)

You need to remember that the word *to* in the infinitive phrase (the infinitive marker) is sometimes omitted.

Missing Infinitive Marker (To)

Please help me *find* the missing equations.

Go *see* Professor Phillips immediately.

Have you heard her *tell* her version of the incident?

Let's *complete* this set of graphics before we begin another.

This pattern of missing infinitive markers seems to occur when the infinitive serves as a noun. In all of the above sentences, the infinitive phrase is the direct object of the real verb.

A REMINDER

When *to* joins with a verb to create a verbal (to find, to see, to tell, and so on) it is not the same as the preposition *to*. The preposition *to* is not immediately followed by a verb, but it is followed by a noun or pronoun with their appropriate articles and modifiers: *to the store, to the factory, to a very large audience, to you and me.*

PARTICIPLE

Participles (and gerunds) don't have markers in front of them. Their markers are attached to the end of the verb-like word. The usual marker is *ing* although *ed* occurs when the participle refers to past time. There are only two participle forms: present and past. Again, from conjugating verbs, you probably remember reciting the present participles of the verb: for example, *going, reading, learning, speaking, writing, communicating.* A past participle ends in *ed* when the verb is regular.

Like infinitives, participles aren't strong enough to function as the verb of a sentence. Participles are used as adjectives; as such they modify nouns and pronouns. They are easier to describe than infinitives because they function only as adjectives. Here are some examples.

Present Participles as Adjectives

Laughing, Rona picked up the specimens and left our office. (*Laughing* modifies the subject noun *Rona*.)

The *freezing* rain made it impossible for our plane to take off for Washington. (*Freezing* modifies the subject noun *rain*.)

NomaLubi found her *programming* job *boring*. (Both *programming* and *boring* modify the object noun *job*.)

Past Participles as Adjectives

The *exhausted* astronauts left the space capsule. (*Exhausted* modifies the subject noun *astronauts*.)

Delighted, Provost Plonko accepted the invitation to speak at commencement. (*Delighted* modifies the subject noun *Provost Plonko*.)

Disgusted, we handed in our resignations and left our prototype lab forever. (*Disgusted* modifies the subject pronoun *we*.)

All the preceding examples of past participles use verbals derived from regular verbs. Regular verbs form their past tense with *ed*. However, past participles derived from irregular verbs will reflect their irregular past tenses: *begun, flung, hidden, understood, struck*, and so on. Consequently, you may have a bit more difficulty recognizing a past participle verbal.

Irregular Past Participles

Beaten with a host of meteors, the planet nevertheless survived.

Proven correct, the mathematician proceeded to enlarge on his theory.

Flung into orbit, the satellite began to transmit images back to Earth.

GERUND

Gerunds are the easiest of all verbals to recognize. Like participles, they end in *ing,* but they have no past form. And unlike infinitives, they serve only one function. The gerund is a verbal noun. When you see an *ing* verbal beginning a sentence, you are safe in guessing that it introduces a noun phrase that serves as the subject of the sentence. Gerunds can also stand alone as nouns, and they often do. The following examples illustrate both situations.

Gerund Nouns

Hacking is Norbert's favorite hobby.

Studying is hard work.

Teaching at MIT is highly gratifying.

Gerund Phrases

Saying that number sets are time-consuming is true.

Completing multiple number sets quickly is easy for François and his friend Jean-Pierre.

Wieske loves *contemplating the fact that her grade point average is the highest in her class.*

SOME INTERIM TIPS

TIP   1: Search for the real subject of every sentence so you can check that the verb agrees with the right word(s).

TIP   2: Watch out for prepositional phrases that come between subjects and verbs.

TIP   3: Use subject⇒verb⇒object sentence order for sentence clarity.

TIP   4: Treat collective nouns as singular in American English.

TIP   5: Review the four situations that call for passive voice.

TIP   6: Think about where you place modifiers, not just which modifiers are best to use.

TIP   7: Review the three verbals until they are totally familiar.

TIP   8: Never use verbals to replace genuine verbs in sentences.

TIP   9: Distinguish between *to* as a preposition and *to* as an infinitive.

TIP 10: **A Bonus Tip:** When keyboarding mixed case titles, write the infinitive *to* with an initial cap but keep the preposition *to* in lowercase. Examples follow.

Infinitive *To*–Part of a Verb, an Important Part of Speech

"A Plan To Establish Quick and Easy Internet Access"

Preposition *To*–An Unimportant Part of Speech

"A Plan for Quick and Easy Access to Internet"

Transitive and Intransitive Verbs

Moving from verbals to verbs, first we'll briefly review what makes a verb transitive or intransitive, and second we'll provide you with a handy reference sheet on the most elusive of all verbs in English. Because an ESL breakdown of verbs would concentrate on regular and irregular verbs, you may not have had an opportunity to review the nature of transitive and intransitive verbs.

TRANSITIVE VERBS

A transitive verb takes an object—a noun or pronoun that states who or what completes the action of the verb. The important part of that definition (one that's not sufficiently emphasized in traditional grammars) is that the transitive verb must have an object to complete its meaning. (Giles threw the ball.) Without an object, the sentence lacks complete meaning. (Giles threw.) You'll find yourself asking what in a sentence with a transitive verb that is lacking an object.

INTRANSITIVE VERBS

An intransitive verb doesn't take an object; it's complete without one. (Alex walked.) (Alex walked slowly.) Although some verbs tend to be transitive more often, and some verbs are more often intransitive, many verbs can be used in either a transitive or an intransitive sense. (Meg won. Or, Meg won first prize.)

TWO TRICKY VERBS

Two verbs with different forms distinguishing transitive and intransitive states are *to lay* and *to lie*. Even native speakers of English can't remember which verb is which, or how to form the tenses of each. *To lay* (transitive) means to put or place an object down. *To lie* means to recline one's self. Figure 7.1 is intended as a handy chart that you can photocopy and paste onto the slider of your desk for quick reference.

CONJUGATION OF TO LAY AND TO LIE*

TO LAY (transitive)—to put or place an object* down

LAY takes an object. For example: He lays the book on the floor. He lays the body in its coffin.

Principal parts: lay, laid, laid, laying

Present:	I lay	we lay
	you lay	you lay
	she lays	they lay

Past:	I laid	we laid
	you laid	you laid
	she laid	they laid

| Future: | will lay | |

| Perfect: | have laid | |

TO LIE (intransitive)—to recline one's self; to reside in

Lie does not take an object. For example: I often lie down for a nap. The answer lies within you.

Principal parts: lie, lay, lain, lying

Present:	I lie	we lie
	you lie	you lie
	she lies	they lie

Past:	I lay	we lay
	you lay	you lay
	she lay	they lay

| Future: | will lie | |

| Perfect: | have lain | |

*One conjugates verbs and declines (n. declension) nouns.

FIGURE 7.1   To lay and to lie.

A Who-Whom Review

Like *to lay* and *to lie*, *who* and *whom* also present occasions for confusion. The confusion over *who* and *whom* is not in any way an ESL issue. It concerns all speakers of English, including those who believe they know when to use one form and when to use the other. In fact, those most knowledgeable about *whom* often err through overcorrection.

When an aspect of word choice or grammar becomes extremely difficult to unscramble, it will eventually resolve itself. Just how long the resolution will take is not predictable. Sometimes language pundits artificially preserve an especially difficult item long past its time of usefulness. Examples of such artificial preservation are the taboos against final prepositions and split infinitives. (In Chapter 8 you'll learn about the taboo against possessive case for inanimate objects.) The *who-whom* dilemma is, in fact, already resolving itself. More and more often, the use *whom* is dropping away as speakers and writers can't take the time to unscramble the two words, or don't really care to do so. While the two forms are moving toward fusion into one form—true to language movement, the simpler form will prevail—the movement is neither final nor fully accepted at this time. Consequently, as professional writers, you are still expected to make the correct choice, and you need to understand the syntax behind your decisions.

SPEAKING AND WRITING

Before plunging into a syntax analysis, think about separating usage in speech (discourse) from usage in writing. Some writing teachers exhort their students to write the way they speak. This is wrong. We do not write the way we speak, and we shouldn't try to do so. Writing and speaking are two distinctly different skills. What is acceptable in speaking will often not be acceptable in writing. Writing offers many opportunities to revise and correct whereas speaking is spontaneous.

With respect to *who* and *whom*, in speaking, use the form that seems more natural to you. You have a 50 percent chance of being correct. In fact, you have more than a 50 percent chance if you use *who* because more sentences have subjects than have objects. If you overcorrect by using *whom* where it's not appropriate, you'll sound stilted in addition to being wrong. This is not unlike the use of *I* after prepositions, where the more exotic form makes the speaker sound pompous in addition to being incorrect. Rarely does discourse allow enough time for you to unscramble the syntax of a sentence you've not yet produced. Thus, you won't have many opportunities to make the *who-whom* choice with deliberation. In speaking, when in doubt, use *who*.

In writing and especially in technical writing, a different set of priorities prevails. You are expected to write grammatically correct prose. You are not expected to be spontaneous. You have time to revise. You have resources where you can check areas of doubt. The *ESL Resource Book* is one such resource.

SUBJECTIVE AND OBJECTIVE CASE

Who is the pronoun for the subject position in a sentence. Traditional grammar books call that position *nominative*. In English, *m* is the marker for the objective case. *Whom* (who + m) is the pronoun for the object position, regardless of whether the object is direct or indirect. The case is called *objective. Who* and *whom* introduce relative clauses. They also connect a clause to the noun or pronoun to which the relative pronoun refers or for which it substitutes.

> Do not concern yourself with the case of the noun to which the pronoun refers. Trying to match the case of the relative pronoun to the case of the noun it refers to is a frequent error in selecting *who* or *whom.*

THE MOST IMPORTANT RULE

The form of the relative pronoun is always determined by its function in its own clause. In the following examples, the relative clause is italicized in each sentence.

Who As Subject of the Relative Clause

The man *who wrote the code for that software* is my son. (*Who* is subject of the verb *wrote* in the relative clause.)

Benjamin is a good worker *who has no trouble at review time.* (*Who* is subject of the verb *has* in the relative clause.)

Whom As Object of the Relative Clause

The visitors *whom we expected* did not come. (*Whom* is object of the verb *expected* in the relative clause. The clause is inverted from *we expected whom.*)

These travel orders are for the deputy *whom I will designate later today.* (*Whom* is object of the verb *will designate* in the relative clause. This clause is inverted from *I will designate whom.*)

Your sentence analysis becomes more difficult if a phrase or clause other than the relative clause invades the main sentence. The usual position for this invasion is between the subject and the verb of the relative clause. Use a process of elimination in such a case. First, identify the invading phrase or clause. Think of it as a serious distraction from the main idea of the clause. Then temporarily block it out of the clause, remembering that it does not affect the case of the relative pronoun. In the following sentences, the invading phrase or clause is in boldface type and the relative clause is italicized.

Invading Clauses

We invited only the people *who* **Okonkwo said** *held Top Secret clearance.* (*Who* is subject of the verb *held* in the relative clause.)

She is the woman *who* **I think** *received her clearance yesterday.*

Frieda spoke to the draftsman *who* **Karl said** *was his friend.*

It's easy to spot the objective pronoun following a preposition, even if it's separated from its preposition. Not only can the prepositional phrase contain separated elements, it can also be inverted. The elements of the prepositional phrases in the following sentences are italicized. Note that the relative pronoun is objective because it's the object of the preposition.

Whom As Object of the Prepositional Phrase

Scott is the man *for whom* we are looking.

For whom are we looking?

Whom are we looking *for?*

The prepositional phrase rule can make you stumble. Remember that if the relative pronoun is the subject of its own clause, you should use the nominative case even though the entire clause may be the object of a verb or of a preposition. In the following sentences, the relative clause is italicized.

Relative Clause As Object of the Verb

No one can predict *who will be laid off next.* (*Who* is subject of the relative clause; the entire clause is object of the verb *can predict.*)

They should punish *whoever is found guilty of planting the Trojan horse in the software program.* (*Whoever* is the subject of the relative clause; the entire clause is object of the verb *should punish.*)

Here's the construction that causes the most trouble. It's also where overcorrection is most likely to occur.

Relative Clause As Object of the Preposition

Our section chief offered a bonus to *whoever debugged the software first.* (*Whoever* is the subject of the relative clause; the entire clause is the of object of the preposition *to.*)

The corporation will probably give an award to *whoever names the culprit.* (*Whoever* is the subject of the relative clause; the entire clause is the object of the preposition *to.*)

I will exchange software with *whoever has virus protection.* (*Whoever* is the subject of the relative clause; the entire clause is the object of the preposition *with.*)

Earlier in the chapter you were alerted to distinguish between *to* as a preposition and *to* as an infinitive marker. Apply this distinction to relative pronouns: The infinitive form of a verb takes the objective case. That's why *whom* is the correct relative pronoun in the following examples.

They did not know *whom to name to the investigation team.*
(*To name whom* is the inverted infinitive clause.)

Dr. Cunningham is the nuclear engineer *whom they wish to nominate for this year's Congressional Award.* (*To nominate whom* is the inverted infinitive clause.)

You can test your grasp of how to use *who* and *whom* in the following 15 sentences. Remember that these relative pronouns always refer to people, and *which* and *that* usually refer to things.

1. The president of WorldWide Operations didn't know (who) (whom) to select for the assignment.
2. The woman (who) (whom) sold you your computer peripherals shares my office.
3. Dr. Cetiner is just the robot engineer for (which) (whom) we've been looking.
4. Our consultant will offer configuration management training to (whomever) (whoever) wants to sign up for it.
5. Let me welcome the new CFO (who) (whom) you all met at the annual forum.
6. (Who) (Whom) did you say is attending the symposium?
7. (Who) (Whom) are we waiting for?
8. Our vice president for finance asked me (who) (whom) I supposed would be best able to assist him with the company's financial reengineering.
9. The department controller offered dinner for two to (whoever) (whomever) sold the most U.S. Savings Bonds.
10. (Who) (Whom) do you think will earn the prize of dinner for two?
11. Hughes' CIO had a big smile for (whoever) (whomever) he met this morning.
12. At (who) (whom) did you smile?
13. The systems project officer is a person (who) (whom) you can be sure will be able to keep everything on schedule.
14. That's an opinion that's held by anyone (who) (that) has reviewed the facts carefully.
15. Just (who) (whom) does the government auditor think he is?

Answers: 1-whom, 2-who, 3-whom, 4-whoever, 5-whom, 6-who, 7-Whom, 8-who, 9-whoever, 10-Who, 11-whomever, 12-whom, 13-who, 14-who, 15-who

Some Confusing Words

English words that are commonly confused plague both native and nonnative speakers of English. Long lists of such words can be found in many books. The following short list includes only commonplace words that are likely to occur in your routine writing tasks. The list is compiled from entries in the "Grammar Hot Line" journal of a large R&D center, and with reference to The Random House Handbook.[3] Its focus is on meaning, not on spelling. The first, a military term, is included because it has been the topic of frequent Hot Line inquiries. The remaining entries are general in nature.

material, materiel. *Material* means matter that has qualities that give it individuality and by which it can be categorized: What sort of material did you use for making the plane's surface stealthy? *Materiel* is the equipment, apparatus, and supplies used by an organization or institution: Materiel Command is in charge of organizing everything that will be shipped to Kuwait.

affect, effect. As a verb, *affect* means to influence or to change: Her decision affected the outcome of our meetings. The verb *effect* means to cause or bring about: She effected a new policy for the department. When *effect* is a noun, it means result: The effects of mammalian exposure to nuclear energy cannot always be determined until after months or years have passed.

all ready, already. The two words *all ready* mean that everything is ready; *already* is an adverb meaning so early: They are already at the front entrance; our documents are all ready for them.

amount (of), number (of). *Amount of* describes mass items, and *number of* describes count items: The large number of people using the Corporate Information Server surprised the Computer Center staff. However, the amount of information available from the server is surprisingly small.

a while, awhile. *While* is a noun, as in a while ago: We toured Emanon's plant a while ago—probably two months if not more. *Awhile* is an adverb: I worked awhile on my new computer until it was time for lunch.

beside, besides. *Beside* means at the side of; *besides* means in addition to: Besides a colleague and a mentor or two, no one stood beside Randolph during his time of need.

---

[3] Frederick Crews. *The Random House Handbook*, Third Edition. New York: Random House, 1980.

compare, contrast. *Compare* means to make a comparison or to show a resemblance. Sometimes it's used carelessly to show a difference. *Contrast* always emphasizes differences: Let's compare notes for similar points of interest. We will contrast one system against another before we conclude which one to implement.

complement, compliment. As nouns, *complement* means something that completes or accompanies, and *compliment* means an expression of praise: As a complement to the software that Digital contributed to the school, several sets of ClickArt were included. DEC complimented the purchasers on the excellent configuration they devised.

continual, continuous. *Continual* means recurring at intervals; *continuous* means uninterrupted. Continual engagement of the toggle will wear out the switch. The noise from the engines was continuous.

convince, persuade. *Convince* means to win an agreement; *persuade* means to move to action: If Charles convinces you that the Emanon teleconference equipment is best, Jack may be able to persuade you to buy it.

disinterested, uninterested. *Uninterested* means not interested; *disinterested* means impartial: We need a disinterested person to settle the dispute. Garcia is uninterested in studying cognitive science.

doubtful, dubious. Someone who feels doubt is *doubtful*: Judith was doubtful that Joseph knew the status of distributed product data at our company. An outcome or situation may be *dubious*: George would not accept dubious data.

every one, everyone. *Every one* means each one: Every one of your arguments is false. *Everyone* means all the people as a group: Everyone is going to Sam's retirement party.

flaunt, flout. To *flaunt* is to display arrogantly: They flaunted their superior ability to design compact circuit boards. To *flout* is to defy with contempt: Our mathematicians flouted all the rules of good graphic design.

good, well. To look *good* means you have an attractive appearance. If you enjoy good health, you look *well*.

imply, infer. To *imply* is to create an impression or to insert an implication; to *infer* is to extract or take out an implication: Ronda implied that the laboratory's radon level fell well within safety guidelines, but Sue inferred from other sources that it might be borderline.

in to, into. The two words *in to* combine direction with purpose; *into* indicates direction only: After the plenary session, we went into town. Let's probe in to the bottom of this problem.

it's, its. *It's* (with an apostrophe) is a contraction of *it is*; *its* is a possessive pronoun: It's fascinating to see how the radar compensates for human deficiencies.

lay, lie. *Lay* usually means to set down, and it always takes an object: Please lay the pointer on the podium when you've finished your presentation. *Lie* means to rest or repose: Why don't you lie down after you've finished packing for your trip.

oral, verbal. *Oral* means by mouth (spoken); *verbal* means in words, whether written or spoken: The students were assigned an oral presentation for the second week of classes. Their mastery of verbal communication was impressive.

precede, proceed. To *precede* is to go ahead of; to *proceed* is to go forward: The chief engineer preceded his colleagues as they proceeded toward the test site.

predominant, predominate. *Predominant* is an adjective; *predominate* is a verb: What is the predominant characteristic that makes this monitor superior? Our products predominate in both quantity and quality.

prescribe, proscribe. *Prescribe* is to dictate or order whereas *proscribe* is to forbid as harmful or unlawful: Physicians are authorized to prescribe medicine for their patients. Judges may proscribe actions by writing them into law.

rebut, refute. To *rebut* an argument is to answer it; to *refute* an argument is to prove it wrong: Senator Kennedy will rebut his opponent's argument next Friday evening although I doubt that he'll be able to refute it.

replace, substitute. To *replace* uses the old item as its object: We plan to replace our current laser printer with a color printer. To *substitute* uses the new item as its object: However, we will not plan to substitute an extended keyboard for our regular-size board.

toward, towards. Both words mean in the direction of. *Toward* is preferred in American English.

usage, use. *Usage* is overworked in technical writing. It's often used where *use* will suffice. *Usage* implies customary or conventional use: English language usage requires that you punctuate sentences and questions with end points.

Use is simply the act or practice of employing something: Proper use of the protocols will enable the two machines to interact.

who's, whose. Who's is a contraction of *who is*: Who's afraid of our competition? *Whose* is the possessive pronoun used in asking questions: Whose theory of extraterrestrial intelligence will prevail?

This short list can serve as a basis for your own record of confusing words. A much longer list is available in *Words into Type* which offers 23 small-type pages of commonly confused words.[4]

You can test your command of these frequently confused words in the following 15 sentences.

1. (Who's) (Whose) technical report is entitled "Phased Array Sequencing"?
2. I can't understand what you mean to (imply) (infer) in your opening paragraph.
3. You should (precede) (proceed) with your briefing after a short break.
4. Certain similarities caused Jeffrey to (compare) (contrast) the research facility with a college campus.
5. You won't (affect) (effect) the course of events by failing to prepare your Performance Appraisal Report.
6. The United States has an early warning system buried deep inside (it's) (its) mountain range in Colorado.
7. Please (lay) (lie) down your pencil and leave the testing room when the timer bongs.
8. The U.S. Marine Corps specifications list describes (material) (materiel) requirements in detail.
9. The graphics presentation package will (complement) (compliment) the spreadsheet software.
10. The project report is (all ready) (already).
11. System (use) (usage) is overextended.
12. Large-scale integrated circuits are our (predominant) (predominate) product.
13. Federally funded research and development centers serve as (disinterested) (uninterested) parties to vendor selection.
14. Fiber optics are (replacing) (substituting for) conventional wiring.
15. That we'll stay within our budget for the current fiscal year is a (doubtful) (dubious) possibility.

Answers: 1-Whose, 2-imply, 3-proceed, 4-compare, 5-affect, 6-its, 7-lay, 8-materiel, 9-complement, 10-all ready, 11-use, 12-predominant, 13-disinterested, 14-replacing, 15-dubious.

---

[4] Marjorie E. Skillin, Robert M. Gay, et al. *Words into Type*. Englewood Cliffs, NJ: Prentice-Hall, Inc. Look for the most recent edition.

Some Pretentious Words

Confusion of one word for another will result in an error. While not an error of grammar, the wrong word in a document or presentation is an error of diction. A wrong word can cause a greater failure of understanding than a grammar error. That's why word choice is a topic that shouldn't be relegated to the appendixes of books about writing, where it's too often found.

Less serious than the wrong word is the pretentious word. While pretentious words won't cause you to misunderstand the text you're reading, they can blur an issue or decrease a document's overall readability. Although this item of diction relates to style more than grammar, it's nevertheless a big problem in the fields of technical, business, scientific, and legal writing.

Sometimes practitioners of medicine and law resist the movement toward simpler prose. Engineers and businesspeople use expressions inherited from an earlier era when more elaborate style was admired. And many ESL writers in the United States come from countries where belletristic (beautifully ornate) prose is not only admired but also encouraged. Notwithstanding the reluctance of all these writers to use plain prose, the movement toward simplicity is encompassing American English. It's especially important for engineers and scientists to use clear, simple expressions. You will send very mixed signals if you describe cutting-edge technology in Victorian terminology!

SOME SHORT TIPS, A LIST, AND AN EXERCISE[5]

TIP 1: Limit your long words to less than 10 percent to keep your writing at a high school level.

TIP 2: Keep necessary jargon that your audience expects.

TIP 3: Challenge each long word (three or more syllables) not capitalized. Keep those that have no good short word substitute.

TIP 4: Do not use long words to impress. Readers resent being sent to the dictionary.

TIP 5: Avoid words ending in -ize: prioritize, finalize, conceptualize, utilize, actualize.

[5] These tips and the exercise are used with permission from Judith H. Graham and Daniel O. Graham, Jr. *The Writing System Workbook*. Fairfax, Virginia: Preview Press, 1995.

Some Multisyllable Words with Simple Replacements

Pretentious Word	Replacement	Pretentious Word	Replacement
accomplish	do	fundamental	basic
accordingly	so	generate	cause, make
accurate	correct, right	identical	same
actual	real	implement	do, carry out
additional	more	inception	start
advantageous	helpful	incorporate	merge, join
aggregation	group	initiate	start
allocate	put, place	limitations	limit
anticipate	expect	magnitude	size
apparent	clear	methodology	method, way
appreciable	many	minimum	least
ascertain	learn	modification	change
assimilate	merge	nebulous	vague
assistance	help, aid	necessitate	cause
capability	ability	numerous	many
commence	start	objective	aim, goal
component	part	obligate	bind, compel
consolidate	combine	operate	work, run
constitutes	makes up, forms	operational	working
demonstrate	show, prove	optimum	best
denominate	name	preliminary	before, first
designate	appoint, name	prioritize	rank
disseminate	spread	probability	chance
eliminate	cut, drop	proficiency	skill
encounter	meet	promulgate	announce
endeavor	try	recapitulate	sum up
enumerate	count	relocation	move
equitable	fair	remuneration	payment
equivalent	equal	requirement	need
establish	set up, prove	selection	choice
expeditious	fast, quick	stratagem	plan
expertise	skill	subsequent	later, next
facilitate	help, ease	substantiate	prove
feasible	workable	terminate	stop, end
finalize	complete, finish	utilize	use

Now test yourself by replacing the following long words with short, one-syllable words.

1. accurate	26. fundamental
2. actual	27. implement
3. additional	28. initiate
4. allocate	29. limitations
5. aggregation	30. magnitude
6. apparent	31. methodology
7. ascertain	32. modification
8. assimilate	33. nebulous
9. assistance	34. necessitate
10. capability	35. numerous
11. commence	36. objective
12. constitutes	37. operational
13. demonstrate	38. optimum
14. denominate	39. preliminary
15. designate	40. prioritize
16. disseminate	41. probability
17. eliminate	42. proficiency
18. enumerate	43. recapitulate
19. equitable	44. remuneration
20. establish	45. requirement
21. expeditious	46. selection
22. expertise	47. stratagem
23. facilitate	48. substantiate
24. feasible	49. terminate
25. finalize	50. utilize

But Graham and Graham note, "You and the reader are stuck with some long words that have no good short word substitute: *civilization, computer, continuous, dangerous, helicopter, satellite, zirconium. . . .* You also use long words that take the place of many short words. For example, *management* = the people who watch over the firm's daily affairs."[6]

Fashionable Words and Phrases

In addition to confusing words and pretentious or multisyllable words, you might find yourself using fashionable words and phrases that will needlessly increase the word count of your text. Fashionable words and phrases seem to

[6] Graham and Graham. *The Writing System Workbook.* p. 108.

add an air of authority to your writing, but they really reveal that you're using other people's trite expressions. This, in turn, suggests that you can't think of your own words to express your ideas.

Fashionable phrases invade business writing more often than technical writing, but technical and scientific prose is not immune. Usually referred to in grammar and rhetoric books as *clichés* (from the French verb meaning *to stereotype*), these expressions spare the writer the burden of expressing exact meaning. If you use clichés in the belief that they sound authoritative, you're revealing that you're naive about using English. Both ESL and native writers of English err by using these expressions to make their writing sound more robust.

The first 10 of the following sentences are from memos and the second 10 from technical reports.[7] Review the sentences, identifying the fashionable word or phrase. Then substitute a simpler expression. Some of the clichés can be eliminated. There is no one correct way of improving the sentences, but suggested improvements follow the exercise.

An Exercise on Clichés

1. We are advancing our deadline due to the fact that funding will lapse at the end of the fiscal year.
2. Please respond to this memo at your earliest convenience.
3. We are calling a department meeting for the purpose of discussing our new contract.
4. I'm submitting this chit in lieu of an official receipt.
5. Please be advised that all personnel action reviews are due in the main office by June 30.
6. We are crediting your project as per your instructions.
7. Despite the fact that our informational meeting has been canceled, we are expected to prepare an action plan within 30 days.
8. Our office is in receipt of your memo #432, dated August 6.
9. Please be advised that the attached memo is a draft that has not been assigned a log number.
10. I am taking the liberty of expressing my concern through the corporation's Letter to the Editor column.
11. The proposed model uses a video accelerator chip to provide enhanced graphics capabilities.
12. The program will have a modular structure to enable enhancements and changes.
13. There are three parameters to be taken into account: flow-rate, pressure, and temperature.

---

[7] The second 10 sentences are derived from an exercise held at MIT's annual summer program: Communicating Technical Information. Their use is not restricted by copyright, but the program is credited as a courtesy.

14. Abrasive resistance has been a most difficult parameter to measure effectively.
15. The database will record the parameters of temperature tolerance.
16. The pitch datum chaser is activated, thereby inhibiting the attitude error signal.
17. The recommended system incorporates the following functions: error recovery with immediate or deferred error handling for error localization and inhibition of faulty elements.
18. Operation of the Stop Pulsing push button inhibits the main thyristor bridges, cutting the output pulses.
19. Improvements were several orders of magnitude greater than in the beta test.
20. The purpose of this report is to provide a summary of the work done to date for implementing Emanon's financial reengineering plan.

Answers:

1. *due to the fact that* is the fashionable phrase. Replace it with *because*.
2. *at your earliest convenience* is the fashionable phrase. Replace it with *quickly*.
3. *for the purpose of discussing* includes the fashionable phrase *for the purpose of*. Replace the entire phrase with *to discuss*.
4. *in lieu of* is the fashionable phrase. Replace it with English: *instead of*.
5. *Please be advised that* is the fashionable phrase. Eliminate it.
6. *per your instructions* is introduced by the fashionable Latin word *per*. Replace the phrase with the single word *instructed*.
7. *Despite the fact that* is the fashionable phrase. Replace it with the single word *although*.
8. *Our office is in receipt of* can be simplified to read *We received*.
9. *Please be advised* can be replaced by the single word *Note*.
10. *taking the liberty of* is both fashionable and ornate. Eliminate it.
11. *to provide enhanced* can be replaced by the simpler words *for improved*. Be wary of *enhanced*. It is extremely fashionable in technical writing.
12. Rewrite this sentence to read, *The program's modular structure supports enhancements and changes.* You might consider changing *enhancements* to *improvements*.
13. Eliminate *There are*. Replace *to be taken into account* with *should be considered*.
14. *has been a most difficult parameter* can be replaced by *is difficult*. *Parameters* is currently the most fashionable word in technical writing.
15. *the parameters of* can be eliminated. If you are uncomfortable with that decision, then replace the phrase with *the limits of*.
16. Simplify this sentence to read, "Activating the pitch datum chaser inhibits the attitude error signal." Be careful of *inhibit*, however. It's

competing with *enhance* for first place among the fashionable words of technical prose.

17. Replace *for error localization and inhibition of* with *to locate errors and discourage*. Here's *inhibit* again. You decide whether to keep it, or to replace it with some clearer word, perhaps *discourage* or *arrest*.

18. Rewrite this sentence. *Use the Stop Pulsing push button to bypass the main thyristor bridges, thereby cutting the output pulses.* You may have a better version.

19. *several orders of magnitude* is the most fashionable phrase in technical writing. It has a genuine mathematical meaning, but is usually written carelessly to mean *a lot of*. In this sentence, replace it with *much*.

20. *The purpose of* is highly fashionable in abstracts and in introductions to technical reports. Don't write about the purpose; simply state it: *This report summarizes current plans for implementing Emanon's financial reengineering.* Watch out for *implementing*, another high-fashion word.

Work very hard to avoid using *enhance, parameters, inhibit,* and *implement.* Unwatched, they will take over your laboratory.

Wordy Phrases

In addition to confusing, pretentious, and fashionable words, you should be alert to popular phrases that substitute for single words or simpler phrases. These phrases are deeply rooted in writing and speaking. Like multisyllable words, they can contribute to a pretentious tone. They will surely increase your writing's word count. Replacing them with single words will advance your progress toward plain prose.

Some Wordy Phrases

Wordy Phrase	*Replacement*
adjacent to	next to
a number of	some
as a means of	to
as prescribed by	under
at the present time	now
by means of	by, with
close proximity	near
due to the fact that	because
for the purpose of	for, to
has the capability	can

Wordy Phrase	Replacement
in accordance with	by, under
in addition	also
in an effort to	to
in conjunction with	with
incumbent upon	must
in order that	so
in order to	to
in regard to	about, concerning
in the amount of	for
in the course of	during, in
in the event that	if
in the near future	soon
in view of	since
it is essential	must
it is requested	please
limited number	few
provided that	if
provides guidance for	guides
take appropriate measures	please, do
until such time as	until
with reference to	about
with the exception of	except for

Nominalization

Another means of increasing your word count needlessly is through the technique known as *nominalization*: transforming verbs into noun phrases. A single word—the verb—grows into a string of three, four, or more words clustered around the noun taken from the subject-verb-object statement. Instead of saying, "He cancelled the flight," the nominalized sentence begins, "His cancellation of the flight. . . ." Nominalization sometimes creeps into your text without your awareness.

Nominalization not only pads your prose with needless words, but it adds a sense of vagueness. Because clarity and accuracy are the hallmarks of scientific and technical prose, vagueness is undesirable. If, however, you need to introduce a distancing factor to your prose, nominalization is the technique for you. Nominalization often teams up with passive voice to produce a really blurred picture for the reader. Fortunately, once you become aware of nominalization, you wonder how you ever tolerated it.

Find the nominalized word clusters in the following exercise, and convert them to their simple forms. Change the nominalization into a concrete verb.

1. A thousand Emanon employees will be in attendance at the MFA exhibit.
2. Avoid a confusion between elusive and allusive.
3. Large offices are a representation of corporate status.
4. The accountant's tabulation of the figures is correct.
5. A correction of security lapses is necessary.
6. Our manager is scheduled for a presentation of awards to long-service employees.
7. The Emanon library has announced the cancellation of overdue fines.
8. Mustapha provided a translation of the Arabic Peace Shield motto for me.
9. Emanon's board of directors voted for the reorganization of the corporation.
10. I volunteer for the orientation of new members of our group.
11. Some employees are in a state of confusion about the new matrix management structure.
12. The encouragement of good working relationships between Emanon Corporation and neighboring colleges and universities is a corporate practice.
13. Our lab environment is characterized by its commitment to individual research.
14. Emanon's educational unit is generous in its payment of tuition fees.
15. Departments Z30 and Z35 are carrying out flow property measurements on the unit.

Answers: 1-change *will be in attendance* to *will attend*, 2-change *avoid a confusion between* to *don't confuse*, 3-change *are a representation of* change to *represent*, 4-change *tabulation of the figures* to *tabulated the figures* (*correctly*), 5-change *a correction of security errors* to *correct security errors*, 6-eliminate *is scheduled for*; change *for a presentation of* to *will present*, 7-eliminate *has announced*; change *the cancellation of* to *will cancel*, 8-change *provided a translation of* to *translated*, 9-change *for the reorganization of* to *to reorganize*, 10-change *for the orientation of* to *to orient*, 11-change *in a state of confusion* to *confused*, 12-change *The encouragement of* to *encourages*, 13-change *is characterized by its commitment to* to *is committed to*, 14-change *is generous in its payment of* to *pays generously*, 15-change *are carrying out flow property measurements* to *are measuring flow property*.

8

GRAMMAR AND

STYLE FINE

POINTS

The Metaphor of Music

To be a polished writer, you will want to advance beyond the rudiments of correct grammar. Writing is a craft that needs to be practiced over many years before you can consider yourself an accomplished writer. You shouldn't let that realization daunt you, however, because high-quality writing, like any craft or skill, can be achieved more quickly by lots of practice and by careful attention to details.

Achieving writing competence is like learning how to play a musical instrument. The more you practice, the better you become. ESL writers must first familiarize themselves with the patterns of their target language. This is like doing finger exercises on a piano. Then, all those who write as part of their job learn how to fulfill the special expectations of their trade or profession. As a scientist or engineer, you write complete technical reports or journal articles. That's like being able to play entire musical compositions.

Finally, as a writer you'll shift your concern from what's correct and incorrect to what's good, better, and best. The shift from what's right and what's wrong to what's best is the route to virtuosity. A virtuoso musician develops fine shadings of sound and produces concert-quality music. Similarly, to become a virtuoso writer, you must fine-tune your prose so that it has balance and grace.

The Rhythm of Parallelism

Parallelism is an ancient technique. It's said to have been developed by the Greek rhetoricians in the Golden Age of Pericles. It was used by the famous Greek orators to enthrall their audiences. It also helped them memorize their speeches more easily. Parallelism was later adopted by the medieval European minstrels who used it for the same reasons. And it's used by speakers and writers today for the same reasons.

Parallelism means using the same grammatical structure for all logically similar parts of a sentence. It is heavily patterned, and, as such, is intentionally applied by the writer. Parallelism holds sentences together, adds emphasis, and provides a smooth, rhythmic flow to writing. If used more extensively, it can relate sentences to one another and even provide effective coherence between paragraphs. It's usually economical, because fewer words are needed to express ideas if they're grammatically parallel. However, a writer must occasionally add a word or two to reinforce his or her parallelism. Once undertaken, parallelism is a conscious commitment to rhythm that the writer must maintain throughout a chosen passage.

Here are five sentences from the workplace that use parallelism. They are followed by 10 general sentences with faulty parallelism. Correct the faulty parallelism. There are usually several ways of bringing two or three elements into conformity with one another. Suggestions follow, but your version may be better.

Good Parallelism

Emanon Technical Report #900 is out of stock and out of print.

Terry's ambition is to win a promotion and to earn a raise.

Outside office hours, Camilla has served the Girl Guides as a troop leader, an administrator, and a secretary.

Emanon staff members sometimes come to meetings with pens and pencils, notebooks and calendars, beepers and laptop computers.

To reach the simulation lab, you can take either the indoor tie corridor or the outdoor service route.

Note the perfect balance of the intentionally parallel units. In the fifth sentence, for example, *either the indoor tie corridor* and *or the outdoor service route* are perfectly symmetrical. Parallelism is contrived, and if you elect to introduce it then you are expected to edit very carefully to make sure you've achieved perfect symmetry. If the fifth sentence read, *you can either take the indoor tie corridor or the outdoor service route*, there would be a flaw. The position of *either* in front of the verb throws off the balance of the two symmetrical elements. If you were to diagram the sentence, it should look like this.

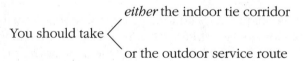

Note that the two halves of the correlative conjunction (either/or) are in exactly the same position in each of the two parallel phrases. Now apply these rigorous standards to the following sentences. Some of the corrections will be quite small. If you read each sentence aloud, you will probably be able to hear a dissonance.

1. Logical thought, coherent organization, and the ability to express oneself clearly are the major features of good writing.
2. The technical editor at the spectroscopy laboratory couldn't decide

whether she should ignore the technical report or to write an unfavorable review of it.

3. If you use Lotus 1–2–3, you can construct a database, analyze the data in a spreadsheet, present the data in graphical form, and the software can export results into a word processor.
4. The northwest corner office needs painting, to be cleaned, and a patch job.
5. The symposium committee requires that you be either prepared to submit your application on Friday or that you apply again in August.
6. The client not only is well funded but is also quite generous.
7. With our software you can write technical reports, enhance them with graphics, check spelling and grammar, and your screen will also display their color photographs.
8. A good manager not only works well with people, but also he does not compromise his ideals.
9. Having lost his contract and unable to find another, Omar charged his time to overhead.
10. Haystack Observatory will continue to refine geodetic-VLBI (Very-Long-Baseline Interferometry) instrumentation and to develop geodetic-VLBI technique and it will continue to freely distribute its work worldwide.

Answers:

1. Logical thought, coherent organization, and clear expression are the major features of good writing.
2. The technical editor at the spectroscopy laboratory couldn't decide whether she should ignore the technical report or review it unfavorably.
3. If you use Lotus 1–2–3, you can construct a database, analyze the date in a spreedsheet, present the data in graphical form, and export the results to a word processor.
4. The northwest corner office needs painting, cleaning, and patching.
5. The symposium committee requires that you be prepared either to submit your application on Friday or to apply again in August.
6. The client is not only well funded but also quite generous.
7. With our software you can write technical reports, enhance them with graphics, check their spelling and grammar, and display their color photographs.
8. A good manager not only works well with people but also preserves his ideals.
9. Having lost his contract and not having found another, Omar charged his time to overhead.
10. Haystack Observatory will continue to refine geodetic-VLBI (Very-Long-Baseline Interferometry) instrumentation, develop geodetic-VLBI technique, and distribute its work worldwide.

The Syncopation of Syntax

Sentence structure (syntax) offers another way of displaying your virtuosity as a writer. With a good command of syntax, you can add a varied beat to your writing. Sentence variety is a subtle way of keeping your reader interested in your prose. Nothing is more disturbing than reading an article in which every sentence has the same beat. All very short sentences produce a staccato effect. This is what's called primer prose—the sort of sentences found in the first reading books (primers) given to young school children. Typical primer prose sentences read, "See Jane run." "Spot is a dog." "Spot is black and white." "Spot has a ball." "See Spot chase the ball." After a while, your reader will either have an attack of nerves or will start to wonder what sort of person wrote the article. Neither response contributes to a good communication relationship.

Conversely, all very long sentences are boring. Your reader will soon become lost in the flood of information coming his or her way. Even though sophisticated subject matter sometimes requires sophisticated syntax, if all the sentences in an article are exceedingly long you run the risk of losing your reader. This reader will not become nervous or distracted. He or she will become bored or even befuddled.

Writing experts advocate using all medium-length sentences. This is the safe path. You will neither irritate nor befuddle your reader if you write everything in sentences of a certain number of words. Doing so, however, severely limits the sentence structures you can employ. Most likely you'll use simple sentences or compound sentences, the latter having short independent clauses. Your communication relationship with your reader is well served by this plan of action. However, you won't be using the full range of structures available in English. Safe writing isn't the same as excellent writing.

Recall that the four sentence structures of English are simple, compound, complex, and compound-complex. Simple sentences have one independent clause, and compound sentences have two or more independent clauses.

Simple Sentence—One Independent Clause

Researchers at MIT's spectroscopy laboratory have successfully operated a laser using a single, isolated atom.

Compound Sentence—Two (or More) Independent Clauses

(1) Researchers at MIT's spectroscopy laboratory have successfully operated a laser using a single, isolated atom, and (2) they expect to use the laser to advance their study of light and its interaction with atoms.

Complex sentences are not evenly balanced like compound sentences. Their clauses have a different relationship to one another. A complex sentence must include one independent clause and any number of dependent clauses. In the interests of clarity, technical writers usually create complex sentences of one independent and one dependent clause. As the definition implies, the dependent clause exists to support or expand the independent clause. Often, only the kind of conjunction used differentiates a compound sentence from a complex sentence. However, the kind of conjunction used influences the meaning of the sentence in a powerful way.

Compound Sentence

Kyungwon successfully researched the microlaser for his Ph.D. thesis project, and Professor Feld supervised his research effort.

Complex Sentence

Because Professor Feld supervised his Ph.D. project, Kyungwon successfully researched the microlaser for his doctoral thesis.

You can see that the meanings of these two sentences are clearly different even though the sentences use the same vocabulary. The first sentence indicates that Professor Feld's supervision was useful whereas the second sentence implies that it was highly supportive. The verbs in both clauses of both sentences are full verbs, so that's not the factor that introduces dependency. The significant factor is the kind of connector—the conjunction. In the preceding example, the subordinating conjunction is *because*. Compound sentences use coordinating conjunctions and complex sentences use subordinating conjunctions. There are only a few coordinating conjunctions: *And, or, but* are the most important ones. There are many subordinating conjunctions. Here's a list of the most frequently used ones.

Subordinating Conjunctions

after	since
although	so that
as	though
as if	unless
because	until
before	whether
if	when
provided	while

Subordination rarely has any problems associated with it. The only possible danger is excessive use, simply because it's such a useful structure. Excessive use could mean that you used complex sentences to the exclusion of other types, or that you piled up a great many dependent clauses in one sentence.

Compound-complex sentences are what the name indicates: a combination. You would need at least two independent clauses and one dependent clause to create a compound-complex sentence. The placement of the various clauses depends on you, the writer.

Compound-Complex Sentences

Because Dr. Ramachandra Dasari was a leader of the microlaser research team, Kyungwon An pursued the project for his doctoral thesis and Dr. Michael Feld supervised Kyungwon's research.

The research is supported by the National Science Foundation and has been performed at the Spectroscopy Laboratory's Laser Research Facility although future development of the microlaser may be conducted at a different laboratory.

Because of the semantic (meaning) difficulties you can get into with these hybrids, you will probably not use very many compound-complex sentences in your technical writing. But you needn't feel that they're not a usable item for your repertory.

The real point of this discussion isn't to review the four types of sentence structure because that would fall under a lesson in basic grammar, not a chapter on fine points. The lesson here is that you should be sensitive to the musical beat of your writing. Just as there is intonation in speaking, there is a texture or beat in writing. An advanced writer will stop occasionally and look over a piece of writing to see what sort of sentences he or she has composed. You may be surprised to discover that you favor one type of sentence. Your choice of sentence structure (syntax) is closely allied with your overall writing style. Sometimes you need to assess your syntax choices, and sometimes you may have to free yourself from overuse of one type. If your sentences lack variety, then rewrite some of them. A good mix of simple, compound, and complex sentences is the mark of a versatile writer.

Stress in Sentences

Another way of classifying sentence types is according to where the stress falls. Stress or emphasis in sentences refers to where you place the most important information. Stress position is also culturally influenced. For example, American English tends to distribute stress throughout the sentence, whereas British English often places the stress at the end. Specialists in discourse analysis explain that many sentences in written English are constructed with the old information at the beginning and the new information at the end. This is a slightly different interpretation of stress. Old information at the beginning of a sentence is material that's been introduced earlier in a conversation or in the preceding sentences of a report. Placement of old information at the beginning of the sentence gives listeners or readers time to orient themselves before the new information appears.

The new-information-at-the-end sentence pattern is useful for technical and scientific writing. It's especially useful for briefings because it helps the audience keep up with information that isn't being delivered in printed form. The placement of new or important information in each sentence isn't necessarily correlated with simple, compound, or complex structure.

If you find this fine point of writing interesting, you'll want to know that there are three general types of sentences classified according to stress position: *periodic, cumulative*, and *balanced*.

- A periodic sentence reserves its main idea until the end. The sentence type is named for the punctuation mark (period) that comes at the end of a declarative sentence.
- A cumulative sentence, sometimes called a loose sentence, completes its main idea and then adds subordinate details. Think of the word *accumulate* because that's how these sentences convey their information.
- A balanced sentence is a compound sentence in which the clauses are nearly parallel. Think of a seesaw with both sides ridden by children of equal weight.

Your choice will be guided by the emphasis you wish to create. Periodic and balanced sentences are usually planned by their writer. Sometimes they're produced during revision and don't occur in first drafts. As the periodic sentence is especially emphatic, you should use it with discretion. Balanced sentences are less important when you're thinking about where to place your stress because they don't emphasize one piece of information over the other. Consider the following examples:

Periodic

His vugraphs criticized, his presentation ridiculed, and his proposal rejected, Ernesto returned to his office in defeat.

Cumulative

Ernesto returned from his briefing with his vugraphs criticized, his presentation ridiculed, and his proposal rejected.

Balanced

Ernesto returned to his office, but he came back in defeat.

A skillful writer will use both periodic and cumulative sentences in the same piece of writing. Changing from a number of cumulative sentences to one periodic sentence is a very effective way of tightening your prose and quickening its pace.

The following exercise involves three steps. You may wish to go through the set of sentences three times, completing one step each time, or you may wish to complete all three steps for each sentence before going on to the next.

- First, underline the part of the sentence that contains the core idea—what you might call the main idea or the most important item.
- Second, identify each sentence as either periodic or cumulative (loose). There are no balanced sentences included in the exercise.
- Third, rewrite each sentence in its opposite stress pattern.

1. Martine showed great patience when her group leader revised her feasibility study four times and her secretary questioned her choice of words.
2. Our sponsor has rigorous requirements like those illustrated in the sample specifications.
3. While the technology center was establishing its identity and formulating its objectives, a major corporate reorganization left it obsolete.
4. Raoul was promoted because he raised employee morale, reduced expenses, and completed a major task successfully.
5. It's disturbing to realize that whenever we write a purchase order, it costs the corporation $60 to process it.
6. Because Emanon does not manufacture equipment, written reports are its most important product.
7. After three meetings, one briefing, and an interview, I ate my lunch.
8. What is needed in the research environment is a combination of patience, skill, and objectivity.
9. The project neared its final milestone with the engineers working frantically and the technical assistants writing furiously.
10. After much practice, many mistakes, and some embarrassment, the new employee learned how to use a personal computer.

Answers: 1-Cumulative: Martine showed great patience; 2-Cumulative: Our sponsor has rigorous requirements; 3-Periodic: a major corporate reorganization left it obsolete; 4-Cumulative: Raoul was promoted; 5-Periodic: it costs the corporation $60 to process it; 6-Periodic: paper is its most important product; 7-Periodic: I ate my lunch; 8-Periodic: needed . . . is a combination of patience, skill, and objectivity; 9-Cumulative: The project neared its final milestone; 10-Periodic: the new employee learned how to use a personal computer.

Opposite Stress Pattern:

1. Although her group leader revised her feasibility study four times and her secretary questioned her choice of words, Martine showed great patience.
2. The sample specifications illustrate that our sponsor has rigorous requirements.
3. A major corporate reorganization left the technology center obsolete even while it was establishing its identity and formulating its objectives.
4. Because he raised employee morale, reduced expenses, and completed a major task successfully, Raoul was promoted.
5. It costs the corporation $60 whenever we write a purchase order.
6. Written reports are Emanon's most important product because it does not manufacture equipment.
7. I ate my lunch after I attended three meetings, a briefing, and an interview.
8. A combination of patience, skill, and objectivity is needed in the research environment.
9. With engineers working frantically and technical assistants writing furiously, the project neared its final milestone.
10. The new employee learned how to use a personal computer after much practice, many mistakes, and some embarrassment.

Clauses As Chords

The skillful use of clauses in a sentence also marks you as an accomplished writer. Just as there are various ways of classifying sentences, there are several ways of classifying clauses. In an earlier chapter on ESL problems, relative clauses were introduced as a feature available in English but not available in all languages. To refine your use of relative clauses, you need to differentiate between essential clauses and nonessential clauses. After that, you can punctuate your writing to help your readers understand messages that may be embedded in your prose.

Sentences often carry meaning beyond the combined meaning of their words. Some of the meaning is implied, some may be only partially expressed, some is absolutely necessary for the full understanding of the sentence, and some is additional information that's good to have but not essential.

Nonessential meaning can be useful in a technical document. You mustn't feel compelled to eliminate from a sentence every word that expands its usefulness. Sometimes you'll find yourself trying to decide in favor of economy (fewer words) or clarity. Although economy is highly regarded in technical writing, clarity must never be sacrificed in the interest of economy. It'll be easier for you to make editing decisions about economy and clarity if you understand which information is essential and which is useful. After distinguishing between essential and useful information, you can decide how useful the nonessential information is.

Phrases and clauses that aren't essential to the meaning of a sentence are called nonrestrictive: They don't limit the meaning of the sentence, they enhance it. These phrases and clauses merely add information about a word already identified. On the other hand, a restrictive phrase or clause is essential to the meaning of the sentence. It contains information that limits or restricts the meaning of the word it modifies.

There are punctuation signals and sometimes word signals that you can transmit to your readers to help them interpret your sentences. First, we'll look at samples of sentences containing restrictive or nonrestrictive elements, and then at punctuation signals. Finally, we'll consider word signals.

Nonrestrictive Clause

Nam, whose office is across from mine, is our expert on artificial intelligence.

Restrictive Clause

The man whose office is across from mine is our expert on artificial intelligence.

In the first sentence you learn that Nam is the local expert on artificial intelligence. The fact that his office is across from mine is simply additional information. The clause *whose office is across from mine* is not essential to the core meaning of the sentence (Nam is our expert on artificial intelligence) and could be deleted. For that reason it's separated from the main clause by a pair of commas. In general, items inside a pair of commas can be viewed as additional but nonessential sentence elements.

In the second sentence you learn that the man whose office is across from mine is our expert on artificial intelligence. The clause *whose office is across from mine* identifies the expert. It is essential; therefore, it's restrictive and should not be separated from the rest of the sentence by a pair of commas.

The same sentence can sometimes be written either with a pair of commas or without, depending upon the author's intended meaning. In such sentences, only the writer knows the true meaning of the sentence, and that's why it's imperative that writers know how to punctuate meaningfully for restrictive and nonrestrictive use.

Restrictive Clause

Emanon's Vice President, Angus MacPherson, was selected to chair the National Academy of Sciences task force on educational reform.

Nonrestrictive Clause

Emanon's Vice President Angus MacPherson was selected to chair the National Academy of Sciences task force on educational reform.

In the first sentence, the writer surrounds the name *Angus MacPherson* with commas, thereby signaling that although there is only one vice president at Emanon, the reader might like to know his name. In the second sentence, the writer designates which of Emanon's various vice presidents was the one selected to chair the Academy task force. The comma indicates the difference in meaning between these two sentences.

The following chart may be helpful.

Restrictive	Essential to sentence	Omit commas
Nonrestrictive	Useful but not essential to sentence	Use commas

A further way of signaling restrictive or nonrestrictive use is through the words *which* and *that*. Here's an area of potential danger because when technical editors engage in "which hunting," replacing *which* with *that* whenever possible, they can distort the meaning of the author's sentence. Generally, if you intend a relative clause that does not refer to people to be nonrestrictive, you use *which* and punctuate the clause with commas. Alternatively, if you intend a relative clause to be restrictive, you use *that* and omit the commas. Because commas are used carelessly in English, sometimes a writer will use *which* and omit the commas for a nonrestrictive clause. This amounts to sending crossed signals. The following chart expands on the preceding one.

Restrictive	Essential to sentence	Omit commas	*that,* who, whom
Nonrestrictive	Useful but not essential to sentence	Use commas	*which*, who, whom

It's difficult to create an exercise for restrictive and nonrestrictive clauses and phrases because so much of the meaning of sentences is determined by writers. And in all created exercises, sentences or paragraphs are usually stilted and can be unrealistic. But if you'll take these limitations into consideration, you may find the following exercise helpful. Try punctuating the sentences to indicate if the italicized clause or phrase is restrictive or not.

1. The article *that is being submitted for publication* has been reviewed carefully.

2. The article entitled "Nemesis, The Death Star" *which is being submitted for publication* has been reviewed carefully.
3. This document *which is entitled "Nemesis, The Death Star"* is being submitted for publication.
4. The document *"Nemesis, The Death Star"* is being submitted for publication.
5. Dr. Muller's interim report about a prehistoric catastrophe *"Nemesis, The Death Star: The Story of a Scientific Revolution"* has been submitted for publication.
6. The deadly star *which is orbiting the sun* will set loose a barrage of comets.
7. The comets *that will barrage the earth* will do the damage.
8. The Nemesis hypothesis explains the disappearance of the dinosaurs *which requires data from geology, astronomy, and paleontology.*
9. Dr. Muller first expounded his hypothesis to Luis Alvarez *who served as Dr. Muller's mentor* before engaging in painstaking research and experimentation.
10. Nobel Laureate Luis Alvarez learned from his father *Dr. Walter Alvarez* that the key to discovery is not to be lazy.

Answers: 1-Restrictive, no commas; 2-Nonrestrictive, commas; 3-Nonrestrictive, commas; 4-Restrictive, no commas; 5-Nonrestrictive, commas; 6-Nonrestrictive, commas; 7-Restrictive, no commas; 8-Nonrestrictive, comma; 9-Nonrestrictive, commas; 10-Nonrestrictive, commas.

Sentence Combining

When your draft documents have been returned after copyediting, you'll often find long sentences separated into two or perhaps three shorter sentences. The primary concern of editors is readability, and their favorite technique for promoting readability is by breaking long sentences into short sentences. Writers are also interested in producing readable text, but readability is not their primary concern. Writers are interested in relaying information. The difference is that writers focus on content whereas editors focus on technique.

In this respect, writers and editors can be in conflict. They pursue similar but not identical goals. As you gain greater self-confidence as a writer, you'll be able to work more fruitfully with editors because you'll be able to better explain and if necessary defend some of your writing decisions. One of the issues you'll be prepared to discuss is that of sentence length. Often short sentences are better for readability, but too many short sentences equate primer-like prose.

English has many sentence structures available. These varied structures enable you to incorporate parts of one sentence into another (relativization, as an example). You can also express closely related ideas in structures that reinforce the close relationship of the ideas. Sometimes sophisticated ideas are best expressed in sophisticated sentences. By combining simple and separate sentences into one slightly more sophisticated sentence, you can frequently economize on words and also clarify a relationship between words. In the spirit of the music metaphor, you can compose more symphonic prose by a judicious use of sentence combining.

Here are two very simple sentences that can be written as a single sentence.

Separate

Walter Jones wrote an executive summary.
It is 20 pages long.

Combined

Walter Jones wrote a 20-page executive summary.

By combining the two sentences, you eliminate *it is* and *long*. And by placing the modifier *20-page* before the noun *executive summary*, you clarify the relationship between the adjective (20-page) and the word modifed (executive summary). You've produced a more integrated sentence and you've economized on overall word count. However, you have certainly written a longer sentence. This example probably oversimplifies the technique of sentence combining, but it may serve as a model for your future decisions.

Here's another example of effective sentence combining.

Separate

Peter Hagelstein invented a soft X-ray laser.
He invented it at Lawrence Livermore Laboratory.
He is an American.

Combined

Peter Hagelstein, an American, invented a soft X-ray laser while working at Lawrence Livermore Laboratory.

You can combine sentences in numerous ways.[1] Regardless of how you decide to do so, the primary purpose should be to show the relationship

---

[1] Sentence combining is an involved subject because there are so many ways of combining clauses. An excellent book that gives details for forming combinations is by Katie Davis, *Sentence Combining and Paragraph Construction*. New York: Macmillan Publishing Co., Inc., 1983.

between ideas. In each of the following groups of sentences, note the directions for combining the sentences.

1. Combine the following three sentences into a single sentence.

   Atlantis' astronauts captured a German satellite.
   They retrieved the satellite just north of Antartica.
   The satellite carried measurements of Earth's ozone layer.

2. Combine the following two sentences by using a subordinate conjunction to show the relationship between the ideas.

   The corporation did not hire the candidate from California.
   He was not qualified for the job.

3. Combine the following three sentences by adding a coordinating conjunction. Use *but* to indicate a contrasting relationship.

   Magnetic lines of force can pass through any material.
   They pass more readily through magnetic materials.
   Some magnetic materials are iron, nickel, and cobalt.

4. Combine the following five sentences into one sentence. Keep the same sentence order and employ parallelism.

   Atlantis Astronaut Ellen Ochoa captured a German satellite yesterday.
   The satellite is equipped to measure Earth's shrinking ozone layer.
   It tested experimental heat pipes.
   Its infrared telescopes collected 15 million images.
   It analyzed up to 14 atmospheric gases per second.

5. Try combining the following five sentences into two sentences, each with different structures. You can retain the same order of ideas and general order of words.

   The crew's most important decision had to be made.
   It was early on December 24.
   Apollo was approaching the moon.
   Should the spacecraft simply circle the moon and head back toward Earth?
   Should it fire the service propulsion system engine and place the craft in orbit?

Answers:

1. Just north of Antartica, Atlantis' astronauts retrieved a German satellite carrying measurements of Earth's ozone layer.
2. The corporation did not hire the candidate from California because he was not qualified for the job.

3. Magnetic lines of force can pass through any material but they pass more readily through magnetic materials like iron, nickel, and cobalt.

4. Yesterday, Atlantis Astronaut Ellen Ochoa captured a German satellite that was measuring Earth's shrinking ozone layer by testing experimental heat pipes, collecting 15 million telescopic images, and analyzing up to 14 atmospheric gases per second.

5. The crew had to make its most important decision early on December 24 as Apollo was approaching the moon. (complex sentence) Should the spacecraft simply circle the moon and head back toward Earth, or should it fire the service propulsion system engine and place the craft in orbit? (compound sentence)

TIPS FOR FINE POINTS

TIP   1: In refining your writing, think about improvement instead of correction. ·

TIP   2: When applying parallelism, be thoughtful; don't just drift into it.

TIP   3: Using parallelism is a style decision; producing flawed parallelism is a grammar problem.

TIP   4 Reading a sentence aloud helps you hear if its parallelism is flawed.

TIP   5: Counting the number of simple, compound, and complex sentences in a report you've written helps you understand your personal writing style.

TIP   6: Mixing types of sentence structure produces more interesting paragraphs.

TIP   7: Developing skill at writing periodic and cumulative structures enables you to position emphasis effectively.

TIP   8: Learning the difference between restrictive and nonrestrictive clauses is essential for an accurate transfer of information.

TIP   9: Punctuating nonessential words, phrases, and clauses with commas differentiates them from essential elements.

TIP 10: Combining sentences clarifies idea relationships and improves text economy.

Possessive Case in Technical Writing

A series of recent usage surveys shows that engineers use possessive case very frequently in technical writing. The nouns used in technical writing are almost always inanimate, and it's these inanimate nouns that are described as possessing attributes and functions. This fact arouses perplexity because technical writers sometimes try to respond to rules about possessive case that were formulated in an earlier era. However, the grammar of the last century didn't have to take into account the multitude of technical documents now published daily, all of which feature abstract or inanimate topics.

Possessive case was formerly known by its Latin name, genitive case, and some grammarians still use that name. Several methods exist for displaying possession. One is by means of the pronouns that show personal possession: my, yours, ours, and so forth. More relevant to technical writing, however, are the two general modes: apostrophe plus s, and the preposition *of*. We'll call the first the *s-possessive* and the second, the *of-possessive*.

s-possessive

The computer's memory was erased.

What is the project's deadline for completion?

The jet's engines could scarcely be heard.

Tell me your microscope's magnification.

of-possessive

The pages *of the book* were torn.

What is the name *of the ship?*

Our entrance is at the back *of the building*.

What is the location *of the radar*?

Because technical documentation is about things and not about people, the preceding sample sentences are about objects: computer, project, jet (plane), microscope, book, ship, building, radar. The choice of s-possessive or of-possessive was random; the governing factor was simply to illustrate the two possibilities.

SOME HISTORICAL BACKGROUND

Grammar books from the late nineteenth century stated the rule that only humans can be attributed with possession. As a result, only nouns denoting human beings were to be marked with the s-possessive. Everything else was to be marked with the of-possessive.

s-possessive

Amanda's brother lives in Liverpool.

The little girl's favorite story is "Peter Pan."

Queen Alexandra's kennel was renowned throughout England.

My wife's favorite nephew is visiting us.

of-possessive

The name *of the house* was Xanadu.

The top *of the table* is made of marble.

We scraped the bottom *of the barrel.*

The handle *of the jug* is broken.

A few items seemed to resist this classification system. For example, children persisted in talking about the *dog's tail* and the *cat's toy mouse.* Adults also referred to favorite horses or faithful hounds with the s-possessive: *Old Dobbin's new blanket* or *Fanny's puppies.* There were even some difficult-to-explain expressions like *today's newspaper* or *the ship's passage.*

Perhaps grammarians had to retrench because the next generation of grammar books stated the rule of possession a bit differently: Only animate objects could exhibit possession. As a result, they could be referred to with the *apostrophe* and *s.* Such a rule made it possible to admit animals (including beloved pets) into the realm of possessing attributes, qualities, offspring, and even names. They were exempted as "higher animals." Inanimate objects were to be designated by the of-possessive. Some difficulty now existed with respect to the "lower animals" who (that?) still had to be referred to with the of-possessive: the scales of the fish, the wings of the bug. Certainly there was no talk of the plane's wings or the computer's keyboard.

If this all sounds antediluvian, you need only to pick up a contemporary secretarial handbook. "As a rule, nouns referring to inanimate things should not be in the possessive. Use an *of* phrase instead." An example is provided: *the lower level of the terminal* followed by a boldfaced note—*NOT the terminal's lower level.*

A HYPOTHESIS

The question arises: What happens when all your technical subjects are inanimate? Do all the expressions of possession use the of-possessive form? Or do engineers consider their topics of sufficient liveliness to merit the s-possessive? Another consideration arises: What is the effect on the length of a document of using of-possessives for inanimate nouns? It surely takes more space and ultimately more paper to render all inanimates into the of-possessive, especially when most technical reports have multiple references to objects and a high rate of genitive usage.

We hypothesized that familiarity with inanimate objects might cause engineers to move away from the of-possessive and toward the s-possessive. Entrenched idiomatic expressions, many of which refer to animate or human nouns, would be disregarded in any test of the hypothesis. We didn't know what other variables might influence the choice. The only variable described in grammar books is that inanimate objects able to move often took the s-possessive.

Without explaining the purpose of the survey, we presented 10 sentences on a related technical subject to three audiences of scientists and engineers who were readily available: students in MIT classes, native English-speaking colleagues in an Research and Development center, and ESL professionals in a corporate on-site course. All the nouns in these sentences, as in most technical reports, refer to inanimate objects: measures, battle, situation, missile, model, computer, plane, bomber, escort (plane), ENHANCEMENT I.

Since this was a usage study, we were interested in learning how scientists and engineers actually use the possessive, not how they think they should use it. Consequently, they were asked to underline their choice of either the s-possessive or the of-possesive in each sentence without trying to remember rules about possessive case they may have learned in school.

We expected to find that late twentieth-century engineers would disregard the early grammar rules about genitive usage. We also expected that the MIT undergraduates would be even more emancipated in their usage. We had no preconception regarding the ESL group.

Most of the several hundred engineers surveyed chose of-possessive, so our hypothesis was disproven. In general, the engineering writers surveyed were far more conservative than we had expected. (In addition to engineers from the Boston area, engineers working at sites in Arizona and Texas were included in the survey.) As we expected, however, the college undergraduates surveyed showed a stronger preference for the s-possessive. The ESL participants were balanced in their choices.

While more study needs to be done on the use of possessive forms in technical writing, some interesting observations resulted from this survey. You might gain insights from these observations as you continue to refine your own writing.

- Rigid grammar rules prescribing markers for possession are not useful for technical writing.
- Habitual use of the of-possessive is more wordy than either varied use or s-possessive preference.
- Objects in motion (trains, planes, missiles) attract the s-possessive.
- The author's desire to emphasize, rather than a grammar rule, often promotes a preference for the of-possessive.
- Complex or lengthy modification (typical of technical writing) encourages use of the of-possessive.
- Associated modifiers can affect the choice. For example, *hostile* is a human-like characteristic; when applied to planes, it stimulates preference for the s-possessive.
- Style choices can supersede grammar rules when the writer or editor tries to avoid two adjacent *of* phrases.

- Aspects of former rules remain valid. For example, code words and acronyms elicit the of-possessive. Their highly abstract nature provides no suggestion of motion or animation. (The code name *ENHANCEMENT I* in one of the sentences is too intangible to yield to the s-possessive.)
- S-possessive and of-possessive are not viewed by technical writers as perfectly interchangeable.
- Cohort (age and education group) appears to be an influence in communication situations involving choice of grammar or style.

The study demonstrated that current writers of technical material describing inanimate nouns do not depart significantly from established rules. This suggests that a conformity factor may be in operation. If your particular work environment stresses conformity (the team player approach), you may need to bend your style choices to fit workplace norms. This issue becomes more important in collaborative writing settings. However, if your work environment encourages individualism (the creativity approach), you now know that enough reasons exist for you to depart from old rules regarding genitive usage. Like the law, rules of grammar are sometimes slow in adapting to new realities. This is true for both descriptive and prescriptive grammars.

Gender in Scientific and Technical Writing

In the last two decades, women have increased their efforts to gain fair treatment in society, and especially in the workplace. They have extended their struggle to include a reform of sexism in English. Their concern is that a bias in favor of men has been built into English. This bias is expressed in a number of ways, but the primary way is by using masculine pronouns wherever a gender reference is unclear. This is known as the rule of masculine by preference. This grammar rule was created to work around an inherent problem in the language. It provides a quick and easy solution to the lack of a singular pronoun that includes both sexes.

Masculine by Preference

Each manager is to turn in his monthly report on Friday.

An electrical engineer cannot complete his degree without a firm understanding of circuit theory and electromagnetic theory.

Understandably, women felt that sentences like these implied that only men are managers and that only men could matriculate for electrical engineering programs. When the small number of women in management and the very few women matriculated in engineering programs were noted, it became clear that there was a relationship between language usage and social reality.

GENDER IN TECHNICAL TEXTBOOKS

How to handle gender references is not a popular topic in technical writing textbooks. The great titans of technical writing—Robert Rathbone and Herbert Michaelson—wrote their books before gender in writing came to be examined more closely. Many current authorities on technical writing have neglected the topic in their textbooks.[2] It can't be found in the indexes of such outstanding textbooks as Michael Markel's *Technical Writing: Situations and Strategies* (now in its third edition) or his new IEEE guide, *Writing in the Technical Fields*. Huckin and Olsen's comprehensive textbook *Technical Writing and Professional Communication for Nonnative Speakers of English* offers no guidance for how to handle references to gender in technical documentation. Even the most recent edition of the *Government Printing Office Style Manual*, the most valuable resource for employees in U.S. Government agencies, doesn't include help with this perplexing issue.

Gender bias in English is an issue that perplexes technical writers for whom English is a first language as well as their ESL colleagues. It's especially troublesome to scientists and engineers from countries that have not yet become engaged with gender treatment in language, or whose first languages pose no gender problem.

GRAMMATICAL GENDER AND NATURAL GENDER

Some ESL writers have first languages that assign gender to all nouns in the language. This grammatical gender, which is artificial, arbitrarily designates each noun as feminine, masculine, or neuter. German is an example of such a language. Some languages assign masculine or feminine gender to all nouns, including inanimate objects. French is an example of such a language. English differs because it no longer has grammatical gender.

English relies only on natural gender: female creatures are feminine, male creatures are masculine, and inanimate objects are neuter. This is another way of saying that in English, gender for animate creatures is determined by sex. A lack of grammatical gender in English is part of the modern problem with gender assignations because there isn't grammatical facade behind which pronoun choices can be rationalized.

There is in English a sort of common gender that applies to certain general terms like boss, supervisor, employee, friend, and cousin, but this isn't the same as neuter case. The sex of these common gender words will be revealed if they are subsequently referred to with pronouns.

The second grammatical item that contributes to the current perplexity over

---

[2] Robert A. Day deserves credit for including a chapter on "Sexist Writing" in his recently published *Scientific English: A Guide for Scientists and Other Professionals*. Phoenix: Oryx Press, 1992.

gender references is the absence of any singular pronoun that can be used for both sexes. This peculiarity can be seen in four of the eight types of pronouns. (The other four of the eight types of pronouns are not involved: relative, demonstrative, interrogative, indefinite.)

Personal	he, she, it
Reflexive	himself, herself, itself
Possessive	his, hers, its
Intensive	himself, herself, itself

Plural pronouns, on the other hand, encompass all genders. You might think of them as gender-free. That's why casting problematic singulars into plurals has become one of the best ways of handling the gender issue. Words like *they, their, theirs, themselves* are devoid of any built-in gender bias.

THE PLURAL SOLUTION

The plural solution is the most graceful of the several ways devised to move away from the masculine by preference rule. It does take some rethinking of sentences to make it work, and sometimes it just won't work. You might approach this solution by writing as naturally as possible, and then go back to see if you can convert any of your noun-pronoun combinations that involve an needless gender reference into plural number. Obviously, if the named nouns are all male, you will continue to use masculine case. Here are a few revisions that you can use as models for the plural solution.

Plural Nouns and Pronouns

All managers are to turn in their monthly reports on Friday.

Electrical engineers cannot complete their degrees without a firm under-standing of circuit theory and electromagnetic theory.

THE ELIMINATION SOLUTION

Closely related to the plural solution is the technique of eliminating the gender-bearing pronoun. In this way, you can use either singular or plural number.

Pronoun Eliminated

Each manager is to turn in a monthly report on Friday.

All managers are to turn in monthly reports on Friday.

An electrical engineer cannot complete a degree without a firm understanding of circuit theory and electromagnetic theory.

Electrical engineers cannot complete degrees without a firm understanding of circuit theory and electromagnetic theory.

COMPOUND PRONOUNS

Often substantives (words and word groups that act as nouns) and their pronouns don't respond satisfactorily to plural number, or you really do wish to retain singular number. College faculty members have learned to lecture using the compounds *he and she, he or she* whenever this situation occurs. It's surprising how quickly you can accommodate to this style. At first you think about it for each reference, and very soon it becomes part of your speaking style. With writing, you have the same option. Yes, it does add words to the text. But so do many other technical writing techniques, and this technique has an commendable motive.

This option also yields another possibility. You can sometimes arbitrarily alternate *he* or *she* and *his* or *her* in the text. This alerts the reader to the fact that the writer does not favor the masculine by preference rule. Of course, this technique only works if the noun doesn't refer to a specific person.

Compound Pronouns

Each manager is to turn in his or her monthly report on Friday.

An electrical engineer cannot complete his or her degree without a firm understanding of circuit theory and electromagnetic theory.

Alternated Pronouns

Each manager is to turn in her monthly report on Friday

An electrical engineer cannot complete his degree without a firm understanding of circuit theory and electromagnetic theory.

Alternating male and female pronouns is more risky than using compounds. Taken out of context, a masculine pronoun appears to follow the old masculine by preference rule. The technique has a certain shock value that is quickly dissipated if you overuse it. Please do not use the truly ugly forms: he/she or (s)he.

WORD CHOICE

The issue of occupational words ascribed with masculinity or femininity has received more public attention than any other aspect of gender bias in writing.

It's helpful to remember that gender bias means stereotyping people by gender. When you speak of *airline stewardesses* you recall an era when women serving passengers were often treated by businessmen as geishas. When you write about *man-machine interfaces* you are suggesting a technical environment that values only men. When you issue memos that refer to a certain number of *man hours,* you ignore the existence of women who work alongside of men. It may take some time to become accustomed to using words like *human-machine interface* or *staff hours,* but using these terms shows that you're in the advance guard of the language revolution.

SYNONYMS

Here are a few synonyms that will help you overcome the gender gap. Some female designations can be eliminated altogether.

Occupation	Synonym
businessman	professional
chambermaid	housekeeper
fireman	fire fighter
foreman	supervisor
middleman	broker
poetess	[eliminate] [use poet]
policeman	police officer
postman	letter carrier
salesman	sales representative
stewardess	flight attendant
waiter	server
waitress	server

MR., MRS., MS., DR., PROF.

By this time, most professionals in the United States workforce have accepted *Ms.* as an impersonal courtesy title for a woman professional. This form was introduced when women realized that *Miss* or *Mrs.* as courtesy titles were appropriate for social situations but not for professional use. A woman's marital status should be no more significant in the workplace than a man's, which is always shielded by the courtesy title *Mr.*

Woman professionals appreciate it when their educational rank is acknowledged. Sometimes women with doctorates are considered unpleasant if they prefer not to be called by their first names in the workplace. If their male colleagues are addressed as *doctor,* then they should receive the same courtesy. For correspondence, you can solve the Miss, Mrs., Ms. problem by addressing a woman as Dr. or Prof. if she has a doctorate or if she holds academic rank.

Without question, awareness of gender bias has made our writing tasks more difficult and more time-consuming. Masculine by preference saved a lot of time. However, since that grammar rule is unlikely to survive in American English, you should plan your replacement strategies now.

Spelling in the United States

For centuries, English spelling was an inexact craft. At first, only wealthy people were educated and only educated people could write. If a university-educated scholar spelled the same word differently in various documents or in the same document, nobody questioned the matter. Unfortunately, some scientists adopted a similar attitude today. They relegate spelling and grammar to the care of secretaries or technical editors. Similarly, many university students challenge faculty who insist upon correct spelling and polished writing. The students relegate spelling to spell-checking software. Both scientist and student claim that "it's the idea that counts" and they leave their work for someone else to tidy up. Without a secretary or a software package, these modern-day aristocrats are helpless.

Today's business managers have attitudes about correct spelling that differ dramatically from those of the scientist or student described in the preceding paragraph. Managers expect their employees to produce letters, advertisements, and reports that are grammatically and orthographically correct.

Spelling is too often used by managers as a means of judging a piece of writing. Because spelling is so visible, it's easy to seize upon it as a measure of quality in writing. This measure of writing rapidly translates to a measure of the writer: Incorrect spelling is the mark of a careless employee. Since all engineers are educated, only careless engineers will spell incorrectly. The equation looks like this: incorrect spelling=poor quality writing=undesirable employee.

Employees from overseas who are trying hard to learn English are often the employees who work hardest at their spelling. They could serve as models for U.S.-educated professionals who dismiss correct spelling as an unimportant aspect of documentation. Because documents are often the first and sometimes the only deliverable a client receives, their quality must be nothing short of perfect. Perfection includes correct spelling. If for no other reason, pride of authorship should motivate technical and scientific writers to produce perfect documents.

SPELLING AIDS

HARDCOPY DICTIONARIES

Dictionaries remain the ultimate resource for learning, checking, and correcting spelling. The better the dictionary, the more information it will provide for each entry. Most dictionaries provide information about variant spellings (often British English spellings), but only some dictionaries will help you with spelling past or progressive tenses of verbs. Not everyone can afford a personal laptop computer with a spell checker, but everyone can afford a hard copy dictionary. Even an abridged, paperbound dictionary that can be carried to class is better than no dictionary.

SPELL-CHECKING SOFTWARE

Spell-checking software, popularly known as *spell checkers*, is widely used. It is extremely useful although it has notable limitations. First, the electronic dictionary incorporated into any one software package is never as complete as a good hard copy dictionary. Further, if you customize the dictionary by adding words from your professional vocabulary, you can easily add misspelled words that the checker won't know are incorrect.

Second, the software won't know if the word you're checking is misused. It only knows if a word is misspelled. The software will accept any possible spelling even if you've selected the wrong word. For example, many people confuse *preceding* and *proceeding*. The spell-checking software will tell you that both words are spelled correctly. It's only when you look up the word in a genuine dictionary that you can be sure you've chosen the right word.

Third, when running a general check for spelling, the software won't know if you've mistyped a word. If, for example, you've written *that* when you mean *than*, the software will not catch it. You can't rely completely on either spell-checking or grammar-checking software to proofread your document.

Fourth, spell-checking software weakens your ability to spell. It's like the calculators and computers used in banks. If a bank teller misplaces a calculator, he or she can't total your deposit. Bank tellers used to be able to add, subtract, multiply, and divide. If the bank computer is down, no transactions can be processed. The bank becomes dysfunctional because none of the branches has records of past transactions.

SPELLING RULES

If you don't have spell-checking software, you're more likely to learn the patterns of correct spelling. Any real language has a grammar of predictable patterns that are called rules. The rules have a high degree of reliability even though they do have exceptions. For example, here is a rule for adding suffixes to the end of certain groups of words:

> In words of one syllable and words accented on the last syllable, ending in a single consonant letter preceded by a single vowel letter, *double the final consonant letter* before a suffix beginning with a vowel letter.

This sounds overwhelming. But if you analyze it, you'll learn how to add -ed and -ing to many words without looking up the new spelling. Let's break down the rule to make your analysis easier.

1. This rule applies to short words of one syllable: *get, hit, drop, cut.*
2. It also applies to longer words in which the accent is on the final syllable: *prefer, submit, equip, begin.*
3. It does not apply to words that are not accented on the final syllable: *promise, benefit, offer, visit.*

Note that all these words end in a single consonant with a single vowel before it. This particular rule applies only to suffixes (additions to the end of a word) that begin with a vowel: a, e, i, o, u.

> This rule is especially useful because the greatest number of suffixes in English begin with a vowel: -ed, -ing, -ent, -ant, -able, -ible, -ence, -ance, -ous, and others. (For the record, some suffixes that do not begin with a vowel are -ful, -hood, -less, -ly, -ship, -some. These consonant suffixes are used far less frequently than the vowel suffixes.)

Now to see these directions applied to two categories of sample verbs, look at the following lists.

One-Syllable Words Ending in One Vowel Plus One Consonant

beg	begging	begged	begger
bid	bidding	bidden	
brag	bragging	bragged	bragger
cram	cramming	crammed	
cut	cutting	*irregular*	
drag	dragging	dragged	
drop	dropping	dropped	
get	getting	*irregular*	
plan	planning	planned	planner
quit	quitting	quitted	quitter
rob	robbing	robbed	robber

sin	sinning	sinned	sinner
snap	snapping	snapped	snapper
stop	stopping	stopped	stopper

Exception: do not double final *w* or *x*: *throw, throwing, fix, fixing, fixed*

The rule also applies to words that are not verbs. For example, *clan* and *man* are nouns; *glad* and *sad* are adjectives. They also double the final consonant if you add a suffix beginning with a vowel: *clannish, mannish, gladdest, saddest.*

Now, to apply the rule to some two-syllable verbs, also ending in one vowel, followed by one consonant. These words are accented on the final syllable and they double the final consonant when adding a suffix beginning with a vowel.

Two-Syllable Words Ending in One Vowel Plus One Consonant Accent on Final Syllable

ad**mit**	admitting	admitted	
be**gin**	beginning	*irregular*	beginner
com**mit**	committing	committed	
con**cur**	concurring	concurred	
con**fer***	conferring	conferred	
e**quip**	equipping	equipped	
oc**cur**	occurring	occurred	
pre**fer***	preferring	preferred	
sub**mit**	submitting	submitted	
com**pel**	compelling	compelled	

*Note: Do not double the final consonant if the accent shifts away from the final syllable when you add a suffix: confer⇒**con**ference; prefer⇒**pref**erence

If the accent falls on a syllable other than the final one, the rule about doubling the final consonant when it's preceded by a vowel before you add a suffix beginning with a vowel does not apply

Two- (or More) Syllable Word Ending in One Vowel Plus One Consonant Accent Not on Final Syllable

benefit	benefiting	benefited	
happen	happening	happened	
offer	offering	offered	
profit	profiting	profited	profiteer
visit	visiting	visited	visitor

The final permutation of the rule applies to suffixes that begin with a consonant when all the other factors are the same. Do not double the final consonant.

One- (or More) Syllable Words Ending in One Vowel Plus One Consonant Suffix Begins with a Consonant

equip	equip**ment**
glad	glad**ness**
man	man**hood**
profit	profit**less**
sin	sin**ful**

This analysis of a spelling rule may help you realize that spelling in English is not as haphazard as it may appear. Understanding this rule can lessen your dependency on spellcheckers and perhaps even on the dictionary. You can learn other similar rules later.

CHECKLISTS

A completely different approach to overcoming spelling weaknesses is to begin a list of words that you use frequently but about which you feel insecure. Many grammar books include prewritten lists of commonly misspelled words. However, you will improve more quickly if you create your own list. You'll have greater involvement with the words in such a list, and you can develop your own program for conquering each one. To make this *Resource Book* even more useful, you can use the following box for recording your personal spelling demons.

A Personal Spelling List

9

THE WRITING

PROCESS

Any piece of writing is greater than the sum of its parts. You master style and grammar to express the contents of your document, and you conquer grammar troublespots and learn fine points of prose to raise the quality of your writing. Grammar, style, spots, and points are all components that must be pulled together to create an end product that's greater than their combination. A good means of doing this is by adopting a systems approach to writing.

The systems approach to writing, as with a systems approach to engineering, shifts your way of working from micromethod to macromethod. From focusing on isolated components, you adjust your vision to see the entire system. Within the entire system, you look for the relationship of components to one another. As a result, a systems approach is integrative and comprehensive.

Integrated approaches have been adopted in many disciplines over the past two decades. In manufacturing, for example, the principles of Total Quality Management (TQM) and its corollary, continuous improvement, now inform the entire production process from predesign through post-distribution. In academia, writing-across-the curriculum attempts to integrate writing into all the other disciplines: sociology, psychology, history, language studies, and so forth.

Writing as a Process

In technical writing, this systems approach is called process writing. Writing-as-a-process, like systems engineering, TQM, and writing-across-the-curriculum, is an effort to promote integrative activity. When you adopt the philosophy of systems engineering or process writing, you are attempting to define a broader vision. Applied to writing, the systems approach helps you to explore how each stage of the writing experience relates to each other, while at the same time you keep the total product in mind. This fascinating exercise in simultaneous analysis and synthesis works extremely well in technical writing.

When applied to technical documentation, process writing promotes awareness of the activities that immediately precede writing and those that immediately follow it. These activities or stages in the creation of a document are called prewriting and post-writing. The total system is one of pre-writing, writing, and post-writing.

PROCESS WRITING FLOW DIAGRAMS

Technical writing consultants have borrowed from systems engineering the concept of the flowchart or flow diagram to depict the writing process graphically. Different writing experts have their own visions of the overall writing process, consequently, quite a few flow diagrams of greater or lesser complexity now exist. In addition to helping define an integrative approach to document production, these flow diagrams are also useful for analyzing collaborative writing processes. Collaborative writing as a discrete topic will be discussed in Chapter 11, "The Group Experience." For now, think of the writing process as it applies to your own productivity.

Figure 9.1 shows the relationships between components of the writing process in a clear and straightforward manner.[1] While separating the compo-

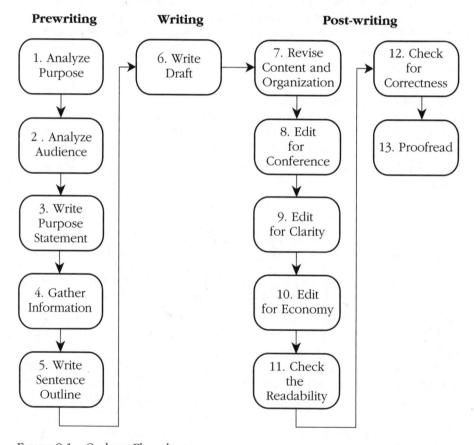

FIGURE 9.1   Graham Flowchart.

[1] Flow diagram used with permission of Graham Associates from "Effective Business Writing." Washington, DC: American Management Systems, Inc., 1991, p. 7.

nents into prewriting, writing, and post-writing activities, at the same time the diagram shows how they relate to one another. Finally, the diagram depicts the overall process. Consequently, it simultaneously takes apart and puts together an author's activity.

A graphical representation of the writing process shows you how to proceed with your writing task, thus alleviating anxiety about the assignment. You can see what you have to do without reading a lot of rhetorical theory. Further, seeing how to break the task into manageable units will do away with the fear that you may not be able to sustain the overall effort. If you undertake the process step by step, all the time keeping the big picture in view, you will feel more confident about your ability to write a substantial report. In addition, by following a flow diagram of the writing process you'll be able to write quickly. Since deadlines are a reality with which we all live, an approach that promises speedy completion is worth trying.

PREWRITING

Before beginning any piece of writing you need to identify the purpose—why you are writing this document—and the audience—for whom you are writing it. In creative writing, a definition of purpose is likely to be nebulous. You write a haiku or a short story to express an artistic urge or to create an object of beauty. Creative writing, from the viewpoint of purpose, can be abstract or vague.

Conversely, utilitarian writing, of which technical documentation is a prime example, always has a clear purpose. You don't write a monthly report or a technical advisory letter just because you feel like it. You write because you must.

Purpose and Purpose Statement

Usually, a technical document fulfills a contract requirement, either completely or partially. So you can assume that there is a clear purpose. Your job is to articulate it. For every document you are about to write, ask the question: "What is the purpose of this document?" Your answer will be your purpose statement. Remember that you will very likely incorporate the purpose statement into the beginning of your document. And you will surely use it at the beginning of any abstract you write after the document is complete. What you want to avoid is a trite expression of the purpose statement. It should be direct and full of information.

Trite Purpose Statement

The purpose of this working paper is to report the status of Emanon's financial reengineering project to date.

This is a typical opening. You have doubtlessly seen such statements many times, and probably haven't questioned their effectiveness. At a minimal level, this opening flags the fact that it is a purpose statement. It also provides a sense of direction to the reader. In that respect, it's useful. The reader should be the focus of the purpose statement, not the writer.

On the other hand, a purpose statement should be evident without being tagged. Your reader will expect the opening statement of a technical document to announce its purpose; it doesn't have to talk about doing so; therefore, eliminate the phrase, *The purpose of.* Second, you needn't identify the document as a working paper or a letter or a trip report. Your reader will know from its format, its identification number, and its manner of distribution what it is. So, eliminate the identifier. In this case, delete *this working paper.* Even the phrase *is to report* is wasting your reader's time. Working papers by their very nature report information. The first nine words of this purpose statement are both trite and unnecessary. In fact, they are merely the writer's way of getting started, of warming up to the writing task. Save this wordy purpose statement for yourself. It's marginally okay for the prewriting stage, but you will need to improve it for publication. Here's an improved version of the same purpose statement. Note that it gets to business more quickly and it also offers more information.

Improved Purpose Statement

Emanon's financial reengineering project was six months behind in its first phase of implementation. Several factors affected the project's schedule, and Department FR16's implementation team has created new software to overcome these factors for the next phase of implementation.

What are the categories of information that a purpose statement should include? As succinctly as possible, it needs to consider the audience, express who is performing the research, development, or implementation, and explain how the action will take place. Information about the probable outcome of the action should be included if appropriate. Future projections are not always called for in an informational tutorial. The decision to include an outcome projection depends upon the purpose of a document; you make the judgment call. Test the preceding purpose statement against these criteria:

Purpose Statement Components

(Implied) audience—internal: officers and employees.
Stated agents—Department FR16 implementation team.
Stated action—created new software.
Anticipated outcome—overcome unexpected factors; get project back onto schedule.

You can't control the audience for whom you're writing, nor can you designate the agents about which you're writing. You can control the vocabulary with which you state the actions and outcome. Of these two components—actions and outcome—action is where you can exert the greatest control. You choice of vocabulary, particularly verbs, gives you control over the impressions your reader gathers. To do so, develop a vocabulary of powerful, clear, and concrete verbs. In the preceding purpose statement, the writer used the verbs *create* and *overcome*. These two verbs convey positive vibrations, those of creativity and successful activity. Too often students and inexperienced writers resort to weak, almost meaningless, verbs to convey action. Words like *do* and *make* are unremarkable. If you're reporting on a project that's behind schedule, you want to convey a sense of energy and optimism. Many technical writers maintain an inventory of action verbs. You will doubtlessly be able to use some of these as you devise purpose statements for your technical writing.

Some Action Verbs

act	apply	assemble
assess	build	classify
compare	complete	conclude
conduct	create	decide
demonstrate	describe	design
determine	develop	enlarge
evaluate	examine	expand
identify	illustrate	implement
increase	indicate	install
observe	overcome	plan
prepare	produce	provide
purchase	reclaim	reduce
regulate	repair	restore
review	select	suggest
summarize	synthesize	test
train	transport	validate

AUDIENCE, SINGLE AND MULTIPLE

When you know why you're writing a document, you very quickly figure out who is supposed to read it. A technical document is rarely written only for the files. It can be, but not often. Even monthly employee reports that are primarily file documents are written from the point of view of the potential reader. Employees always picture how their supervisors will respond to what they have accomplished during the past month. In fact, the sense of the reader is so strong in monthly reports that it often skews how the information is presented.

Audience is the great motivator in technical writing. It goes without saying that user manuals require an enormous amount of research into audience factors before anything is keyboarded into a document. Consultants exist whose full-time job is to convene focus groups to query what readers like and dislike about different publications. Although the everyday laboratory report isn't preceded by focus group surveys, similar concern for the expectations of the report's audience is important. The act of identifying who your reader or readers might be will put you into a frame of mind to think about them as you write. The simple question you ask yourself is, "Who will read this document?" In this respect, writers of technical and scientific documents are far more fortunate than writers of creative prose. Someone who writes a short story for publication may never know his or her audience. That's why negative reviews of a novel sometimes come as a great surprise to the creative writer. Never having examined his or her audience, he or she is unprepared for audience reaction. You, on the other hand, are in a better position to tailor your work to suit your reader's expectations. By so doing, you have a high degree of assurance that your completed document will receive a favorable response.

Writers about to prepare a document in the workplace are able to survey their audience in advance. Even though their audience may be multiple, perhaps consisting of supervisors as well as external customers, the technical writer can start an audience analysis by taking a sentence outline to a supervisor to find out if the direction of the report meets the supervisor's expectations. This is known as testing the waters. If you are in a position to do this, by all means do so, because it can save you an enormous amount of time later. Preparing your supervisor in advance may protect you later from negative criticism. Enlisting your most immediate reader before you begin to write can gain support for your document during subsequent review cycles.

You have asked yourself, "What is the purpose of this document?" to steer yourself toward a purpose statement. You've also asked yourself, "Who will read this document?" to define your reader. Next, you need to ask, "Why will the reader read this document?" If your reader works for a funding agency, he or she intends to find out if the funds have been well placed. The funding agency may also use this information later to decide whether to continue funding. If your reader is a customer expecting delivery of a product, the customer wants to know if delivery will be as scheduled. If a client has asked your organization to come up with a feasibility study, he or she needs the information to project budgets for money and staff commitments. The possible reasons for reading a report are myriad. Some of them are almost self-evident. Others need your thoughtful attention.

SORTING MULTIPLE READERS

Thinking about this question (Why will the reader read this document?) will help you choose a proper level of expertise for presenting scientific or technical detail. A reader who wants funding information will probably not need a deep level of technical detail. A reader who must assess future staff commitments will need a higher level of technical detail for matching staff capabilities to project requirements. A reader who has issued an RFP will want to compare your level of expertise with that of your competitor. If your document will be read by more than one person, you must sort out who is most important, less important, and least important.

At the same time, you have to bear in mind the internal reviewers who can seriously delay your document if their needs are not met. To suit internal readers, you must write defensively in order to get your document into distribution without enervating delays. Satisfy their expectations while simultaneously satisfying the information needs of your target reader. No scientist or engineer writing in the workplace really has a single audience. At the very least, you are writing to pass internal review as well as to inform a target reader. Your reader analysis might end up looking like this:

Internal Reader(s)	*External Reader(s)*
Supervisor	Primary target reader
Peer reviewer	Secondary target reader
Technical editor(s)	Tertiary target reader

Internal readers are easier to predict because they are usually familiar people. You'll know if your company uses both hierarchical (management chain) and collegial (peer) reviews. While keeping internal readers in mind, you must direct your writing to primary target readers. If you know why the primary reader will read your document, then you know the level at which to write. In brief, write to the level of your most important reader. Others will have to fall into place. If you know that secondary or tertiary readers will have different reasons for reading your document, try to add some details to satisfy their interests, but add them after you've completed your first draft.

Multiple readers make your writing task very difficult, but knowing their reasons for reading your document will increase the probability of its achieving its purpose.

GATHERING INFORMATION

Gathering information constitutes the lifework of scientists and engineers. They perform experiments, create prototypes, and conduct research to gain information. Usually the information necessary for a report has already been collected by the time you are called upon to write. It would be presumptuous to tell a scientist or engineer how to gather information.

What you do need to think about, however, is how to sort through and select from the information at hand. You are more likely to have too much information rather than not enough for your report. Obviously, if you don't have enough, you aren't ready to write. If you have a great deal of information, you have to exercise discipline. The report does not exist to provide a forum for everything you know about topic ABC. The report exists to convey specific information to an identified audience. For this reason, your purpose statement will help guide you in selecting what information to incorporate into your document. Just as when you wrote research papers for secondary school and college, some of your information will be discarded. The best way to translate your purpose statement into the matter of a document is to prepare some sort of outline that will both select and order the information you have at hand.

OUTLINES

As an example, when this *Resource Book* was conceived, it was seen as a compendium of useful information for the English as a second language professional engineer or scientist working in the United States. The audience was manifestly clear in the mind of the author. The purpose of the *Resource Book* was *to fill* a gap in the materials available to this audience. It was *to provide* critical information in a comprehensive manner. To be functional, the purpose needed fuller expression in an outline that would impose structure on the large amount of information that a resource book could contain. The outline would also help to determine which details the author wanted to use, and by omission which details were already adequately covered in other books.

Unlike the recommendation in the Graham flow diagram, the author's outline was not always in the form of complete sentences. Sometimes words and phrases were all the author needed to trigger a subset of information that would fit into the slot indicated by the outline. In other instances, full sentences were used. Sometimes short paragraphs were better for capturing topics.

Authors respond differently to outlines, and you might find phrase, sentence, or paragraph outlines are the best approach for your purposes. There's no reason why you can't combine them. The more experienced you become as a writer and the more knowledgeable you are about your subject, the less regimented your outline can be. Although you may not care to work with outlines, don't refuse to do so. They enable you to get all your information into logical relationships, and they prevent you from forgetting important material.

After reviewing the outline for the *ESL Resource Book*, the publisher next requested a brief synopsis of the book's chapters. This request forced the author to add another dimension to her outline. Not only did each synopsis require full sentences, it revealed how some aspects of the outline had to be altered. Items that fit together were combined into a single chapter. Some chapter synopses were longer than others, suggesting that some chapters would be longer than others. You might keep this observation in mind as you structure your technical report. You will be structuring major sections instead of chapters, and you need to think about how much weight to give to each section. Some sections may contain less material than others because there may be less to say or the information is less important. Trying to make every section of your report the same length will tempt you to add needless fill.

PROPORTIONS OF TIME INVESTED

The flow diagram of the writing process shows a surprisingly large investment of time for the prewriting stage. All the work of determining your audience and preparing a useful purpose statement, of gathering information and arranging it into logical order takes place before you even think about writing a draft. The post-writing stage is also time-consuming. In fact, post-writing takes more time than composition. Of the three stages, the actual writing takes the least amount of time. This insight elicits surprise from most technical writers. Various estimates have been made about the proportion of time allocated to each of the stages. These estimates vary, but a realistic estimate might apportion 25 percent to prewriting, 25 percent (plus) to writing, and approximately 50 percent to post-writing. Budgeting a large amount of post-writing time allows for your own revisions as well as for the multiple reviews through which all documents pass in a research center.

The Writing Stage

The scientist as writer has a long tradition in European history. An engineer composing at a computer is a descendant of the medieval scribe writing in his study. The monk who tried to capture in writing the truths of the universe is forefather to the scientist who writes up the results of an experiment to be read by colleagues around the world. When the preparation for a writing task is complete, the actual writing must begin. Here's where you'll find the sentence outline (and if you have one, the paragraph outline) enormously helpful. Each of those sentences will launch a new subsection, eliminating the problem of getting started. Getting into a new section is the hardest part of writing. That's why so many purpose statements and topic sentences sound like engines warming up. The sentence doesn't start to move until the fifth or sixth word. But the cold start is avoided if you can plug in your prepared section openers and then develop each one with supporting statements, examples, and technical details.

WRITING AS RAPID PROTOTYPING

The secret to writing a document is the secret of rapid prototyping. Plunge in and move through the text quickly. This technique is very, very difficult for scientists who have been trained to move with exquisite care and for engineers who are arch-conservatives when documenting their work. This may be the only time in your life when recklessness is encouraged. You mustn't stop to check your punctuation and spelling although you may pause to arrange a sentence more gracefully if that act gives you satisfaction. The point is that you mustn't tinker with your writing as you produce your first draft. You'll have up to 50 percent of your budgeted time to go back to change words, insert better examples, check subject-verb agreement, and work out your punctuation later. As one writing consultant advises: sprint.

Unfortunately, office routines being what they are, you sometimes can't stay with a writing task. Meetings, visitors, and emergencies call you away. Even lunch and coffee breaks get in the way. However, you should fight to stay with your writing task as long as you can. The more you write, the better you'll feel about your productivity. Success feeds upon success.

Not all writers have the same needs. But all writers do need to stop writing when they feel they've exhausted themselves. If you believe you're starting to write inferior text, it's time to stop. If you've allocated enough time to your writing task so that you can spread it over a couple of weeks, return to your task the next day. A new day gives you a fresh outlook. You'll be able to summon crisp words and clear sentences.

THE OTHER AUTHOR

When engaged in a writing project, you should have some scraps of paper and a pencil handy on your bedside table and on the dashboard of your car. If you drive back and forth to work from the suburbs, as many do, you'll find that stops at red lights and delays in traffic offer excellent opportunities for capturing vagrant ideas that can buttress something you wrote the day before. These gratuitous ideas will appear without your forcing them. You only need to capture them. This is probably the opposite of the so-called writer's block. Recognize writer's gush when it happens, and don't ever ignore it. It's possible to jot down a few key words without going off the road. You can even compose beautiful sentences while waiting at a red light.

Your subconscious is your co-author. As a writer, you work on several levels of consciousness. Just because you've turned off your computer doesn't mean that you've turned off your mind. When you are resting, often when you are sleeping, your mind continues to work over problems you've been trying to solve. That's why you need a paper and pencil on your night table. If you wake up and find that you've gained a new insight while sleeping, you must write it down before it disappears. Sometimes these fugitive ideas have a lifespan of a few milliseconds. As Jack Ryan's wife says in Tom Clancy's *Debt of Honor,* "If you don't write it down, then it never happened."

THE INCREMENTAL METHOD

This discussion of the writing phase has assumed that you'll write your technical or scientific report at the completion of a project. This method is both conventional and acceptable. An exception to the "total report at completion of project" method is a milestone report, where you'll be writing about work in progress until the time of a critical milestone. You may afterwards write a completion report to cover the entire project.

Milestones mark important junctures in the progress of your experiment. When everything is finished, they remain as the landmarks in your research. Milestones may be artificially defined by a client as time requirements: a monthly report, a six-month report, an end-of-year report. Or they may be determined by natural breaks in the continuum of the project: completion-of-research report, implementation report, follow-up report. Similarly, major stages in a long-term project may be written as a report on the prototype, a report on the beta test, a completion report.

The idea of milestone reports for documenting significant stages of a project or experiment suggests an alternate way of pacing your writing. Rather than writing your material conventionally at the completion of your work, you might consider writing your material in incremental sections. This methodology was first suggested by Herbert Michaelson in the first edition of his groundbreaking text on technical writing, *How to Write and Publish Engineering Papers and Reports*, now in its third edition.[2] Michaelson calls his method "The Incremental Method." It merits consideration.

Michaelson recommends that instead of waiting until you've completed your project before beginning to write, you write throughout the course of its progress. The major advantage of such a method is that you're not hit with the entire task at one time. Further, as he points out, practicing engineers are often quickly reassigned to another project without being given time to write up the results of an earlier job. When you do get to writing the report, you may have lost some of your enthusiasm about the experiment. Loss of immediacy and enthusiasm can be reflected in your prose. Further, the longer you delay your report, the less likely it will be to represent state-of-the-art technology.

The incremental method does have some built-in problems. If you use it in a literal way, you'll end up writing a chronological report of your experiment. Following a time line is certainly one way of structuring a body of information. It's always the most simple way but rarely the most effective way. The time line dominates the material so that every aspect of the experiment or project assumes equal importance. An effective report highlights important aspects and deemphasizes unimportant ones. Michaelson recommends that you avoid this problem by writing an outline at the beginning of your project rather than at the beginning of your writing, as in the conventional method. He claims that in this way your writing may even influence your research. It is questionable that conducting an experiment or setting up a project to follow a report outline, including possible outcomes, represents good scientific methodology. Perhaps the incremental method works better for engineering than for scientific research.

Notwithstanding, the incremental method can be useful if you feel threatened by the prospect of writing a long report all at one time. You might adapt the incremental method, refusing to permit a predetermined outline to force your research decisions. Writing up whole sections as you proceed with your assignment can't help but capture the excitement of the moment, and may even remind you of some steps that might otherwise escape your memory. You might look upon the incremental method as keeping a journal. After the experiment or project has been completed, you can excise information that hindsight shows to have been less important or even irrelevant. And you can

---

[2] Herbert B. Michaelson. *How to Write and Publish Engineering Papers and Reports*, Third Edition. Phoenix, Arizona: The Oryx Press, 1990.

develop more fully those sections describing procedures that turned out to be of paramount importance.

In summary, use any tricks and stratagems that will aid you during the writing phase. If you write conventionally, sprint without fixing up your text. If you write incrementally, keep a journal or write up chunks of prose for later use. In either method, be prepared at all times to capture vagrant ideas and insights.

This list of tips summarizes the prewriting and writing phases of the process approach to documentation.

TIP   1: See your documentation task as an integrated process including pre- and post-writing.

TIP   2: Use the flow diagram in Figure 9.1 to guide you through your writing task.

TIP   3: Determine the purpose of your document before you create an outline.

TIP   4: Write a purpose statement and use it as a point of reference throughout your task.

TIP   5: Identify as clearly as possible the audience for your document.

TIP   6: Recognize the members of a multiple audience and try to appeal to all.

TIP   7: Write at the technical level of your most important reader.

TIP   8: Add information for secondary readers after you write your rough draft.

TIP   9: Analyze why readers should be interested in your document.

TIP 10: Prepare an outline for your document, using any form that works for you.

TIP 11: Choose a sentence outline if the form is immaterial to you.

TIP 12: Write quickly without regressing to correct spelling and punctuation.

TIP 13: Fight for time to dedicate to your writing task. Write as long as possible each session.

TIP 14: Stop writing only when you become exhausted and your prose becomes limp.

TIP 15: Learn to capture unexpected ideas and insights that appear during odd times.

Post-Writing

Post-writing is the most time-consuming part of the writing process. It can equal that needed for production and printing. When viewed from an even broader perspective, the writing process is a process within a process. The larger picture might be called the writing and production process. If publication of your document is urgent, you must make it your business to plan far ahead. Not only must you factor in the post-writing phase, which falls partly under your personal control, but also the production process, which is largely beyond your control. Engineers and scientists sometimes abdicate from responsibility for their documents once they've written the draft text. If urgency is an issue, you may find yourself having to step out of the role of writer and into the role of production supervisor. The systems approach means that you'll involve yourself in the entire process.

Post-writing is really revising and editing. And at the very end of the process, it's even proofreading. Some brief definitions are in order.

THREE DEFINITIONS

Revision is from the Latin *revidere*, to see again. In English it means to look over again, and it usually applies to a whole document. Revision is the umbrella term that includes under its purview both major and minor changes that will improve your document. Major changes might include reorganizing parts of the document and adding, deleting, or expanding material. The Graham flow diagram in Figure 9.1 allocates a separate step for revision of content and organization. Some authors divide this review into two separate steps: one for content and one for organization. Most of us review and revise best when we're concentrating on one aspect of the manuscript at any one time. It's necessary to separate this larger function of the post-writing phase from the smaller functions included in editing.

Editing, or copyediting as it's sometimes called, requires that you revisit your manuscript, sometimes several more times, to catch style inconsistencies and to check grammar correctness. You might consider one review for style issues and a separate review for grammar. The grammar review is sometimes referred to as a review of mechanics. If you've reviewed your document twice, once for content and once for organization, and you now review for style and for grammar, you are revisiting the manuscript four times after completing the draft. These multiple reviews explain why so large a proportion of your time has been allocated for post-writing. It's during the fourth review of your document that you can permit yourself to double-check your spelling and punctuation, those items that so often delay authors during the drafting stage of writing.

Proofreading, which is the last step of the revision process, is intended to perfect the physical text. Here, you or a professional proofreader look for missing or unnecessary spaces between words, words that have been typed twice, uppercase and lower case letters that need to be changed, mishandled acronyms, inconsistent headers, and all such typographical details.

THE ESL FACTOR

Prewriting, with its gathering of information and identification of audience and purpose, presents no special problems to the writer from overseas. As educated professionals, you know how to conduct research and organize its results just as well as your American counterparts.

Writing is a personal experience for each author, regardless of his or her native language. Writing with speed will elicit errors of grammar from all writers, and at the writing phase don't concern yourself with these errors. Your responsibility is to put your information onto paper in a logical manner. Thus, as an ESL engineer or scientist, you are at no special disadvantage.

Post-writing will be the most difficult stage of the writing process for the ESL professional. It will certainly be more time-consuming than for an American counterpart. Keep this in mind. Any insecurities you may have with word choice, with phrasal verbs, idioms, verb tenses, and article usage will have to be confronted during post-writing.

The aspect of post-writing for which you must reserve an especially generous amount of time is editing. Let's look at why this is so. During the first step of revision for the larger elements, you'll be able to review the effectiveness of your document's organization and the completeness of its content as well as any colleague. Having a different first language shouldn't have a major influence on decisions about content. Regarding organization, if you've had your supervisor review your outline before starting to write, you probably have an acceptable scheme of organization. At the minimum, you have an approved scheme of organization. ESL writers do, however, have to make sure that the logic of their outlines conforms with western notions of logic. Finally, the proofreading step of post-writing can be relegated to a professional proofreader or to your secretary.

It's the central phase of post-writing—the editing phase—that will cause the most difficulty. Failure to recognize this fact is where an ESL scientist or engineer can get into serious trouble. On the other hand, recognizing the fact may motivate you to develop personal compensatory strategies. In sum, the editing step of the post-writing phase of the writing process poses the greatest threat to an ESL scientist or engineer. You may need additional help with editing decisions, but first try to cope with editing by yourself before handing your document over to a technical editor. Regard the technical editor as your safety net. If you simply hand your document over to a technical editor after reviewing it for organization and content, you may never learn how to correct certain errors without help. Reading this *Resource Book* indicates that you believe in the philosophy of self-help. So, first do the best you can with your editing task, and only then enlist the aid of a technical editor.

Role Change: Author to Editor

Just as you had to shift your role from engineer to author, you now have to shift from author to editor. Most companies maintain editorial services for their authors, but before turning your document over to a service representative, plan to edit it yourself. You, as engineer-author or scientist-author, are the best editor for content. Technical editors develop impressive expertise in their company's specializations, but they aren't qualified to judge scientific methodology or experimental validity of your experiment. Difficult as it is to distance yourself from your own writing, you must disengage yourself from the role of author to achieve objectivity. Many academicians set aside a completed piece of writing for several days before returning to it as editor. If you're on a tight publication schedule, insist on at least an overnight break before reapproaching your document for editing. ESL professionals are especially urged to create a physical break between writing and editing. If you can afford the time, set your manuscript aside for a week.

Revision for Content

You can elect to review content first or organization first. It's a bit easier to edit for organization. However, if you find afterwards that you've had to revise content, that could affect the document's structure. When you tackle a content edit, check to see that you've included all salient parts of the research, have eliminated extraneous elements, and have buttressed assertions with supporting detail. It's acceptable to include negative results, alerting readers or other experimenters to unsuccessful techniques and warning other professionals away from attractive but nonproductive paths of inquiry. Of course, you don't want to over-emphasize the negative. As mentioned earlier, you need to check that you've given proportional attention to processes: longer explanations about more important factors. One enormously important content element you must check is the conclusion. Many technical papers have conclusions that simply do not follow logically from the information provided in the body of the paper. This is the most common failing of papers by experienced authors submitted to an annual competition held by a large research and development center in New England. Leaps in logic may be acceptable in metaphysics, but not in electrical engineering.

Content includes your choice of a title. Most writing consultants advise writing a title after the document is complete. This precludes writing a title that promises something that the paper fails to deliver. If you like to create a title in advance, think of it as a working title—a title that may guide you but which can be altered or replaced after—writing.

Creating interesting titles is one of the most satisfying parts of an author's job. Two-part titles are commonplace and useful. They indicate the nature of the contents in one part and the nature of the format in the other. A two-part title can also name and further qualify the content of a report.

Two-Part Titles

Emanon's Financial Reengineering Project: A Plan for Early Initiation

Lotus Notes: An Information Sharing Tool

Scientific English: A Guide for Scientists and Other Professionals

When checking your title, keep in mind that it should not be written as a sentence. Omitting normal sentence elements saves words and also gives greater vivacity to your title. Also keep in mind that the content of a title should not be sacrificed for brevity. Many authors write titles that are too short to convey sufficient information to prospective readers. Related to this issue is the usefulness of a title in electronic retrieval systems. Include enough concrete key terms in your title to help a reader anywhere in the world find your paper based on title alone or on title and abstract.

A content review will also ensure that prior research has been credited and sources of data acknowledged. As author, you must make frequent decisions about which facts are in the common knowledge of a discipline and which facts must be attributed to other scientists. Aside from being an ethical decision, this is a judgment call that you are best equipped to make. A technical editor, for example, is unlikely to know the state of prior art, what is widely known, what has been recently discovered, and by whom. Forms of crediting sources vary, and you can discuss them with your technical editor. Your responsibility in a content review is to identify material and references that merit citation.

A responsible content review revisits the issue of a document's audience. While you do analyze audience in the prewriting phase, you need to reconsider if the completed document will satisfy the identified audience. Also, find out if the audience has changed while you've been gathering information and writing text. If new players have come aboard, you may have to add details to the contents. Further, this is the stage at which you add the technical details for secondary readers. Having written to the technical level of your primary reader, you must now look to see where you can appropriately provide the details that second- and third-level readers need.

Not only must you consider adding material when you're revising content, you must take the plunge and eliminate extraneous detail. As writers, we often get carried away with the details that interest us. A reader-oriented revision will make sure that such details will also interest the audience. If not, minimize or eliminate them. For some authors, this is the hardest part of revision. Authors develop protective feelings toward the material they write and find it disturbing to destroy anything. This might be the Frankenstein complex where the creature escapes from the creator's control.

A checklist will help you with your content review. Use the following checklist to stimulate checkpoints of your own.

- ❑ Have you stated the subject and purpose of the paper early in the paper?
- ❑ Have you included sufficient detail to support every major assertion?
- ❑ Have you alerted readers to unsuccessful techniques and nonproductive procedures?
- ❑ Have you made absolutely sure that your conclusions follow from the information provided in your paper?
- ❑ Have you created an informative and interesting title?
- ❑ Does your title lend itself to electronic retrieval?
- ❑ Have you credited other professionals and cited sources of data?
- ❑ Have you checked to see if your audience has changed during fact-finding and composition?
- ❑ Have you added information needed by secondary and tertiary readers?
- ❑ Have you eliminated material that interests you more than the audience?

Add five of your own checkpoints for reviewing content.

- ❑ _____
- ❑ _____
- ❑ _____
- ❑ _____
- ❑ _____

REVISION FOR ORGANIZATION

The organization of a document is built into it according to principles of logic and then displayed by means of titles, section headers, and subheadings. In other words, there is correspondence between what is included in the paper and how it is designated. Nontechnical writing doesn't use such elaborate display of structure, usually confining itself to chapter numbers and titles. The assumption of nontechnical writing is that the book or article will be read from beginning to end.

Unfortunately, authors of technical books and articles have learned this is not the case for their documents. Scientific and technical readers search for the elements that interest them, and often skip the other parts of the text. Technical readers are probably more likely than scientific readers to read in this hunt-and-peck manner. Readers of user manuals are the most flighty of all audiences. When the user of Microsoft Word wants to know how to set up a three-column table that's centered on the page with internal and external borders, he or she isn't going to read the manual from cover to cover. He or she will look in the index for an entry that addresses that need, and then turn directly to that page. The rest of the manual will be read on an as-needed basis, and probably the entire manual will never be read.

Technical readers demand both ordered content and visible markers. Consequently, your review task is twofold. You must ascertain that your organizational design is logically complete and correct, and you must make sure that the organizational divisions are clearly and consistently marked.

Your organizational line of reasoning should be stated early in the document so that your reader knows he or she has a map in hand. Keep your purpose statement displayed on a clipboard next to your monitor so that you can refer to it frequently. If you keep your preapproved outline equally accessible, you can check against it to make sure you haven't strayed from your plan of organization.

The easiest task in organization review is to check for a full and distinct introductory section as well as for a full and logical concluding section. You can call these sections *Introduction* and *Conclusion*, or you can create more imaginative titles. If you choose the latter option, make sure that the notions of introduction and conclusion are conveyed by the wording. It's safe to assume that the rest of your document is the body. Of course, you don't simply call everything else *Body*, so if you haven't provided interesting and appropriate subtitles throughout the body, this is the time to write them.

When creating titles and subtitles for the body section of your document, keep them parallel. If you use words for the first subdivision, then continue with that format. If you decide to use phrases, not only should you continue to use phrases, but you should also create phrases that all reflect the same syntax. In this chapter, the author has decided to break the major sections with one-word subtitles: Prewriting, Writing, Post-Writing. She has decided, however, that subsections would be more informative in the form of phrases: *Revision for Content, Revision for Organization, Editing for Coherence, Editing for Clarity*, as examples. Note that not only are the words parallel, but so too are the formatting elements.

A somewhat clumsy way of checking the overall consistency of your header scheme is to duplicate your document and strip away all the text on the duplicate. You'll be left with titles and subtitles that you can more easily evaluate. If you are fortunate enough to have an outlining feature in your software program, you can view your outline without seeing the associated text. An outlining program also enables you to move a chunk of your text along with its header, and have the move register in the outline. You can see immediately if you violated the integrity of your outline when you moved the chunk of text. However, many people can't write using an outline program. If you find the program inhibiting, don't force yourself to use it.

Most companies provide templates that format sections and subsections without your having to set them up. This enormously helpful support software wasn't always available. However, you still have to do a little work. You have to plug in titles that go beyond generic designations like *Subsection One, Subsection Two,* and so forth. And you do have to keep in mind the hierarchical relationship of information. You decide when your material dictates a drop to a lower level in the document's structure. And remember the old outline rule that once you've introduced a subsection one, you need to introduce a subsection two (or more). If you find you really don't have enough information for a subsection two, reformat the section, eliminating subsections, and keeping all your information at the section level.

Beneath all this armature, of course, you must have developed your subject in the most logical manner possible. Some people have greater talent than others for doing this. Some people see things hierarchically while others see them in global perspective. This is often a cultural factor, but it can be a factor of cognitive style or even gender. Engineers are eminently good at seeing outline patterns. This may be the result of training, or it might be that a preference for logical structure is an influence in propelling students into engineering. Whatever the reason, if you think your logical vision doesn't conform to the expectations of your workplace, seek help. You can turn to your officemate for a quick structure check. You can ask your instructor in a corporate class to take 20 minutes to review this single aspect of your document. A peer review will probably uncover a problem here, but you might want to take care of it before circulating your document for general comments.

A checklist for review of organization will get you started. Because revision for organization is easier than revision for content, you won't need as many checkpoints.

After completing your next edit for organization, you can add your own checkpoints to the following list. Perhaps you won't need to add any.

- ❏ Have you stated your line of reasoning early in your document?
- ❏ Do you have full and distinct introduction and conclusion sections?
- ❏ Have you provided informative and interesting subtitles throughout the body of your document?
- ❏ Are your section titles and subtitles parallel in syntax and parallel in format?
- ❏ Have you confirmed the hierarchical relationship of each section and subsection?
- ❏ Have you used transitional words to indicate these relationships?
- ❏ Have you introduced a second subsection whenever you've introduced a first?
- ❏ Is there a correlation between each subsection's length and the importance of its contents?
- ❏ Have you checked to see if reorganizing any one section has affected other sections?
- ❏ Have you taken time to try outlining programs and format templates?

EDITING FOR STYLE

Shifting from revising content and organization to editing for style and grammar entails a somewhat different level of attention. The former tasks are inclusive, whereas the latter will be more particular. In the first chapter of the *Resource Book* you learned that technical writing style in the United States is quite standardized. Its characteristics are clarity, accuracy, comprehensiveness, accessibility, conciseness, and correctness. It emphasizes plain prose and simple word choice. Whenever possible, it favors brevity of expression, although brevity must never take priority over clarity. Many technical and scientific reports that circulate widely do not conform to these standards. You'll find that convoluted sentences and multisyllable words are often preferred over plain prose and simple word choice. Some of these mannerisms may have crept into your own prose, so watch for them as you edit for style.

Many software programs exist to to help you write simply and directly. At first they were separate packages that you had to buy and install on your computer. Writer's Workbench is such a program. Most of these programs focus on similar aspects of style, but they can only handle elementary aspects of style, and sometimes confuse style and grammar. They all identify passive voice and suggest active verbs as replacements. Most of them search for nominalizations and recommend revisions of such noun phrases. They will highlight overused words, and attempt to spot sentences that they call run-ons. Such style-checking software is now part of most word processing packages, so everyone can invoke the grammar and style tools.

However, these electronic programs can never replace the author, a secretary, a technical editor, or a writing specialist. Human experts understand syntax in a way that artificial intelligence probably never will. The tone of your writing, possible ambiguities, and inappropriate digressions are a few of the features that won't show up in an electronic edit. Therefore, you should use your style- and grammar-checking software with reservations. Don't obey it slavishly. Sometimes it will be useful, and sometimes it won't.

All this points out that you are your own first line of defense, and you must develop your own editing strategies. To make your third review (after content and organization reviews) of a draft document manageable, focus exclusively on style, ignoring grammar. At first, limit yourself to those aspects of style with which you feel comfortable. Before undertaking a comprehensive sweep for coherence, clarity, and economy—stylistics cited in the Graham flow diagram—first ask yourself a few general questions as you reread your draft. This checklist contains only questions about style. You will undoubtedly want to add checkpoints as you think about more elements of style.

❑ Have you chosen words to express your meaning exactly?

❑ Do you generally choose simple (Anglo-Saxon) words over ornate (Norman) words?

❏ Have you distributed your modifiers so as to enhance understanding?
❏ Will both primary and secondary readers understand your sentences?
❏ Have you used a variety of sentence structures?
❏ Have you broken up very long sentences into shorter units?
❏ Have you used acroynms only where necessary?
❏ Have you limited professional jargon to the level of your readers' usage?
❏ Have you eliminated clichés and other prepackaged expressions?

COHERENCE, CLARITY, AND ECONOMY

EDITING FOR COHERENCE

Paragraph coherence is discussed in detail in Chapter 2. To review, general coherence in documentation is reinforced by two distinctly different methods. You should use both for any long or medium-length document.

• Prose chosen to show relationships between thoughts.
• Visual devices inserted to show relationships between topics.

The following do's and don'ts of documentation coherence refer to the first method.

Do's of Coherent Style

Do repeat key terms as often as needed.
Do create noun-pronoun reference patterns.
Do use transitional words and phrases.
Do choose the right transitional word to convey an intended relationship.
Do link ideas with demonstrative adjectives: *this, that, these, those.*

As you progress through your coherence edit, here are some negative items to look for.

Don'ts of Coherent Style

Don't substitute new words for terms already introduced.
Don't abandon parallel structure within sentences or between sentences.
Don't write sentences in isolation.
Don't fail to link graphics with text.

You will have already encountered some visual devices for coherence during your review for organization. Coherence in the format of a document is reinforced if you are consistent in setting up its segments. Although writers are too frequently charged with the crime of inconsistency, 100 percent consistency is essential in designing and positioning visual elements. But while visually consistent elements reinforce coherence between document segments, they mustn't be used to establish false relationships.

Visual Consistencies in Documentation

The document title must be consistently worded throughout the document.

Chapter (or section) headers must be consistent.

All level headers must be consistent.

Figure captions should be consistent.

Table captions should be consistent.

Bibliography items should be parallel.

Table of Contents items should be parallel.

Table of Contents items should replicate their format in the document.

Each time you revise during editing, you may be introducing new problems. To be safe, limit revisions to what is really necessary. When you *must* revise in order to correct or improve a document, double-check to see if you've disturbed coherence. This applies especially to changes in the order of sentences in a paragraph. Assuming that the sentences originally had a logical flow, you can disrupt that flow when you delete a sentence or shift its position.

Editing for Clarity

Clarity in documentation refers to meaning that is easily understood and free from ambiguity. Editing for clarity involves word choice and sentence structure, both of which you studied in Chapter 4, "Special Style Notes." The following short checklist will serve as a review.

- ❏ Use active verbs to express actor, action, and result clearly.
- ❏ Present facts in positive form; reserve negative for exceptional use.
- ❏ Use English words; replace Latin and French terms.
- ❏ Limit modifiers; rearrange them for optimum clarity.
- ❏ Remove gender bias; devise a graceful system for gender references.
- ❏ Replace abstract words with concrete words.
- ❏ Replace vague words with specific words.
- ❏ Make verbs indicative for statements and imperative for directions.
- ❏ Omit rhetorical questions—questions without real answers.
- ❏ Avoid shifting verb tenses without cause.

An issue that you have not read about earlier is ambiguity. Ambiguity means that a word or sentence can have at least two meanings. An ambiguous statement lacks clarity. Although ambiguity is often confused with vagueness, it isn't the same, nor is it the same as abstractness. Vagueness is sometimes introduced intentionally in correspondence or during a conversation if the writer/speaker is trying to avoid making a commitment. But vagueness should never be introduced into a technical document. When it occurs accidentally in technical writing, it represents a failure of clarity. Fortunately, it's easily overcome. Vague expletives like *there is* and *there are* as sentence openers should be replaced with the real subject of the sentence. Vague pronouns that don't have a noun preceding them need to be strengthened. Here are examples of these two kinds of vagueness.

Vague Expletives

There is going to be a meeting in the new conference room tomorrow.

There were system upgrades promised for both centers.

Vague Expletives Replaced

The department will meet tomorrow in the new conference room.

Xanadu Systems promised system upgrades for both Cambridge and Washington.

Vague Pronouns

What is *this* all about? (What is *this*?)

Because Emanon didn't support financial reengineering, *it* failed. (What failed, Emanon or the reengineering project?)

Vague Pronouns Replaced

Snow is predicted for later today.

What is this argument all about?

Because Emanon didn't support financial reengineering, the company went out of business.

Ambiguity is a more serious problem than vagueness. And editing for ambiguity is more difficult than editing for vagueness. Once you've been alerted to the usual carriers of vagueness, you can quickly replace them. But ambiguous terms or sentences are far more elusive than those that are merely vague. Since clarity by definition is absence of ambiguity, you'll need to learn how to recognize ambiguity. To cure ambiguity, you must first learn to diagnose it.

Two kinds of ambiguity are *lexical ambiguity* and *structural ambiguity*.

Lexical refers to words; words with two or more possible interpretations are ambiguous. Structural ambiguity is a result of how words are arranged in a sentence. Not any of the words in a structurally ambiguous sentence are troublesome. But an ambiguous sentence is prone to misinterpretation—a dangerous situation, especially in a scientific context. Each of the sentences in the first two sets of examples has one ambiguous word that gives the sentence two possible meanings. No one word in the sentences, including the ambiguous word, is difficult to understand, nevertheless, the meaning is unclear.

Lexical Ambiguity

Junko couldn't *bear* children.
(Junko is incapable of giving birth.
Junko doesn't like children.)

Nam found a *bat* in his laboratory.
(Nam found a mammal with wings in his lab.
Nam found some sports equipment in his lab.)

After the computer scientists complained, their managers decided to give them more *power.*
(The managers gave the scientists more influence in management decisions.
The managers gave the scientists more powerful computers.)

Lexical ambiguity is rarely found in technical writing because so many nouns and verbs are deeply embedded in the context of a description. Nouns and verbs also often have multiple modifiers that quickly clarify an intended meaning. Structural ambiguity is more likely to occur. English has a high incidence of structural ambiguity. You may not always see it in a sentence, and you're less likely to see it if you've written the sentence because you know what you meant to say. But your readers may sometimes be baffled by what seems to you to be a straightforward statement.

Structural Ambiguity

Flying planes can be dangerous.
(Are townspeople at a zoning board meeting remarking about the danger of airplanes flying over their town?
Are aviators applying for life insurance commenting on occupational risk?)

In the preceding example of ambiguity contained within the structure of a sentence, the problem is solved when the sentence is put into a larger context. Thus, you may not have too much trouble with this kind of ambiguity. However, the really problematic sentences are those that remain ambiguous even when placed into a reasonable context.

Structural Ambiguity

We saw a pretty little girls school.
We saw a school for little girls. The school building is pretty.
We saw a school for girls. The school building is small and it's pretty.
We saw a school for girls who are all pretty and little.
We saw a school for girls. The building is moderately small.
We saw a school for girls who are moderately small in size.

You can find many more possible interpretations for this one sentence because it is deeply ambiguous from a structural point of view. In addition, it contains one word that exhibits lexical ambiguity: *pretty*. *Pretty* can be understood in this sentence from the standard meaning of *attractive*, and it also makes sense from the colloquial meaning of *somewhat*. The ambiguity is greater in this sentence when spoken, because careful punctuation can help improve the written version. However, punctuation is not as complete a solution to structural ambiguity as technical editors believe. In fact, commas can make the matter worse. If you are successful in identifying a structurally ambiguous sentence, the best thing to do is to rewrite it. Don't just load it with commas. You'll have to add more words and phrases to make your meaning clear. When ambiguity is an issue, you mustn't hesitate in sacrificing economy in favor of clarity.

EDITING FOR ECONOMY

When you edit for economy, you edit to bring your document up to the technical writing standard of conciseness. The practical purpose of conciseness is to encourage your reader to really read your document. Extraordinarily long documents usually discourage readers. As noted several times earlier, however, your pursuit of conciseness must never be at the expense of clarity. You do have to explain every aspect of the system, object, or service described in your document. Your task is difficult because you have to find a balance between clarity and conciseness.

Your goal is to express the most information in the fewest possible words. First, you have to decide if you've included information that isn't necessary. Remember your readership test. Write to the needs and interests of your readers, not to your own. Granted, you as author and engineer must sometimes decide for the readers what they need to know. In such a case, clarity comes first.

Second, you need to pare back your manuscript. Your experience as an author-editor will demonstrate that you'll always remove more material from a draft than you add. The joy of editing is the joy of deleting unnecessary phrases, using economical forms, selecting short words instead of long words, and liberating yourself from lengthy clichéd expressions.

Editing for economy is the easiest of your revision tasks because many techniques exist, all of which are simple and straightforward. They include cutting out redundant expressions (those that say the same thing twice), converting nominalizations to action verbs, excising *there is, there are, it* sentence openers, eliminating needless prepositions, among others. As you become more analytic about your own writing style, you'll learn where you get into trouble with wordiness. Not all writers commit the same crimes against conciseness.

See Chapter 7, "Grammar Troublespots," for help with recognizing pretentious words and fashionable expressions that you can eliminate from your writing. That chapter also lists multisyllable words that have single-syllable replacements and wordy phrases that have concise equivalents. In addition, the chapter contains information about active and passive voice with illustrations of wordiness associated with the passive voice. At the end of the chapter, you'll find an exercise on nominalization.

You read about meaningless sentence openers earlier in this discussion of editing for style, but redundant expressions and needless prepositions still need to be addressed.

ELIMINATE REDUNDANCY

One form of redundancy includes expressions that contain the same idea stated in two different ways. These short phrases are often clichéd. They appear more often in correspondence and memos than in technical or scientific reports. Look for the repetitiveness in the following examples. Every one of the following expressions can be reduced to one of the two terms.

absolutely essential
advance forward
advance reservations
basic essentials
cancel out
cease and desist†
close proximity
completely eliminate
consensus of opinion
end result
enter into
eradicate completely
first and foremost†
full and complete†

mutual cooperation
null and void[†]
personal opinion
tried and true[†]
unexpected surprise
utter destruction

Doublings (those examples followed by the dagger symbol) are a close relation of redundancies. They actually have a very impressive ancestry; Shakespeare is a famous doubler. His plays and sonnets contain many examples of expressions that are half Norman French and half Anglo-Saxon. The balance is highly poetic. It satisfies the human urge for rhythm, much like parallel sentence structure. Doublings are more likely than redundancies to creep into technical documentation because engineers try hard to invest their writing with the highest degree of completeness possible. Be alert, however, because some compounds that look like doublings actually make useful distinctions. These sample sentences may help you see the difference.

Needless Doublings

Miranda Campbell wrote a *full and complete* account of access to the corporate information server through World Wide Web client software.

Once connected to Emanon's networks, *each and every* employee can gain access to the server through appropriate World Wide Web client software.

First and foremost, employees can access the Technology Program Server via the following address: http://www-xxxx/xxx.

Useful Compounds

Users can *view and mail* the documents they retrieve through the database.

Write and read access for project principles will be through AppleShare for Macintosh users and Novell NetWare for PC/Windows users.
World Wide Web's client software offers hypertext capabilities that make
World Wide Web's client software offers hypertext capabilities that make it *quick and easy* to search a full-text index.

Needless Prepositions

Prepositional phrases increase the word count of any piece of writing. The genitive usage study in the Chapter 8 showed how s-possessive is far more economical than of-possessive because the latter format introduces a prepositional phrase. As a rule, engineers are very economical with their prepositional phrases. The unwieldy pileup of modifiers in front of nouns illustrates the extent to which engineers will go to avoid using prepositional phrases for qualification. Scientists may be a bit less inclined to use premodification. Businessmen and businesswomen, scientists, and engineers all need to discriminate between prepositional phrases that are useful and those that are excessive. In the following exercise, delete the prepositional phrases that are excessive and retain any useful ones. In some cases, you may have to rewrite the entire sentence.

1. Irmgard's review of the project on DNA at high resolution first appeared in the Macromolecular Structure and Function Seminar Series introduced by her department head, Dr. Jason Friedman.
2. The Macromolecular Structure and Function Seminar Series was announced in January during the monthly meeting of the laboratory.
3. The Rich Lab reserved Kresge Auditorium in order that all interested students could attend their lectures at the present time as well as in the near future.
4. In the process of reserving Kresge Auditorium, Rich Lab representatives explained that their laboratory seating facilities at this point in time were inadequate for the size of their audiences.
5. In order to satisfy the great interest in the Macromolecular Structure and Function Seminar Series, members of Rich Lab will repeat the first five lectures whether or not a large audience is expected.
6. In making this decision, the laboratory director is mindful of the fact that he may overspend his budget for the current fiscal year.
7. In order to qualify for the exemption from budget review by the oversight committee, Rich Laboratory must conform to certain requirements.
8. In accordance with university policy, the laboratory can seek an exemption because of the fact that its research mission is so critical.
9. With regard to their educational mission, the members of the research team plan to continue the seminar series in spite of the fact that funding is in question.
10. Because they are in the midst of important experimentation in four-stranded intercalated cytosine-rich DNA, the members of the research team will have to put in extra hours in order to prepare their lecture materials.

Check for Correctness

You are now almost finished reviewing your document. The final steps are to check for correctness and then to proofread the final version. Your correctness check includes grammar and mechanics. Grammar includes, among other items, spelling and punctuation. A mechanics check looks at format and typography.

Many authors who don't know how to revise and edit their documents begin with grammar, neglecting the important areas of content and organization. Inexperienced English teachers often follow the same course of action. They add periods and commas and correct spelling because they haven't yet learned how to evaluate style or improve organization. Unfortunately, this doesn't mean that inexperienced teachers or editors simply reverse editing methodology. It usually means that they focus on the easy and obvious tasks, after which they consider the editing job complete.

SPELLING

Your best approach for checking spelling is to buy a recent edition of a good dictionary. *The American Heritage Dictionary* and *Webster's New Collegiate Dictionary* are good choices. If you are using an outdated dictionary, you may find that compound forms have changed since the dictionary was printed. You may even discover that the word you need to look up wasn't in the lexicon five or 10 years ago. Don't plan on using someone else's dictionary. You'll learn through frequent use of a personal copy how to use a dictionary most effectively. For a review of some basic spelling rules and a discussion of how to use spell-checking software, refer to Chapter 8, "Grammar and Style Fine Points."

Many teachers vaunt *Roget's Thesaurus* (or anyone's) as a writing tool. You will do better to invest the additional money in a really good dictionary. If you are feeling extravagant, you might consider buying an unabridged dictionary. In addition to providing multiple definitions, a high-quality dictionary will tell you how a word sounds, its parts of speech, past and progressive tense spellings, historical background, and etymology—language origins, word roots, foreign language variants, English variants. Sometimes dictionaries include illustrations, and they almost always provide extremely useful synonyms. On the other hand, a thesaurus suggests word groupings that often aren't close to the meaning of the target word you're researching. You have to guess about which word grouping comes closest to the word that interests you. If you feel compelled to find a synonym for a word you've already used, you'll do better to use a synonym from a dictionary because it will already be close to the meaning of your original word. Shopping for words in a thesaurus is a fascinating pastime, but it frequently results in quixotic word choices. If you really do wish to use a thesaurus, check to see if you already have an electronic version installed on your computer. An electronic thesaurus offers a less bewildering selection of synonyms and is less likely to lead you astray.

PUNCTUATION

As you edit for punctuation, be wary about apostrophes in possessives and apostrophes in contractions. When checking contractions, see if the apostrophe is in the position of a missing letter or letters. For example, don't = do not, shouldn't = should not, o'clock = of the clock. The most frequent apostrophe error in English is use with the words *its* and *it's*. No writer is beyond making the *its* punctuation error. Overcome this pitfall by reminding yourself often that:

it + apostrophe + s = the contraction for *it is*.
it's = it is

Also, an apostrophe to show possession is *not* used with possessive pronouns. By their very nature, possessive pronouns show possession. Adding an apostrophe is overkill. When *its* is a possessive pronoun, it follows the same rule: no apostrophe.

Possessive Pronouns = No Apostrophe

mine, ours, yours, his, hers, its, theirs, whose

The only time you would use an apostrophe with *whose*-like form is when you intend to contract *who is* into *who's*. In that case, you're using a contraction, not a possessive pronoun.

A comma usage peculiar to technical writing is called the final series comma. Series commas should also be used in scientific documentation to help avoid confusion about sets. In a series comma list, every independent item is separated from every other item with a comma—including a comma in front of the *and* that introduces the last item of the list.

Nontechnical Writing

During our cruise, our ship will dock at Aruba, La Guira, Barbados, St. Kitts and St. Thomas.

Our Thanksgiving dinner menu included soup, turkey, stuffing, mashed potatoes, sweet potatoes, peas, celery, pickles, olives, cranberry sauce and pumpkin pie.

Technical Writing

Applicants for the position must have experience installing and servicing Local Area Networks, Wide Area Networks, T1 links, and fiber optics.

GTE examined its structure and found that each area of its company had its own set of applications, data, and functions.

Users can print items in many formats including Microsoft Word, Power-Point, PostScript, Text, and Hyper-Text Mark-Up Language.

Commas are the most frequently used marks of punctuation in English; consequently, many opportunities exist for error. Further, because commas are weak, unlike the strong end marks—periods, question marks, exclamation points—their usage is more variable. If you are unsure about commas, refer to a good grammar book for an extended discussion of correct comma usage. Your local college book store will have some on the shelves. Your company library, your neighborhood library, or the library at a nearby college also will have grammar textbooks. Also, review the *Resource Book* discussion of non-restrictive commas in Chapter 8. And pay particular attention to quotation marks used with other punctuation, especially the difference between British and American usage. Chapter 6 covers this.

Colons and semicolons are often incorrectly used interchangeably. They are not interchangeable. A colon separates and a semicolon joins.

Colon as Separation Mark

The object technologies satellite broadcast will include interviews with the following experts: Steve Jobs, Bill Joy, Bud Tribble, and Chris Stone.

Industry experts who have reengineered information architectures include such corporate figures as: Ray Lane at Oracle Corporation, Dennis Courtney at Dunlop Tire Company, Jim Woods of GMHUGHES, and George Thompson at Johnson & Johnson.

Note that a full colon often introduces a list that follows a statement. It divides the statement from the list. It can also be used like a dash to complete an unfinished statement. Again, it divides the statement from the completion comment. On the other hand, a semicolon (half colon) serves to join two independent clauses that lack a coordinating conjunction.

Semicolon as Connection Mark

Secretary of Defense Perry will explain the new legislation on streamlining DOD acquisition procedures; he will also announce and explain a new acquisition policy.

The new DOD acquisition policy involves buying more commercial products; it also uses industrial specifications in place of military specifications.

Keep in mind that colons and semicolons are the two most commonly confused punctuation marks in English. Pause before inserting one or the other, and review the preceding guidelines.

MECHANICS

Checking for mechanics includes the visual aspects of your document. Your edit for typography will include checks for consistency in font style and sizes; capitalization schemes in graphics, headers, and text; treatment of numbers and abbreviations. Some of these items will be checked again when you turn your document over to a professional proofreader.

In addition to an edit for typography, checking for mechanics includes larger aspects of your document's appearance. Consistency of appearance falls under layout, a term that includes spacing decisions for all aspects of every printed page—margins, borders, gutters, rulers, and more—as well as indentation, pagination, justification, and spacing. A layout check is imperative for any document that is presented as camera-ready copy. How your graphics are presented, their captions written, figures numbered, graphs annotated are also all aspects of layout. Because layout and typography require expertise, you might have a mechanics edit included in your proofreading review. Although everyone who owns a Macintosh has typographic capabilities at their fingertips, few of us have been schooled in graphics design. If you'd like your document to look good after so much hard work, turn for advice to the graphics art department at your university or corporation. In a few hours, a graphic designer can give your document a highly professional appearance.

Proofreading

Proofreading is one of the specialized skills associated with documentation. Another, even more specialized skill, is index preparation. Although it's advisable that you hire an index expert to prepare a lengthy or complex index, you can train yourself to proofread your document. A second pair of eyes will always be needed for proofreading, but you will have a better grasp of the entire writing process if you understand the difference between editing and proofreading. Further, many companies now have such serious budget constraints that they expect their authors to assume responsibility for larger segments of the post-writing and production processes.

Most textbooks of technical writing include a list of proofreader's marks. College textbooks for freshman composition will have them inside the front or the back cover. The *GPO Style Manual* devotes several pages to marking systems. You can also find a full column of them in *Webster's Ninth New*

Collegiate Dictionary, listed under Proofreader's Marks. Learn to use a few of the most commom marks, such as insertion, deletion, new paragraph, no paragraph, transpose letters, close space, open space, and so on.

Recognition of typographical errors is more important than knowing which marks to use. Typographical errors are mostly mechanical, although a few verge on the grammatical. Proofreaders, unlike editors, are not authorized to change text. Their authority extends to advising authors of errors by marking them with appropriate symbols. If you are your own proofreader, you are likely to overlook some of the manuscript errors that a different reader will catch. Secretaries who serve as proofreaders are trained to proofread with another secretary. Some proofreading systems have been developed requiring you to look at your text backwards, in chunks, or in zig-zag patterns. Seeing the text differently frees you from too much familiarity with it. If you know what your text is supposed to say, you'll read what's in your mind rather than what's on the page. The following exercise was developed by the head proofreader of a corporation's printshop. It illustrates some of the most common typographical errors.

Proofreading Exercise

A series of symbols have been developed to communicate changes with the prooofreader. These symbols are called proofreader's marks. The marks are usually placed in the margin of page and in a different color as an aid to the compositor. Leaders or lines may be dreawn from the mark mark to the arae needing correction. a more popular application of proofreaders' marks is to use the correct symbol to identify the poent of the error in the copy and the the symbol defining the type of error in the margin. Symbols are red from left to right, with each new symobl defining the next errorin the line.

Role Change: Author to Production Manager

Earlier in the chapter, you were alerted that you might have to shift your role from author to production manager if your document is on a tight schedule. Actively guiding your manuscript through peer and hierarchical reviews will often get it off people's desks more quickly. Otherwise, your paper can sink down into a pile of other papers needing a colleague's or manager's attention. You may also have to alert your graphics teammate that your document is on a particularly tight schedule. Illustrators and designers are usually pleased when an author wants to work directly with them. Their job is made easier if you can explain the effects you would like to achieve. Otherwise, you may have to return several iterations of a design concept. After that, printing and distribution employees can help you. Unfortunately, reproduction facilities are always expected to make up for slipped deadlines. If you are tactful about your emergency, you may be able to get your document out on schedule after all. Printers can move your document forward in the printing queue if other jobs are not urgent. All these efforts require your best people skills. Requesting will work better than demanding. And reserve your shift from author to production manager for the most urgent publication occasions.

Other Editing Approaches

Several taxonomies exist for editing. Having followed the Graham flow diagram, you might also look at two other approaches to editing. All three approaches assume that editing is part of post-writing. They represent a difference in method, not philosophy. Basically, these methods all divide the editing task into layers or divisions.

AN EDITORIAL DEPARTMENT APPROACH

In a busy writing and editing department, the staff member in charge of document flow will ask what level of edit a client wishes. The choices available are not very exact. They're worded vaguely: a light edit, a medium edit, a heavy edit. As a client, you need to ask what's included in each level. You have several reasons for asking this question.

- First, the more editing you sign up for, the more money it's going to cost your project; publications departments are usually run as cost centers.
- Second, the more editing you sign up for, the longer it's going to take before you get your document back, thereby slowing down the whole production cycle.
- Third, the more editing you sign up for, the greater will be your loss of control over your own document.

A heavy edit gives the editorial group permission to do whatever they think will improve your document. Their intentions will be honorable, but you may not be prepared for the document that comes back to your desk. A heavy edit includes possible reorganization of the entire body of material, and it covers everything down to proofreading.

A light edit is usually defined as a review of spelling, punctuation, and grammar. It will probably not cover style, but may cover format and mechanics.

A medium edit will depend upon the editor's interpretation of the word *medium*. It obviously covers more than a light edit; it may include a check for conformity of the document with corporate standards. It may mark deviations from company policy. It will not include reorganization of the document or an evaluation of its contents.

LEVELS OF EDIT AND QUESTIONS FOR EACH TYPE

Content—Knowledge of subject matter and transfer of that knowledge, information, or message

1. Is information or a message being transferred to the reader?
2. What is the message?
3. Are specific details provided to explain or prove generalizations?
4. Have the best materials been selected to explain the message?
5. Are the ideas fully explained?
6. Are unnecessary materials included?

Structure—Organization of whole piece of writing, of each section, and of each paragraph with clear beginnings, middle parts, and endings

1. Can a definite structure be seen?
2. Is that structure logical?
3. Is another structure better for the material?
4. Does the introduction set up all the parts?
5. Do the middle sections fulfill the promises of the introduction?
6. Is there logical coherence between the parts?
7. Does the conclusion summarize all the parts?

Style—Pattern of sentences and use of words

1. Is the writing clear?
2. Is the writing concise?
3. Is the writing strong?
4. Are the style of sentences and use of words appropriate to the subject?
5. Does the style interfere with the intended message?
6. Is the language appropriate for the intended audience?
7. Does the writer use effective parallelism, subordination, and coordination?
8. Is there an absence of wordiness, compound phrases, and redundancy?
9. Is there good use of agents for action to avoid passive constructions?
10. Is there good use of specific verbs, adverbs, and adjectives to suggest action?
11. Is the diction clear, concise, and connotative?

Format—Specialized physical arrangement and appearance

1. What format is used?
2. Is the format appropriate for the material?
3. Is that format the correct format for a report, a memo, an article, a proposal, a thesis, or a class paper?
4. Are the graphic aids effectively prepared and placed?
5. Are the headings used correctly and spaced correctly?
6. Is the material referenced correctly?
7. Are footnotes or citations used correctly?
8. Is the bibliography or list of references set up correctly?
9. How can the general appearance of the writing be improved?

Mechanics—Use of language according to established rules of grammar

1. Is the grammar of all the sentences correct?
2. Are the sentences structured correctly?
3. Are all the words spelled correctly?
4. Are punctuation marks used correctly?
5. Are typical errors avoided such as subject-verb disagreement, dangling modifiers, incorrect pronoun reference, pronoun-antecedent disagreement, incorrect parallelism, and poor subordination?

Tone—Voice or persona of the writer

1. Is the tone appropriate for the subject and the audience?
2. Is the writer present in the writing?
3. Should personal pronouns be used?
4. Is a persona created for the writer in the writing?

Policy—Conventions that the writer should follow for a journal, company, or organization

1. What policy conventions should the writer be following for the publishing agent or for the intended audience?
2. Are those conventions followed?
3. Is the writing non-sexist?
4. Is the writing free of other prejudices, biases, and imbalances?

FIGURE 9.2   Taxonomy of editing tasks.

A Comprehensive Taxonomy

Ten years ago, a Professor of English at New Mexico State University developed a highly useful taxonomy of editing tasks (see Figure 9.2).[3] His comprehensive summary provides a systematic approach to editing. It serves as an aid in defining light, medium, and heavy edits. It includes high-level editing like content and organization revision, as well as matters of style, grammar, format, and policy. It does not include proofreading. You may find some of the questions helpful as you undertake your post-writing tasks.

[3] R. E. Masse. "Theory and Practice of Editing Processes in Technical Communication," *IEEE Transactions on Professional Communication*. March 1985, p. 34 ff.

10

SPEAKING AND

LISTENING

In addition to refining your writing skills, as an individual contributor you need to spend time developing and improving speaking skills. By studying the first nine chapters of this book, you've worked hard on improving your writing skills. But writing is only part of technical communication. In fact, ESL professionals often have more difficulty with oral communicating in the workplace than with writing reports. Whereas many in-house aids exist to support written products, speaking and listening skills are usually taken for granted. As a result, you may have to become proactive in helping to bring ESL speaking and listening courses to your workplace.

At one Massachusetts research center, an ESL advisory group was convened to investigate the need for such courses. The advisory group developed a questionnaire for distribution to all technical employees at the corporation's headquarters. The purpose was to have the ESL professionals assess their own language needs and priorities.

Most of these professionals held Masters degrees and quite a few held doctorates. Some of the doctorates were earned overseas, but more of them were earned in the United States. Any ESL courses that would be brought to the research center would have to be constructed at a much higher level than ordinarily offered by commercial vendors. Upon reviewing the array of commercial companies offering in-house ESL courses, the advisory group discovered that the highest level of commercially packaged courses targeted bank tellers. If became evident that the corporation would have to customize courses if the survey indicated a need and desire for them.

The survey examined which language skills needed to be addressed first, how much time employees would be willing to devote to coursework, how long the courses should last, what sort of sequence would constitute an integrated program. The questionnaire could be completed anonymously, or respondents could identify themselves if they wished to have results of the survey mailed to them. If you would like to launch such a survey at your workplace, you may use the questionnaire found in Figure 10.1 or adapt it to your laboratory or company. The advisory group has not restricted its use.

The advisory group appointed a statistician from its membership to analyze the survey returns. The group wisely decided that its report to the corporation would have to have maximum reliability and credibility. The results clearly indicated that there was a desire for ESL coursework, and that more ESL respondents wanted (and needed) coursework in speaking than in writing.[1] (Some responses also came from native-speaking supervisors who lauded the effort, identified what they thought was needed, and offered to nominate

[1] The first course, Improving Spoken English, was offered six months after the completion of the survey with 20 professional employees enrolled.

Emanon Institute

To help us assess staff interest in possible ESL (English As a Second Language) coursework, please complete the following short questionnaire and return it by 31 May to mailstop E078. If you would like to receive a tabulation of the returns, include your name and mailstop. Otherwise, the questions may be answered anonymously.

Name _____   Mail Stop _____

1. Is English your second language?

   Yes _____
   No   _____

2. If Yes, what is your first language?

   Answer _____

3. How do you rate your English language skill in each of the following areas? (E = Excellent, G = Good, F = Fair, and P = Poor)

   Speaking   _____
   Writing   _____
   Reading   _____
   Listening _____

4. Rank the above areas according to your interest in improvement.

   Speaking   _____
   Writing   _____
   Reading   _____
   Listening _____

5. How long (in years) did you spend in acquiring the language skill in each of the areas?

   Speaking   _____
   Writing   _____
   Reading   _____
   Listening _____

6. Under what circumstances did you learn English as a second language?

   As a high school student _____
   As a 4-year college student _____
   With private tutor(s) _____
   At a language school _____
   Informally (e.g., from friends) _____
   Others _____

7. What problems do you encounter while speaking English?

   Pronunciation _____
   Incorrect grammar _____
   Poor sentence structure _____
   Inflection _____
   Idiomatic expressions _____
   Others _____

8. What problems do you encounter while writing English?

   Incorrect grammar _____
   Poor sentence structure _____
   Problems with tone _____
   Poor choice of words _____
   Improper punctuation _____
   Idiomatic expressions _____
   Others _____

9. Are you currently trying to improve your English?

   Yes _____
   No   _____
   If yes, how _____

10. Would you be interested in Emanon Institute courses to improve your English speaking or writing?

    Yes _____
    No   _____

11. If so, what kind of course arrangement would you find most suitable?

    8 wks, twice/wk, 2 hour/session _____
    12 wks, once/wk, 2 hour/session _____
    Other _____

12. Would you attend off-hour tutorials?

    Yes _____
    No   _____

Please return to Emanon Institute mailstop E078 by Wednesday, 31 May 19XX.

FIGURE 10.1   Professional staff ESL questionnaire.

employees to participate.) Of the four language skills, the identified need for in-house courses was in the following order:

   first: speaking
   second: writing
   third: listening
   fourth: reading (negligible response)

As noted at the beginning of the *Resource Book*, it is especially important to separate these skills when making judgments about the language abilities of ESL professionals. It's important for your supervisors, editors, and co-workers to realize that the same person can have very different levels of proficiency in each skill area. Unfortunately, it is often assumed that if a foreign-born professional speaks English fluently, he or she will write it well; or conversely, that a professional who writes poorly can't read English fluently. These erroneous assumptions lie behind the simplistic notion that technical texts in English for international audiences must contain neutralized text. Neutralized text is favored by American copy editors who prepare material for overseas readers. Professional vocabulary is often replaced with inadequate words, and sophisticated concepts are distorted by reduction to expression in the simplest syntax. This patronizing attitude ignores the fact that the nonnative English-speaking engineer or scientist overseas has no difficulty reading and comprehending journal articles, technical reports, and professional books. You, as an ESL scientist or engineer, may find it necessary at some time during your career to point out to your editors that their misunderstanding about language skills leads to false assessments about the abilities of foreign-born employees.

Language Production

Producing (speaking, writing) a second or third language is generally more difficult than imbibing it (listening, reading). Not only does language production necessitate learning numerous rules of grammar and conventions of pronunciation, it also involves deeply rooted issues of self-confidence and self-image. In no language skill is the fear of error production more acute than in speaking. Writing offers opportunity for correction, but speaking is immediate and usually face-to-face. The potential for embarrassment is considerable.

The occasions for producing or exchanging speech in the workplace range from military-style briefings, through routine staff meetings, to small group sessions and one-on-one conversations. The range of formality is from strict to casual. Collegial conversations will enable you to practice informal or colloquial levels of American English. Of course, substandard forms of spoken English like slang, vulgarisms, and illiteracies are not appropriate for scientists and engineers. Sometimes professionals from overseas don't distinguish between informal and substandard levels of diction, consequently rejecting conversational English. If you reject anything less than precise and formal English, you'll miss many opportunities for achieving fluency. Using conversational English in its informal and casual modes is an effective way of achieving credibility in native-sounding speech.

BRIEFINGS

Having to speak publicly and formally worries most speakers—concern is not restricted to the ESL population. Some people overcome this trauma in time and with repetition, but for some it remains a lifelong anxiety. However, once you have presented your first briefing, subsequent briefings will be easier. Many companies offer briefing workshops, and if they don't, they should. Both ESL and native speakers of English benefit from them. Dress, presentation techniques, and body language are all covered in briefings seminars. Pay attention to these important areas of nonverbal communication so that your briefing style will not reflect cultural differences.

Curiously, the formal briefing situation is less trying for an ESL presenter than might be expected. The scientific, military, technical, financial, or medical briefing is a highly standardized production. The rituals and expectations are generally understood and widely practiced. Further, you will prepare your briefing ahead of time and practice it thoroughly. But don't memorize it. Memorization will result in a stilted performance, and it may lead you into difficulties of continuity if you're interrupted. In addition, audience behavior is generally governed by certain courtesies. Hence, as an ESL briefer, you are in a good position to compete favorably with any native-language speaker.

GRAPHICS

Many companies and laboratories provide standards for high-quality graphics to be used in preparing word slides, tables, charts, and illustrations. These standards ensure an even playing field for native and nonnative speakers. The physical appearance of excellent briefing charts will act in your favor. A superb title slide sets the stage for success. Have it lighted while your colleagues enter the briefing room. Little touches of professionalism like this add to the overall acceptance of your presentation.

Make sure that you use a consistent pattern of parallelism in your slides. First-level, second-level, and (if necessary) third-level headings should have the same pattern in every slide. Lists under the headings need to display consistent, parallel grammar with all items introduced similarly. Consistent format throughout the slides will enhance the visual flow of your briefing. Have a colleague, friend, or editor review grammatical aspects: subject-verb agreement, spelling, correct use of singular and plural, proper use of articles. You mustn't distract your audience with visual errors. An essential rule to keep in mind is not to put too much prose onto your word slides. By limiting the amount of text on each slide, you will not only avoid clutter but you will also minimize opportunities for errors. In addition, sparse word slides are easier for your audience to read. They also discourage you from reading your entire briefing from your slides.

A Possible Problem

As an ESL briefer, your single disadvantage can be an unfamiliar accent. Note that the verb in the preceding sentence is *can be*, not *is*. Accents by themselves are not disadvantageous. An interesting accent can enliven a dull briefing. Some accents, however, cause interference to audience reception. And remember, some of your audience members may have impaired hearing to begin with.

You might have a surprisingly difficult time getting an honest appraisal of your accent and its potential effect on your audience. Most Americans are very anxious to avoid embarrassing a foreign-born colleague. They don't realize that it's an expression of friendship to tell you that you always say *pronunciation* as if it were *pronounciation*. If you can find a co-worker to analyze objectively the effect of your accent, you will be better able to develop compensating strategies. Without such specific input, however, you can work on your pace of delivery. If someone finds that your accent makes understanding difficult—many Americans are still inexperienced in dealing with Asian accents—moderate the speed of your delivery. Give your listener time to work out small rough spots. The general trend in any briefing is for a nervous briefer to speak too quickly. The more nervous he or she becomes, the more the pace of delivery quickens. An unusually rapid delivery plus an unintelligible accent will lead to a briefing disaster.

Some Tips for Dealing with the Problem During your practice sessions, think about the pace of your delivery. During your practice sessions, you have to time your briefing anyway. Usually you'll have a 20-minute limit, or perhaps 30 or 45 minutes in which to present your briefing. Some situations require two-hour briefings. If your supervisor hasn't told you the length of your briefing, find out in advance. You must have that information in order to structure your material effectively.

TIP 1: Consciously adopt a moderate pace of delivery. If you discover that you can't deliver all your material in the allocated time, revise the scope of your presentation.

TIP 2: Practice maintaining the same moderate pace throughout your presentation. If the session chairperson sends you time signals during the briefing, eliminate some of your material rather than speed up the rate of delivery. Briefers frequently skip over some of their vugraphs during the actual briefing when they see that unexpected factors are influencing their schedule.

TIP 3: Watch for the hard of hearing members of your audience. Sometimes, a helpful person will put a hand behind his or her ear to let you know he or she is having difficulty hearing you. Give these folks a little extra attention—more eye contact, for example.

TIP 4: Augment your delivery with hand signals that can help to clarify meaning. Use your hands, your fingers, the pointer to illustrate basic information.

TIP 5: Before you begin your briefing, make sure there is a glass of water on the briefing stand. Alternatively, bring your own can of juice or soda.

TIP 6: Pause during your briefing at appropriate spots. It helps to avoid the impression of the briefer as a mechanical robot. Take a sip of water to keep your throat from getting dry. The pause for a sip of water is also a good tactic to use if you need a moment to recall a fact or rephrase a statement.

TIP 7: If you hear yourself make a mistake, don't apologize or get flustered. Just pause and then repeat the information correctly. In other words, dissociate your mistake from your accent.

TIP 8: After the briefing, review the videotape of your briefing (if one exists). Seeing yourself on tape can be a shattering experience, but it will also provide some objective data about your voice, pace, and presentation manner.

TIP 9: The first briefing is the hardest. Your briefings will improve with experience.

MEETINGS

Like briefings, meetings also have a ritual quality, although the informal atmosphere of some research departments can mask meeting protocols. Department and group meetings are extraordinarily frequent occurrences in the United States, and many of them are held to settle genuine issues. There are also information-only meetings, and the routine "It's Monday morning, and we will have our regular staff meeting at 9:00 A.M" meetings. Such routine meetings of limited value have become less frequent in the 1990s. The current fashion of one-minute meetings and Stand-up meetings are meant to demonstrate that time is valuable and that your supervisor is up to date on management techniques. These quickie meetings cause no concern to anyone because you're really not expected to participate—just listen and remember.

Genuine technical meetings held to iron out project problems or review timetables and budgets can be stressful for the ESL professional. Such meetings can bring together people who are not concerned with maintaining civilities, and they may pose threats to the self-confidence of insecure members of the group. (Introversion is not limited to engineers from overseas; some native-born engineers find meetings uncomfortable.) But these meetings are where much of the real work of a project takes place. Opinions are expressed and decisions made. It's important that the ESL professional participate freely and in a manner that will gain him or her professional visibility and credibility. In addition to project-related aspects of meeting participation, managers make judgments about their staff members on the basis of how they interact with their peers at meetings. Remember, the only time some managers see their staff is at meetings.

It may not seem fair to judge an employee's contribution to a scientific or technical project on the basis of how voluble he or she is at meetings, but the fact remains that periodic reviews frequently report impressions gained by a manager during meetings. If an engineer is from a culture that has not exposed him or her to the give-and-take of a working group, he or she may simply abdicate from participation. The pain of arguing with co-workers, the potential embarrassment of presenting an idea that could be rejected by the group, and the gnawing realization that more is being judged than straightforward technical competence can combine to render a foreign-born team member mute.

Of course, not all meetings are confrontational. Let's start with routine meetings and work out from there. The informality of meetings in some companies can obscure the pivotal issue that the person who calls the meeting assumes authority for the meeting. If conventional rectangular tables are used, the person who calls the meeting often sits at the head of the table in a display of authority. Some meeting leaders prefer to assume a more democratic attitude and sit at a random seat. This doesn't obviate the fact that that person opens the meeting, closes the meeting, calls for votes, tables issues, and determines follow-up measures.

Working within such a framework, your position in a meeting can become quite comfortable. You needn't be like the person who must dominate every meeting. Most of us know at least one such co-worker. Let the dominators proceed. Their performances are often impressive, but eventually everyone tires of their behavior. As a meeting participant, let the meeting leader direct the discussion, and let the meeting "hog" dominate. You will contribute suggestions and ideas that strike you as reasonably useful, thereby getting yourself onto record as a team player who enriches the discussion without trying to control it.

TURN-TAKING

Turn-taking is a concept that professional development trainers advocate for meeting behavior. The idea is sound, although the execution is usually imperfect. In an American meeting, it's often very difficult to know when to insert your comments. If you are mild-mannered, you may feel rude interrupting someone who dominates the discussion. It's difficult to insert your comments as one person finishes speaking because there seems always to be someone else ready to jump at the chance to speak. That is what *you* must learn to do: Be alert to the flow of the discussion, and be quick at seizing a break, no matter how brief. If you speak up at the same time as someone else, don't automatically relinquish your turn. Just continue with your comments. Perhaps your competitor will remember the concept of turn-taking and let you finish. If not, politely but firmly assert your right to speak. If you haven't contributed to the discussion earlier, you have all the more reason to prevail now.

GATEKEEPING

Gatekeeping is another concept that trainers advocate. A gatekeeper is someone who helps to prevent the meeting from getting out of control. If the person who called the meeting is doing his or her job, it won't be necessary to invoke gatekeeping. However, the meeting organizer sometimes doesn't recognize the need for intervention. Anyone at the meeting can assert the role of gatekeeper, and people who do it skillfully are usually admired. If you can simply interject a comment when necessary to the effect that the discussion has drifted too far from the purpose of the meeting, or that time has run out for the meeting, you can gain points as a diplomat without hurting anyone's feelings. So, you can contribute to the fruitfulness of a meeting in two different ways: by offering technical expertise and by enhancing the productiveness of the meeting. If the meeting leader fails to define the next step, ask politely what it might be or when the group will meet again. Such gentle reminders are good examples of gatekeeping. In sum, if the more rough-and-tumble aspects of meetings discourage you, learn and practice ways of participating without engaging in controversy. As you gain confidence, you will contribute to meetings more frequently and in more diverse ways.

You shouldn't feel that as a nonnative-speaker of English you are an outsider to the meeting game, and that you can only respond to someone else's call for a meeting. If you have volunteered to lead a project team, if you serve on an employee committee, or if you are participating in a study group, you can call your own meetings. Determine a clear purpose for the meeting and conduct it at your chosen level of informality or formality. You have your own meeting style. While observing the general protocols, you can still preserve your personal style. If you determine that you are in a position to call a committee or task force meeting, here are some guidelines.

- Let all invited participants know the time, place, and possible length of the meeting several days ahead of time. You might save yourself some embarrassment by asking your secretary to scan available time blocks in advance.
- Plan an agenda of topics to be covered. If you tend to be formal, you can send a written agenda to each participant ahead of time. If the occasion is less formal, simply announce the items on the agenda at the beginning of the meeting.
- Try to articulate a specific purpose or goal for the meeting. You can also announce this information at the beginning of the meeting so that a participant doesn't upset you later by asking, "Why are we all here?"

- Be prepared to exchange ideas openly. Differences of opinion may arise. You hope that they will be expressed politely, but sometimes they can be expressed in a brusque manner. Don't let an abrasive participant upset *your* meeting. Remember, it's your show.
- Bring the meeting to a close at the expected time. Meeting leaders often neglect this responsibility. If done skillfully, you will gain the respect of your committee members.
- Summarize the results of the meeting so that your group can see that their time has been spent profitably.
- Request suggestions for a follow-up meeting time if another meeting seems necessary.
- Thank your group members for giving their time to attend the meeting.

MEETING PROTOCOLS AND PARTICIPATION TIPS

These tips summarize some of the protocols of workplace meetings.

TIP 1: The person who calls the meeting assumes the responsibilities of leadership.

TIP 2: The meeting leader announces the purpose of a meeting at its beginning.

TIP 3: The meeting leader calls for minutes to be read (if they've been recorded) from a former meeting.

TIP 4: The meeting leader asks for a volunteer or appoints someone to take minutes for the current meeting. Don't assume that a clerical employee will be given this task, and don't assume that a woman will serve as secretary.

TIP 5: All participants are empowered to take part in the discussion unless the meeting is information-only provided by the meeting leader.

TIP 6: Anyone can serve as gatekeeper if the need arises.

TIP 7: The meeting leader should bring the meeting to a close punctually. If he or she fails to do so, anyone can serve as gatekeeper.

Small Group and One-on-One Conversation

Your speaking skills will be put to most frequent use in small group discussions and in one-on-one conversations. Some one-on-ones can be rather formal, as when you request an appointment with your manager to discuss a salary increase or a promotion. Or they can be informal, as when you share ideas with your officemate. Unlike the briefings or presentation situation, small group discussions tend to be free from standardized presentation skills. And unlike the meetings situation, there aren't any protocols for one-on-one conversations beyond the norms of courtesy. Collegial conversations provide opportunities for you to test how well you relay your message. The absence of protocols is a mixed blessing. From a negative standpoint, you can't rely on norms, but on the positive side, you are liberated from strict conventions. Because you aren't concerned with protocols and procedures, you can focus more on realistic speech production.

PRONUNCIATION

Most professionals from overseas have a firm understanding of the structure of English from formal coursework. If you are a bit insecure about your grammar, however, don't become preoccupied with the grammatical correctness of your speech. Grammar, as you've seen in earlier chapters, is rule-driven and can be memorized. Also, some leeway is allowed for speakers of other languages, particularly if it's evident that they are newly arrived. You'll probably be surprised to observe that some of your native English-speaking colleagues are a bit sloppy with grammar during informal conversation. And some of them are even casual about their pronunciation. You might think about the meaning of these tendencies and how they might apply to your own use of English.

This is not to say that it's a good idea to reinforce incorrect grammar. You really should get on top of individual problems within a year or two of arrival in the United States so that you won't be considered illiterate despite your credentials. But at first, concentrate on how well you're being understood. Specifically, how understandable is the sound of your speech. What does your pronunciation sound like to your listeners? If your speech is so highly accented that co-workers frequently ask you to repeat yourself, then you have a problem. Even more detrimental to your job success is interaction with colleagues who are too polite to ask you to repeat yourself. They'll just pretend they understand what you're saying, and that is useless for both sender and receiver of the message. Your primary goal in spoken English is communicative effectiveness.

ACCENT REDUCTION

If you suspect that your accent is interfering with transmission of information, you need to engage in a program of accent reduction. There is nothing wrong with having an accent; for the most part, Americans do not attach any social stigma to newcomers with accents. Newcomers with accents are part of the ongoing history of the United States. Consequently, avoid programs that come under the rubric of speech therapy. You are not sick because you have an accent, and you don't need therapy.

Instead of speech therapy, think in terms of accent reduction. Don't set impossible goals for yourself. You needn't attempt to come out sounding like Prince Charles. You aren't a film actor who has to be tutored in British Southern

Regional English for an artificial role. British English isn't much spoken in the United States anyway, and even BBC commentators are starting to use their natural accents, be they from the Midlands or from working class London schools.

You would be well advised to find or initiate a class in accent reduction, preferably to be held in the corporate classroom. It doesn't matter what diverse speech backgrounds your group represents. You all share a common goal, and effective teaching methodologies exist for a mixed group of students. You will progress more quickly if you have colleagues to work with. Accent reduction is rarely successful when pursued out of a textbook alone. Listening to tapes, the television, and the radio are certainly very useful strategies. But your teacher's expertise in a classroom is the single most important element in an active program of accent reduction.

Many commercial ESL schools recruit untrained tutors or self-taught ESL teachers. Often Peace Corps graduates or people who have worked on an overseas assignment for six months or a year are recruited. Such on-site experience is valuable but it is culture-specific and it lacks a foundation in linguistic knowledge. Your company's education department should prepare a Request for Proposal, (RFP), demanding stringent requirements for the responding teachers. Again, remind your employee education representative that he or she should reject any applicants who propose a speech therapy approach.

Accent reduction is a long-term process. You must not give up if you don't see a dramatic change after the first semester of coursework. You will slowly effect changes. You can't overcome the speech habits of a lifetime in a few months. Also, you need to follow your accent reduction program beyond the corporate classroom, and try to avoid speaking your native language at home after work. If you speak English at home, you and your partner will be helping one another. The aim is not to lose proficiency in your first language: Multilingualism is a skill to be valued. Your aim is to reduce your dependence upon your first language and to reduce its influence over your second language.

A well-trained teacher will have you audiotape a speech selection at the beginning of a course and then have you audiotape the same selection at the end, so you can see what progress you've made. A useful tool is an accent inventory passage. The teacher can use this for individualized help and may share his or her analysis with you so that you can recognize the problems that the analysis reveals. You mustn't memorize an inventory passage or practice reading it repeatedly. What you should record is an accurate representation of your everyday pronunciation. The sentences in the following accent inventory paragraph are numbered to help you locate logical breaks in the passage.

Accent Inventory Passage

(1) When a person from another country comes to study and/or work in the United States, he has to find out for himself the answers to many questions, and he has many problems to think about. (2) Where should he live? (3) Would it be better if he looked for a room, an apartment, or a house? (4) If he is employed, should he rent or buy? (5) Should he spend all of his time working or studying? (6) Shouldn't he try to take advantage of the many social and cultural activities which he is offered? (7) At first it is not easy for him to be confident in speech and manner, but little by little he learns to choose the language and customs that are appropriate for formal and informal situations. (8) Finally, he begins to feel sure of himself. (9) This long-awaited feeling, though, doesn't develop suddenly. (10) All of this takes tremendous willpower.

You will realize, of course, that it takes someone trained in phonology to do a good job of listening to your audiotaped reading of this passage and to analyze it accurately. The problems that the analyst will be looking for fall into the following categories:

- Stress and rhythm
- Intonation
- Pronunciation of vowels
- Pronunciation of consonants
- Vowel and consonant confusion

This exercise is accompanied by three pages of specific points for the teacher to observe, and some of the identifications require systematic training in phonetics and phonology. If you'd like to try a bit of self-analysis of this passage, some specific points for observation follow. Stress and rhythm is the easiest of the four categories to judge. Try to distance yourself enough from your own speech to make useful judgments. Fill in each line with the number of instances the problem arises in the paragraph you've taped.[2]

Stress and Rhythm

1. _____ Stress on wrong syllable of words having more than one syllable.
2. _____ Misplaced stress on nominal compounds.
3. _____ Misplaced stress on two-word verbs.

---

[2] It's helpful if you know the phonetic alphabet when using such materials. In this selection, the phonetic symbol *schwa* is used to indicate the unstressed vowel sound used in words like *but, some,* and *up. Schwa* is an inverted, reversed, lowercase *e*. It's the most common reduced vowel. It often serves as an unstressed variant of a stressed vowel; for example, the *e* of *democrat* becomes *schwa* in *democratic.*

4. _____ Other improper sentence stress.
5. _____ Improper division of sentences into thought groups.
6. _____ Failure to blend well, to make smooth transitions between words or syllables.

_____ Improper insertion of ə to break up difficult combinations of consonants.
_____ Insertion of ə before initial *s* followed by a consonant.
_____ Unnatural insertion of glottal stop.

It would be counterproductive to include the entire inventory analysis tool here. The inventory passage contains, for example, 32 possible substitution problems under consonants. The *Resource Book* describes the inventory and one area of potential trouble to convince you that scientific tools exist for measuring accent errors. When analyzed by a trained linguist, the results provide generalizations about a group of students in a class. The teacher can then assess realistically the difficulty of his or her task as well as the areas most needy of attention in the classroom. Such a skilled linguist was able to make the following report to a corporate education department that had recently convened an accent reduction class of 20 nonnative English-speaking scientists and engineers:

> Seventeen out of 20 participants were recorded. In my opinion, five participants have rather extensive problems with normal English pronunciation and accentuation resulting in occasional unintelligibility; an additional nine have clear difficulty, particularly with stress and intonation leading to varying degrees of inarticulation; the remaining three pronounce basic individual vowel/consonant sounds correctly, but have problems with combinations and with natural American phrasing. In sum, all of the participants have some degree of marked difficulty with correct American English pronunciation.[3]

The report continued with specific data. It provided a clear rationale for the corporate education department to justify the expense of a long-term training program in pronunciation for its professional staff. This report demonstrates that trained and talented resources exist to help you achieve accent reduction.

Basically, you'll find it useful to understand that choices involved in pronunciation are based on firmly established habits. How you place your lips, how you place your tongue in relation to your teeth, in what part of your mouth you sound a letter are all involved in these habitual choices. In order to effect accent reduction you must use the following process:

recognize speech habit, break habit, establish new habit

[3] Christopher Sawyer-Lauçanno, Ph.D. to author. Data collected at beginning of course on Improving Spoken English, January 1990.

Both speaking and listening are essential for hearing new sounds and recognizing old ones. If you participate in a classroom group, you can be guided in understanding how your first language causes you to pronounce a letter or combination of letters. Then you can start to work on erasing that former pronunciation habit, and replacing it with the accepted pronunciation of your environment. You will be guided how to position your mouth and tongue and how to use your throat and lips in new ways. You can then practice your learning during small group sessions on projects and in one-on-one conversations in the office. Further, if your officemate is sympathetic to your efforts, he or she might be willing to identify one or two of your distinctive pronunciations that are irritating or that render it difficult to understand what you're saying. Each small segment of speech that you transform will move you closer to the realization of self-confidence that the accent inventory passage describes.

SUGGESTIONS FOR AN ACCENT REDUCTION PROGRAM

- Offer your corporate education department a questionnaire for distribution to employees to determine if there are enough employees interested to justify organizing an accent reduction course.
- Perform a good statistical analysis of the returns.
- Contribute to the composition of an RFP to recruit a highly qualified teacher.
- Accept that the process of accent reduction may take at least two years.
- Stop listening to yourself speak, and listen more closely to external speech models.
- Encourage the corporate education department to invest in multiple sets of audiotapes. *Pronouncing American English* is an excellent set to use.[4] Its associated textbook is also very good.[5]
- Request a pre-course speech sample analysis.
- Compare a post-course speech sample (same passage) to hear areas of personal improvment.
- Try speaking English more at home even though you like to relax after a day of work.
- Listen to your children. They're likely to acquire unaccented English in school and at play. Sometimes they can provide speech models for you.

[4] Gertrude F. Orion, *Pronouncing American English*, Boston: Heinle & Heinle Publishers. 1988.

[5] Gertrude F. Orion, *Pronouncing American English: Sounds, Stress, and Intonation*, New York: Newbury House Publishers, 1988.

GUIDANCE FOR SELF-HELP

The School of Education at Boston University offers a very fine Master's degree program for those who wish to teach English as a second language (TESOL—Teaching of English to Speakers of Other Languages). Teachers from the United States and from around the world matriculate. In recent years, more teachers have been coming from China where they learned classroom English, which, in turn, they have been teaching in China. As might be expected, the classroom English taught in China is formal and precise. When these teachers are exposed to both the informal speech patterns of their classmates and to the liberal linguistic notions of their faculty, they are shocked.

You may not be quite so unprepared for the casualness of American English as these teachers, but you may not really appreciate how much pauses, dropped endings, and elisions determine the sound of American English. Conversely, unless you learn how to produce some of these patterns, your speech will retain an unfamiliar ring for native-born speakers of English.

While you are waiting for your research center to initiate ESL courses in accent reduction, you might start by purchasing a fairly simple textbook for your personal use. *Clear Speech: Pronunciation and Listening Comprehension in American English* is a good choice.[6] Two audio cassettes are available with the book, and they contribute immensely to its usefulness. The book does not cover grammar and vocabulary; it does deal with issues like voice pitch, stress patterns in sentences, and pauses to indicate thought groups. It also contains some very clear and simply drawn diagrams of mouth positions for American English sound production. Because the book has only 100 pages, it's not daunting. It's a good resource.

Here are some other resources to help you with a self-study program in pronunciation. They are listed in random order. The interlibrary loan system in your city can search for some of these books for you to borrow.

Pronunciation Resources[7]

Speaking American English. Clarice M. Jones and Jean H. Miculka. Dallas, Texas: SouthWestern Publishing Company, 1992.

Phrase by Phrase: Pronunciation and Listening in American English. Marsha Chan. Englewood Cliffs, New Jersey: Prentice-Hall, Inc., 1987.

Professional Interactions: Oral Communication Skills in Science, Technology, and Medicine. Candice Matthews and Joanne Marino. Englewood Cliffs, New Jersey: Prentice-Hall Regents, 1990.

---

[6] Judy B. Gilbert, *Clear Speech: Pronunciation and Listening Comprehension in American English*, Cambridge and New York: Cambridge University Press, 1989.

[7] I am indebted to Marnie Reed Murphy, Ph.D., for this bibliography of titles collected for her course ESL Speaking and Listening II, September 1991.

Say It Naturally: Verbal Strategies for Authentic Communication. Allie Patricia Wall, New York: Holt, Rinehart and Winston, 1987.

Speech Communication for International Students. Paulette Dale and James C. Wolf. Englewood Cliffs, New Jersey: Prentice-Hall, Inc., 1988.

English for Science. Fran Zimmerman. Englewood Cliffs, New Jersey: Prentice-Hall Regents, 1989.

Idiomactive English. Vera Theophil. Montreal, Canada: Centre Educatif et Culturel Inc., 1983.

Mastering American English: A Handbook-Workbook of Essentials. R. Hayden, D. Pilgrim, and A. Q. Haggard. Englewood Cliffs, New Jersey: Prentice-Hall, 1956.

The Culture Puzzle: Cross-Cultural Communication for English as a Second Language. Deena Levine, Jim Baxter and Piper McNulty. Englewood Cliffs, New Jersey: Prentice-Hall, Inc., 1987.

Say It Clearly. Susan English. New York: Macmillan, 1988.

The Sound and Style of American English: Foreign Accent Reduction. David Alan Stern. Los Angeles, California: Dialect Accent Specialists, 1987.

A FEW SPECIFICS FOR SELF-HELP ACCENT REDUCTION Because English has a more complex vowel system than most other languages, many of your pronunciation problems will involve vowels. English uses only five vowel symbols (a, e, i, o, u), but in fact we pronounce many more. The "sound alphabet" of English has 15 vowel sounds which are represented by phonetic symbols. As a concrete example, the vowel *a* might be identified by five phonetic symbols:

Phonetic Symbol	Example
ey	train, taste, paper
æ	hat, axe, sad
ɘ	banana, an, camera
a	father, hard, wallet
ɔ	talk, saw, ball

Vowel pronunciation also involves short and long sounds. Actually, tense and lax are more accurate descriptive terms. Each of the five vowels has this capability of short or long pronunciation. These distinctions also have phonetic symbols, but unfortunately lexicographers (writers of dictionaries) do not use the same set of symbols as linguists for marking short and long. Some examples of short and long pronunciation for the letter *e* follow:

Tense	Lax
recede	bed
freeze	fence
between	pencil
me	met
equal	pretty
easy	peck

SOME ESL PRONUNCIATION TRAPS

REDUCTION Long and short vowels are pronounced carefully in single-syllable words and in stressed syllables. But they are often reduced in unstressed syllables, which means they are given less attention when spoken. Often the vowel is reduced to schwa. This practice may seem like careless speech, and it happens so often that you will not always recognize it when you hear it. However, ESL speakers and listeners must learn to accept vowel reduction. It's a predictable speech phenomenon. For example, note what happens to the word *democracy* when it is changed to *democratic*. The *e* in the first syllable becomes schwa in the second form of the word. The stress is shifted to later in the word, and the *e* is minimized. Similarly, the *a* in *photographic* becomes schwa in the word *photography*. Note that the *u* in *carefully* and the second *o* in *chocolate* are greatly reduced.

Some consonants reduce too. The sound *h* often disappears completely in conversational English. This is particularly true with personal pronouns beginning with *h*.

Examples of H Reduction

Did (h)e go? (pronounced *diddy*)

Would (h)e take me? (pronounced *woody*)

Please give (h)er money. (pronounced *giver*)

Send (h)im a message.

Note, however, that *h* is not reduced when the pronoun begins the sentence.

He did go.

He would take me.

Her money is gone.

His memo was lost.

It hardly needs to be said that no word that is emphasized would be reduced.

We selected *him* to go to the conference.

Where is *her* money?

It was *his* memo that was lost.

He said *he* wouldn't go, but his friend will.

STRESS Generally, important words in a sentence are lightly stressed when spoken, whereas unimportant words are not. Lacking any other information, you can consider the important words to be the nouns, verbs, adjective, adverbs, and interrogations. The unimportant words, usually unstressed, are articles, prepositions, and pronouns. In addition, in verbs of more than one word, the auxiliary verb is not stressed: *have, be, do, can,* and so on.

How you stress syllables in a sentence affects your pronunciation. If you lack a sense of stress patterns, your speech can sound peculiar. Another point to remember is that changed stress can alter meaning. Try stressing different words in this sentence:

I never saw that person.
I never saw that person.
I **never** saw that person.
I never **saw** that person.
I never saw **that** person.

The sentence meaning changes significantly with each change in stress position.

Unless you wish to express a special emphasis, don't give unimportant words equal strength as the one or two words that are important to your meaning. Most important, don't give every word in every sentence equal stress. If you do, you'll jeopardize meaning. And you'll sound like a robot.

THOUGHT GROUPS In addition to stress, we usually introduce slight pauses into our sentences. These pauses are not arbitrarily placed; they usually break the sentence into thought groups. Of course, a native speaker of a language doesn't plan all this ahead of time. It's a natural by-product of communication. There are no rules to guide you here. You must rely upon your perceived meaning of each sentence. Your speech will sound more authentic if you can anticipate thought groups and mark them with pauses. Remember, the pauses are very slight. Don't make the mistake of thinking these pauses represent positions for punctuation. Many ill-informed writers have adopted an arbitrary punctuation scheme based on this premise. The result is over-punctuation and frequently incorrect punctuation. Punctuation has logical positions. It serves as far more than merely pause markers.

Examples of Thought Groups in Sentences

The author of the proposed course / believes that language learning is facilitatied / when students are active participants in the learning process.

For the student of a second language / the sound system provides a variety of problems.

Emanon Institute seeks to provide / a second offering of Improving Spoken English / to further develop the oral skills of its technical staff.

SPECIAL WARNING FOR ESL COMMUNICATORS If you break your sentences with pauses at unnatural places, you may interfere with your intended meaning. Sometimes ESL speakers become so concerned with producing correct sounds that they inject pauses at peculiar spots rather than between thought groups. This also happens when the new ESL professional becomes preoccupied with grammatical correctness and pauses to check each decision.

LINKING WORDS If you've learned English from a textbook or other printed material, you will tend to separate from one another the words you speak as if they were in print. In fact, in spoken English, closely related words are often run together with other words in the same thought group. Sometimes two or even three words will be run together. These are called linkages. It's a bit like liaison in French.

Linkage happens so quickly and often so subtly that you will hardly notice it in native English speech. On the other hand, if you always speak each word distinctly and in total separation from every other word, your spoken English will sound very stilted. Here are some examples of linkages. Practice saying the linked words as one word.

Some Examples of Linking Words in Sentences

If sheᴗanswers the phone, please give her my message.

Weᴗought to receive our holiday bonuses soon.

MayᴗI show you our latest Annual Report?

Howᴗold is this computer?

Sendᴗher the following memorandum, please.

Canᴗyou activate the safety switch on this machine?

He saidᴗit two or three times.

I'll call you whenᴗI leave the office.

DROPPED SOUNDS Throughout this book, we've used many contractions because American English is characterized by shortened forms in speaking and writing. This is especially true in speaking. In addition to traditional contractions, spoken English uses blends that may look suspiciously colloquial when transcribed, but which represent typical speech patterns. These speech patterns include those of educated people. The lessons for you are:

- Don't be too critical of what may sound like careless speech (in contrast to classroom English).
- Consider adopting some of these elisions if you wish to sound more like a native speaker of English.

Here are a few examples of acceptable elisions.

Full Form	Contracted Form
going to	gonna
meet you	meetchu
men and women	men 'n women
tea or coffee	tea 'r coffee
is he busy?	izzy bizzy?
cup of coffee	cup o' coffee
what did you say?	whaddya say?
what do you mean?	whatchu mean?
friend of mine	friend o' mine

You may not wish to use these special pronunciations; nevertheless, you must train yourself to hear and understand them in the natural fast speed of conversational English.

UNHEARD *Is* Certain first language sound patterns make it difficult for foreign-born professionals to hear the word *is* when it follows a sibilant sound like *s, z,* or soft *c*. This also affects similar constructions. If you are from such a language group, you must listen especially hard to the English sentence. Otherwise, your ear will reject the verb *is* because it becomes lost in the general hissing sound. If you reproduce what you think you hear, based on your former speaking and hearing habits, you will produce sentences that are missing a verb; consequently, they will be ungrammatical. Here are some examples (the asterisks precede the erroneous sentences).

Reproduced Unheard Sibilant

He washes the dishes.
* He wash the dishes.

The busses are late.
* The busses late.

The ice is cold.
* The ice cold.

Her dress is pretty.
* Her dress pretty.

The fish is beautiful.
* The fish beautiful.

This phenomenon can also invade other sounds, like D and T. Watch out for sentences with *need, needed* and *visit, visited*.

Many more pronunciation hazards exist. A good ESL teacher will guide you through them. In the meantime, if you look through the books in the preceding biography, you can get a head start on some of the others. In addition to checking out books from the library, you might do some shopping at a college bookstore to learn if any TESOL courses are offered, and to see which text-books are being used. A program combining self-help, classroom learning, and on-the-job practice is your best means of achieving accent reduction.

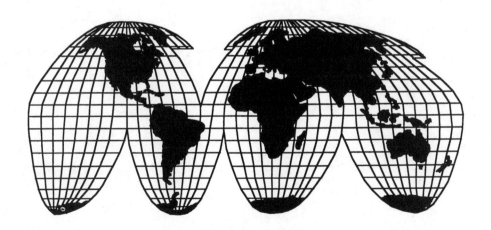

11

THE GROUP

EXPERIENCE

For several centuries, an image grew of the scientist or engineer working alone in the laboratory or drafting table to create designs for the future. Popular mythology portrayed him or her as a genius searching for the cure to a deadly disease or designing a spaceship that would reach the moon. He or she labored in solitude in the lab, study, or workshop. The image would have included a computer, had computers been invented.

There is historic precedent for this image. Metaphorically, the modern scientist is a descendant of the medieval scholar who worked in the quiet world of a monastery. Unlike humanists, scientists and engineers generally didn't engage in debate, oratory, and the perfection of rhetoric. Theirs was a lonely mission, according to the popular image.

The image was given reality in schools of engineering, which were separated from the schools of humanistic studies, when the "nerd" appeared sometime after World War II. Introverted, brilliant, analytic, and seemingly soulless, this person worked day and night at problem sets. For diversion, he or she played a musical instrument—not so much in a band or orchestra as for private pleasure or to become a virtuoso performer. After his or her formal education, there were plenty of jobs in the growing number of American high-tech companies.

Unfortunately, profit-making companies couldn't afford to nurture too many solitary geniuses. Bell Labs existed as an anomaly. The federal government maintained some elite institutes and laboratories, but the majority of graduates were employed by pharmaceutical companies or military contractors to engineer new drugs or space systems quickly and efficiently. They also had to attend staff meetings, work in project teams, and submit their proposals to managers. After a decade or two, commercial companies realized they had a problem: Engineers and scientists didn't fit into the corporate ideal of good team players.

Some companies tried to address the polarities of solitary genius and good team player by instituting dual-ladder tracks. Regular promotion to increasingly higher levels of management would reward good team players. A ladder of special appointments such as Chief Scientist, Chief Engineer, Corporation Fellow, and the like would reward individual contributors to technology. Members of the technical staff soon noted that these special categories were frequently filled by appointees from outside, in which case the technical promotion track didn't offer as many opportunities for internal career advancement as did the traditional management ladder.

Modes of Collaboration in the Workplace

Good team playing is now reinforced by an emphasis on collaboration in the workplace. *Collaboration* became the buzzword of the 1990s. One of its many manifestations is Total Quality Management (TQM)—a push toward integrating employees into a seamless operation. All members of design, development, production, and distribution are now expected to work collaboratively. Division of labor is outmoded. TQM and the collaborative approach are radical shifts from the former assembly line model where each employee became an expert in his or her task which could then be repeated with enormous efficiency. The assembly line model was a distant echo of the specialist working in monastic solitude.

COLLABORATIVE PLANNING

Project collaboration begins in the earliest stages of planning. Frequent meetings bring together members of the extended team as early as possible in the life of a project. The meeting protocols and participation guidelines offered in Chapter 10 will help you participate more comfortably in these collaborative planning sessions. In addition, the following sections describe special strategies of collaboration with observations on how they affect the ESL professional.

BRAINSTORMING

Brainstorming is a valuable technique for probing the creativity of team members early in the planning cycle. It is also a peculiarly American technique that originated at Hughes Aircraft. The offspring of for-profit, corporate America, brainstorming is less often used in academia where the solitary inventor is still honored. Brainstorming is especially popular in research and development companies. Consequently, you are very likely to encounter this technique if you haven't already done so.

It's easy to see how uniquely American brainstorming is. Its basic assumption is highly democratic: In a brainstorming session, everyone is equal and everyone's ideas merit consideration. A typical brainstorming session involves a facilitator who is a master/mistress of ceremonies. First, the facilitator or the project leader will review the problem or issue to be resolved. Each brainstorming session is focused on one issue so that the target concept will not become blurred. Then, the facilitator offers a few simple brainstorming guidelines, and the session begins.

Brainstorming may be accomplished differently from place to place, but the following practices are typical.

- A large display area is required: A classroom with blackboards or white-boards is ideal. Sometimes flipcharts are used, and as each sheet is filled, it is taped around the meeting walls. Flipcharts are less efficient than boards.
- After the facilitator poses the question, the floor is open for suggestions. There are no protocols of turn-taking. Each participant calls out his or her contribution as it comes to mind. Sometimes the facilitator needs an assistant to record the suggestions if they come too quickly for one person to write.
- The facilitator, recorder, and participants express no judgments regarding the quality or usefulness of each suggestion.
- Suggestions may act as springboards for other suggestions; no hierarchy is placed on the relationship of suggestions.
- The timeframe for the brainstorming session is open-ended. The session ends when the participants have exhausted their store of ideas. This aspect of a brainstorming session requires a patient facilitator who will not close down the session prematurely.
- Only after the first phase of collecting ideas is complete are the partici-pants invited to digest, evaluate, and classify all the ideas that have been recorded.

The purpose of such an exercise is clearly to capture as many ideas as possible without discouraging any contribution. The premise is that absence of judgment will promote optimum group creativity. Each participant makes suggestions which may then elicit more ideas as participants react to the suggestions of their neighbors.

Brainstorming technique diverges after the collection of ideas. Some facilita-tors will direct participants to copy down all the suggestions and to give their rankings to the facilitator who will consolidate them after the session. Other facilitators will direct the participants to evaluate the suggestions privately while still in the meeting, and send their evaluations to the facilitator, who will then introduce them for discussion. Still others will immediately open up a second phase of the session where the suggested ideas are evaluated aloud by the group. This last method is the fastest, and it taps into the accumulated energy of the brainstorming session. It also has the best chance of retrieving information before the participants are distracted by project work when they return to their desks. It is, of course, the most likely to cause tension as colleagues organize the contributions, questioning the meaning of some, placing some on a low position of value, or rejecting some entirely.

BRAINSTORMING AND THE ESL EMPLOYEE Brainstorming poses difficulties for many engineers and scientists from overseas, especially those from Asian countries. The mere absence of protocols of behavior during the phase of collecting information is stressful. An ESL participant sometimes has difficulty entering the fray. And because the Asian mode is to withhold ideas until they have been carefully formulated, the seeming irresponsibility of suggesting "half-baked" ideas represents a cultural barrier.

The problem might be looked at from the viewpoint of rapid prototyping. If you can accept the notion of rapid prototyping, you can bring yourself to accept the technique of brainstorming. Don't spend a lot of time examining the philosophy of the technique. Like the theory of learning how to swim by jumping into the water, you must simply plunge in.

To help straddle the cultural barrier, you might think of brainstorming as an exercise in humility. Withholding ideas until you have perfected them protects self-esteem. Alternatively, willingness to contribute imperfect ideas involves considerable humility. So, the ESL scientist or engineer might enter the brainstorming session with an orientation that is totally opposite from that of his or her neighbor. While the U.S.-born contributor might take risks cavalierly—daring to suggest imperfect ideas—the ESL contributor may adopt an attitude of modesty—accepting the imperfection of his or her own ideas. Whatever your orientation, the results are what count.

ROLE-PLAYING

Play is the operative word here. Work as play is an American value. The very best managers believe in having fun at work, and they believe in encouraging their employees to do the same. A lot of management development literature supports this viewpoint. Unfortunately, some managers cannot see how work as play can have serious results. They use the old task efficiency model instead. Often such managers resort to micromanagement which doesn't work well with scientists.

If role-playing isn't used at your company, look upon it as an underground route to problem-solving. Any successful route to solving a project problem is worth a try. If you're not ready to convene a role-playing session, try to participate in one that someone else convenes. Even if you can't see its immediate results, you should learn how it works. There's a likelihood that later in your career, you'll be able to use role-playing successfully.

Like brainstorming, role-playing attempts to get at a problem from a fresh angle. Role-playing is especially effective in sorting out personnel problems. If you are a supervisor presented with a personnel relations problem, you might convene your staff in a role-play session. By forcing yourself and your colleagues to assume different roles, you can often see the other person's position or point of view. Role-playing is also effective in trying to fathom the motivations of a sponsor or client. If you are about to deliver a system or a report, take an hour to meet with your project group and distance yourselves temporarily from your real roles. As TQM involves the client at the beginning of the development process, role-playing can simulate client involvement before you deliver your product. At the far end of the continuum, product reception can be a unknown phenomemon, involving factors you haven't thought about. Role-playing can force such factors to the surface where you can deal with them before they take you by surprise. Here's an example of a personnel problem that would benefit from a role-playing approach.

Dealing with Extended Breaks[1]

Supervisors in a manufacturing company have noticed that the employees are taking advantage of the break policy. The workers have two 15-minute breaks per day. However, they have been stretching their breaks to last up to 25 or 30 minutes each. The workers complain that the factory work is so boring that they need longer breaks. Also, the snack bar is so far away that it takes too long to walk there and back. The supervisors say the company is losing hundreds of work hours per year, and employees should not be paid for time they are not working. The plant manager has called a meeting to discuss this issue.

If you decided to submit this problem to role-playing methodology, you might convene a meeting of just those staff members who will be involved in handling the problem. After stating the problem in the manner of the above paragraph; that's to say, presenting the positions of both the employees and the management, call upon your group to assume the roles involved. This is certainly a creative way of using collaboration to work on an employee problem. Your goal should be determined before you begin the role-play session. In this case, the goal is to decide on the best way to handle the extended breaks. Either the roles can be assigned or meeting members can volunteer. The leader of the discussion might be whoever takes the role of the plant manager. Several meeting members can represent the company supervisors while other meeting members can act as employee representatives.

Try adapting this problem to your own laboratory or project environment. For example, if you are writing a report collaboratively, have your writing team role-play to address the readership problem. Because a report may have multiple audiences, you as a single writer or your collaborative writing team need to identify the various levels of audience. Convene a meeting in which you act as the general editor of the report. Your writing team members can assume the roles of the in-house content reviewer (peer reviewer), the highest level external reader of the report (primary audience), members of that reader's staff, the external financial officer who will approve the report's recommendations (secondary audience), and a general external readership to whom the report is going to be circulated (tertiary audience). If your group actually assumes the roles of these various readers, your role-playing activity

---

[1] Candace Matthews. *Business Interactions.* Englewood Cliffs, NJ: Regents/Prentice-Hall, p. 35.

will ensure that the report is written at an appropriate level to suit the needs of all these readers.

ROLE-PLAYING AND THE ESL EMPLOYEE Graduate students of literature are taught that full understanding and enjoyment of a piece of literature involves a willing suspension of disbelief. As reader, you must accept the terms that the creative writer establishes. If the author invents a main character who can move physically between the eighteenth century and the twentieth century, you must simply accept that condition. If you can't or won't, you will never participate satisfactorily in the novel's action. Of course, much depends upon the writer's skill in enabling you to willingly suspend your disbelief.

Like the willing suspension of disbelief for literature or drama, role-playing requires that you an abandon your own identity. For a scientist who is deeply committed to his or her self-image, role-playing will not be successful. An employee from a very studious European research facility, for example, may find role-playing frivolous. If you bring a condescending attitude to role-playing, your involvement will not be genuine. As a result, you'll deprive yourself of its benefits. As with brainstorming, try engaging in several instances of role-playing problem-solving before pronouncing judgment on its worth. For most employees from overseas, role-playing holds a novelty appeal. If you can utilize that novelty appeal, you will end up by adding one more collaborative technique to your inventory. You might even be able to transport your new techniques of brainstorming and role-playing to consulting assignments overseas.

Last, but definitely not least, role-playing methodology can help you improve your English fluency. A frequently used resource in ESL programs for high-level business executives, role-playing can be taken out of the corporate classroom and into your personal life. Just as you might meet with friends to play dominoes, you can join your friends for role-playing exercises at lunchtime. If your company has an ESL advisory group or an affirmative action advisory committee, you can enlist the membership to establish an ESL table or an AAAC table in the cafeteria. Remember the French table and the Russian table at college?

At either lunchtime or after hours, you and your friends can think of a situation that has stymied them. The situation can be social or work-related. You'll be surprised to learn how many such unsolved puzzles figure in the life of an ESL employee. For each role-play, select one scenario. As in workplace role-playing, decide on the purpose of this particular episode. Don't labor too long over a definition of purpose; your lunch hour is limited. Then, quickly assume roles, and start to enact the situation from the multiple perspectives that your roles demand. You will get caught up by the drama and conveniently forget that you are really expanding your word power. You'll find yourself using fresh vocabulary as you exit yourself from your real-life world. In addition, if you have difficulty expressing yourself, you'll be surrounded by friends. In popular parlance, you'll have a support group around you. Don't underrate such a support group. It's the beginning of a network that can be brought into future play in unexpected ways. There are old boy networks; yours will be a new folks network. Above all, it will help relieve your isolation as someone from a foreign culture. And it will serve as a bridge between your professional and social worlds.

COLLABORATIVE MEETINGS

Imagine yourself attending a traditional meeting. You now know all the devices for enhancing your performance at meetings. But now imagine the parameters for a perfect meeting—a perfect meeting from your point of view as an employee from a very different culture. What attributes might meetings assume that they don't now have? Wouldn't you sometimes like to be able to make your contributions anonymously? Wouldn't you like not to have to figure out where you are in terms of turn-taking protocols? Wouldn't you like to be liberated from the confines of your native culture as well as from the expectations of your new environment? Under such conditions, you would undoubtedly be able to contribute far more usefully to meetings. These attributes are no longer the stuff of dreams. Groupware is coming to market on a competitive basis to implement these new conditions. Groupware is computer software explicitly designed to support the collective work of teams. Entire suites of software are emerging to capitalize on the current enthusiasm for a collaborative workplace.

Collaboration rather than specialization has prompted the creation of new modes of conducting meetings. The hallmarks of these new modes are that:

- They take advantage of available new technologies and continue to refine them.
- They recognize the existence of old reservations about meeting participation.

In this respect, the creators of these software systems acknowledge that not everyone is a happy team player, and that collaborative planning will succeed only if all project members are comfortable in contributing their ideas. This acknowledgment is an enormous boon for the scientist or engineer from overseas. While not designed with the employee from a different culture or language background in mind, electronic meeting technologies have effectively eliminated possible language and culture barriers in the workplace. There are some drawbacks, but they are far outweighed by the productivity resulting from anonymous participation in meetings through electronic media.

ELECTRONIC MEETING SYSTEMS The Ventana GroupSystem 5 exemplifies collaborative software, all of which is generally referred to as groupware.[2] It offers numerous tools in its tool suite, some of which have been developed for group writing and data collection. Those of interest here are the ones that apply to the electronic meeting system (EMS). As *Fortune* magazine noted, "In many meetings, 20 percent of the people do 80 percent of the talking. Those who are shy, junior, intimidated, or just too polite typically shut up."[3] While *Fortune* and even the inventor of EMS, Dr. Jay Nunamaker, haven't commented on the cultural aspects of this observation, the involvement of you, the ESL professional, is an added argument for installing electronic meeting systems. Electronic meeting systems effectively tap the creativity of the silent 80 percent.

Carl Di Pietro, human resources executive at Marriott, has identified another subtle benefit of collaborative meeting software. While not addressing the language and cultural aspects of the meeting milieu, Di Pietro believes that meeting software can enhance cultural diversity. He says, "It's a room of nondiscrimination. You don't know if that idea you're reading comes from a woman or a man, part of the minority or majority, or a senior or junior person."[4]

The typical configuration of an electronic meeting room includes tables in a horseshoe arrangement with perhaps 12 or 14 workstations on the tables. If each workstation can be arranged in such a way as to secure anonymity for each of two participants, such an allocation of workstations can accommodate at least two dozen meeting members. The software itself protects you completely, and a 3M screen, for example, can secure the privacy of each workstation. At the head of the U-shape, a meeting facilitator uses a separate console. In addition, in plain view is a large screen on which the facilitator will display the contributions made by the participants. Additional screens can be added if the session will include videotapes, slides, or other presentation media.

Because these contributions (ideas, comments, suggestions, reactions) can be made simultaneously rather than serially, electronic meetings can process much more information much more quickly. The inhibited and the assertive participants have equal opportunities, and the software sorts their input with objectivity, disregarding who they are—whatever their rank, background, expertise may be. In other words, ideas are treated without regard to their source. Of course, this mechanical disregard for authority can irk some supervisors or managers who have become accustomed to directing discussions.

The process begins when the discussion leader (who can also be the facilitator, but needn't be) states the problem or question. Participants respond

[2] Thanks to Carolyn Johnson at The MITRE Corporation in McLean, Virginia, for explaining the Ventana groupware.

[3] David Kirkpatrick. "Here Comes the Payoff from PCs," *Fortune*, March 23, 1992.

[4] Quoted in "Here Comes the Payoff from PCs," *Fortune*, March 23, 1992.

by typing in ideas and possible solutions. This assumes that all the participants are comfortable with thinking at a keyboard. If not, keyboard-shy participants will be disadvantaged. However, it is very unlikely that practicing engineers or scientists in the United States today would be lacking keyboarding skills.

After the participants have exhausted their comments and reactions, the facilitator can then invoke one of the available sorting tools. He or she can have the computer search for common themes and group them roughly into categories. Or, the computer can be used to aid the participants in evaluating alternatives against a certain list of criteria. Or, the participants can engage in consensus development after all the comments have been exhausted through group evaluation of the issues. GroupSystems V has a Vote tool that orders input in seven quantifiable ways:

rank order
multiple choice
agree/disagree
yes/no
true/false
10-point scale
allocation

At the end of the meeting, the computer creates a printed record of results that is distributed to each participant.

The psychological aspects of this meeting technology are especially important for the professional from overseas. First of all, electronic meeting software creates a level playing field for meeting participation. Patterns of deference can be set aside. Concern about peer ridicule can be eliminated. Fear about worthiness of contributions need not exist. Accent, pronunciation, and grammatical perfection are nonissues. The software is designed to encourage spontaneous delivery of all kinds of ideas from everyone. Indeed, one of the drawbacks of the system is that ideas of little merit share equal place with ideas of great merit. However, the group evaluation process will adjust that unevenness. And the adjustment is made without embarrassing anyone. In sum, electronic meetings have both benefits and shortcomings, but the benefits far outweigh the shortcomings.

The electronic meeting room can be expensive or not, according to how carefully it's installed. Before installation, it's a good idea to take your meetings to an existing electronic meeting room elsewhere to see how well your organization likes the setup. Some colleges and universities have electronic meeting rooms (EMRs) that they rent to outside groups. After two or three visits, you'll probably want to propose one for your own company. (According to *Fortune*, IBM now has more than 50 such rooms all over the world.) If a suitable meeting room is already available in your plant, you can gather from your company warehouse a podium, tables, and however many large display screens you wish to use. Each workstation requires a separate networked, hard disk-based microcomputer. Can you gather these together or do you have to purchase them? A facilitator needs to be trained, but he or she doesn't have to be dedicated to the EMR on a full-time basis. The software itself can be purchased at a lower cost if your organization is affiliated with a college or university. If not, Ventana charges $25,000 to license GroupSystems, according to *Fortune* in 1992.

Other meeting groupware exists. IBM is developing a program called Team-Focus. An Austin, Texas firm offers VisionQuest that sells its license at a comparable price to Ventana's. The move is on; collaboration as a workplace ideal is spawning electronic software that offers meeting relief to nonnative-English speakers. If you find an EMR near you, visit it and try it out.

COLLABORATIVE WRITING

Although it's being promoted as if it were a new discovery, collaborative writing has, in fact, been practiced for quite a long time. Any book that is co-authored is the result of team or collaborative writing. Any anthology of essays or poetry that is co-edited is the product of collaborative editing. And any professional article that lists multiple authors, as many do, has evolved through a process of collaboration. If you've been engaged in research and development anywhere in the world, you've doubtlessly already participated in a form of collaborative authorship. Currently, however, writing professionals are taking a closer look at its characteristics.

THE REALITY OF COLLABORATIVE WRITING

Many of us prefer to write as single authors. But that privilege isn't always available, especially if you are a member of a research team. Essays and textbook chapters on collaborative writing usually begin by advising that the first step to a successful collaborative effort is to carefully select the members of your writing team. You will be advised to look around for people who will work well together—people with compatible personalities or with common research interests. Or you will be advised to look for a mix of desirable talents: someone who is well-known in the field (for prestige), someone expert in the project (for content validity), someone who writes well (for the prose), and someone who is a good editor (for a polished product). Such a mix of talents would doubtlessly ensure success.

Unfortunately, reality rarely permits you to organize an ideal team. More likely, you'll be writing up the results of your experiment in the company of the men and women who worked alongside you during its progress. Your colleagues will be primarily scientists or engineers; their writing, editing, and time management skills (if they have them) will be accidental bonuses. You will be constrained to write with your experimentation or development team.

If your document is a two-person effort, fewer problems arise than if your team includes four or five people. When a group decides to undertake writing a report or article based on the results of their work, certain decisions need to be made before any writing takes place.

A Talent Search

Assuming then, that your team is determined by events rather than choice, an initial writing team meeting should address the skills that each member can bring to the task. These skills are not necessarily the same as the ones you've each brought to the experiment, although there may be some overlap. For example, if one of you is manifestly superior in working on schedule, he or she is the logical project manager for document production and delivery. If another couldn't write well if his or her life depended on it, he or she needs to take responsibility for the mechanical aspects of the document: graphics, overall document design, tables, charts, list of references, table of contents. Many instititutes have rigid standards for document design, so this may not be as overwhelming a task as it appears. Your text will be passed along to a design department for the creation of covers, illustrations, and back matter that conform to standards.

Generally, you're all in the writing boat together. Some of you may be more modest than others about your writing skills; nevertheless, you'll all have to actually engage in composition. Because this is the most typical arrangement for technical documentation produced collaboratively, you need to move beyond the talent search phase. During the first meeting, you'll discuss a division of labor—writing labor. So far, you've not talked about the goal, audience, or time frame for the document. To do so before deciding who does what would be premature.

Task Allocation

Sometimes a prestigious member of the profession is named as part of the document team. That person may not engage in writing any part of the document's body, but he or she should certainly attend the initial planning meeting and be enlisted to write the introduction to the document. He or she can bring a global perspective to the material and endow it with the luster of an outstanding reputation.

There are several obvious ways of dividing the internal chapters.

- Method 1: Agree that after the team has outlined the document (a later meeting), each of you will assume responsibility for writing a section. This has been the most frequently used approach. The sections may simply represent segments of a chronological process, or they may be based on functional aspects of a process. There is latitude here for each writer's technical expertise to be tapped, assuming that the choice of a section is not random. The understanding should be stated that the sections will be roughly equal in length. At no point do you wish to create an impression that some team members are working harder on the document than others. Collaborative writing is, at least in theory, a democratic process. After all the sections are written, one person will serve as editor-in-chief to ensure a consistent style throughout the document. The editor-in-chief is usually a member of the team. However, a technical editor from a service department can serve this function if project funds are available. A technical editor can sometimes smooth out a segment-authored document more effectively than any one member of the group.

- Method 2: You may write each section as a group. This is invariably more time-consuming than the first method because it will involve differences of style and diverse opinions right from the beginning. It will require more meetings, either face-to-face or electronic, and a lot more early editing as accommodations to one another are made. With this method, someone must serve as recorder so that the final version of each section actually represents the group consensus. The recorder can be a member of the group or be a department secretary or technical assistant. But if you write and edit as a group, you shouldn't need an editor-in-chief because the document's style will express the voice of the group. And the resultant document will genuinely reflect every team member's version of what the abstract claims to be the project goal, methodology, and results.

- Method 3: Far less frequently used is the method whereby only one team member is engaged with the writing project at any one time. This method is sometimes used when the members of a project travel frequently and it's unlikely that they'll be able to actually meet together to work on the document. One member of the team will offer to draft the entire document. It is understood that this is a very rough draft meant to get the task "off the ground." After he or she has completed this task, he or she passes the draft to a second member of the team for a thorough content edit. A content edit may involve second and third members because it's of paramount importance. Following the content edit, the third team member passes the document onto a fourth member for a grammar and style edit. The fourth member passes the document to a fifth team member for a policy edit. This form of collaborative writing most closely resembles the single author's subscription to a writing flowchart as described in an earlier chapter. The blessing is that no one person is responsible for completing the entire process.

BASIC CONSIDERATIONS

To review, at the first meeting of a collaborative writing team, it is wise to restrict yourselves to a limited number of items.

- Acquaint yourselves with one another as writing colleagues. This is going to be different from knowing one another as project co-workers.
- Decide which method you are going to use to produce your collaborative paper. Too often a writing team thinks it will drift into some convenient arrangement. And that's just what it does—it drifts. It may take you a bit longer than you think to argue the pros and cons about which method you'll use. Having decided upon a method, resolve to stick to the choice.
- After selecting a method (and you might come up with a configuration other than one of the three described), agree that you all will assume joint responsibility later for writing the conclusion of the paper, article, or report. Too often, conclusions fail to grow out of the body of a technical document. This is a flaw of both single-author and multiple-author products. Because there is additional disjuncture between content and conclusion due to the nature of group writing, an off-target conclusion is a greater hazard in a collaboratively created product. At some future date, then, you will need to reconvene to craft a suitable and logically derived conclusion. Allocate a separate meeting for the conclusion, and if one of you is drawing a timeline for the report, be sure to give the conclusion meeting its own spot on the line.

Before that distant date, however, you will need to meet at least once more as a group to discuss the contents of the report itself. You should postpone drafting prose until after the second meeting. Because everyone has work in progress (usually reports are about completed work), it's psychologically sound to give the team some airtime before reconvening. A week is a good break if your deadline permits you to build in that much leeway at the front end.

While the first meeting was only about the methodology of the collaborative effort, your second meeting will address vital issues relative to content. These are the kind of issues that any single author must settle before writing.

- Firmly establish the audience of the paper.
- Define the level of information to be contained in the paper.
- Designate some stylistic approaches to convey that level of information.
- Agree upon the purpose of the paper.
- Distinguish the paper purpose from the project purpose.
- Make a list of key points to be contained in the paper.
- Decide upon a working title for the paper.
- Establish the deadlines that must be met.
- Rough out an outline of the paper.

Plan on saving plenty of time for the last task: roughing out the structure. You may find that settling the other issues will take up all the time your group can spare for the second meeting, in which case, you'll need to schedule a third prewriting meeting focusing entirely on outlining the paper. Because a solid outline serves as the skeleton for the writing task, you would benefit from factoring into your prewriting schedule some extra time for agreement on the outline.

PROS AND CONS OF COLLABORATIVE WRITING

No discussion of collaborative writing would be complete without reference to its pros and cons. The usual conflicts are mitigated somewhat through the use of electronic groupware: The screen serves as a buffer. But they do not disappear completely. Behind the software are the members of the team. And not everyone has collaborative software to expedite their task.

CON: CONFLICTING STYLES As circumscribed as technical writing is, different writing styles nevertheless emerge. Given the same project to report, no two engineers will write it up in the same sequence and at the same length. Even though they are likely to have the same opinion of where the emphases belong, they will express those emphases differently. Vocabulary may be very similar, but sentence structure will diverge significantly. Personal style can be subtle, but it can also be jealously protected. You can expect different writing styles to emerge during a collaborative writing task. If they are not somehow smoothed, they will be disruptive.

CON: CONFLICTING PERSONALITIES More detrimental to the success of a collaborative writing task is the clash of personalities and opinions. If a lot of electronic interaction takes place during the task, the screen may help to neutralize the clashes. But *flaming* on the Internet has become a topic of real concern, proving that technology doesn't really efface the human element. The most positive aspect of single-author writing is the absence of opposing judgments. Conflicting judgments, personalities, and opinions invest collaborative writing with more hazard than its proponents like to admit.

CON: ADDITIONAL TIME Another negative aspect of collaborative writing is the additional time it requires. Busy professionals have a hard enough time arranging their calendars to fit the demands made on them. Scientists and engineers prefer to concentrate on their projects, but it seems as if management conspires against that goal. We learn to accommodate meetings, travel, and necessary interaction with co-workers. Being asked to add time for writing collaboratively can arouse resentment. Regardless of how successful a collaboratively written document product may be, it takes more time for a group to produce it than to do it alone.

PRO: BETTER PRODUCT[5] It's a cliché to say that the justification for collabora-tive writing is that it produces a sum that's greater than its parts. Creativity is enhanced by combining and coalescing the input of several informed persons. Collaborative writing is a bit like brainstorming without the inclusion of merit-less items. The range of research experience of five people has got to be greater than that of any one. Further, collaboration encourages each writer to contribute to the maximum of his or her abilities. The sense of relief you feel from not having to produce an entire document will encourage you to perfect your assigned section. Quality supersedes quantity.

So, while the argument in favor of single-author writing rests on efficiency and convenience, the argument for multi-author writing rests on a richer, more complete text. Besides a better product—the primary justification of collab-orative writing—a valuable side effect occurs. When the collaborative team has taken the time to acquaint itself as writers and to define its tasks with care, participation in a group writing project results in improved interpersonal skills for all the contributors.

IMPLICATIONS OF THE COLLABORATIVE WRITING EXPERIENCE FOR THE ESL PROFESSIONAL

For the ESL engineer writing collaboratively, a safety net exists in the form of the other team members. No longer must a participant who knows his or her technology but is insecure about his or her English flail about for help with linguistic problems. Your portion of the text will be judged on its technical merit; the smoothing-out process will take place when everyone's contribu-tion is synthesized into one document. Your language irregularities will simply be what needs to be polished in your chapter. The chapter before yours may have serious grammatical errors, and the chapter after yours may be written in an extravagant style. You might look upon a collaborative writing project as providing safety in numbers.

Often, those of us from overseas seek companionship among people from our own country or language group. While personally reassuring, this ten-dency doesn't promote professional advancement. Each venture into collab-oration will encourage you to reach out further to your colleagues.

---

[5] See Mary M. Lay and William M. Karis (eds). *Collaborative Writing in Industry: Investiga-tions in Theory Practice.* Amityville, NY: Baywood Publishing Company Inc., 1991. While weighted in the direction of academic theory about collaborative writing, enough material from industry and the R & D community is included to make this collection of essays interesting for practicing professionals.

Collaborative Communications

The term *collaborative communications* is almost a redundancy, for what are communications if they're not collaborative? Nevertheless, the term carries the special connotation of workplace communications assisted by electronic technology. The range of such communications is fairly broad and it's growing as groupware becomes increasingly available. Collaborative communications includes, among other devices, videoteleconferencing, e-mail, fax machines, and groupware suites of tools.

VIDEOTELECONFERENCING

Only large, well-funded companies are likely to have videoteleconference centers. Those that can afford a videoteleconference system justify it because they have employees working on common projects at large centers that are significantly far apart. Under these circumstances, videoteleconferencing equipment is being used more frequently in the last decade as the quality of its resolution has improved.

A first-level system will use a reserved conference room that has all its chairs lined up behind conference tables facing cameras hidden behind the walls. A typical first-level system seats approximately 20 people. Their opposite numbers are in a similar conference room hundreds or thousands of miles away. The transmission is point-to-point. As in a face-to-face conference, participants take turns speaking. Small microphones embedded in the tables pick up their voices so that their images and their words are transmitted simultaneously. The cameras can project an image of all the participants at the table, three or four adjacent participants, or even the single participant speaking. A well-planned videoteleconference room will be equipped with a fax machine for transmitting text or graphics to the other site, as well as a light table for vugraphs to be projected via the camera. A camera operator is not needed as the few controls to be switched are embedded in a small box on the conference table.

Videoteleconferencing is the next best thing to actual face-to-face conferencing. It's held in real time, it's in color, and it preserves the dynamics of "meeting" your colleagues in Washington, Texas, or wherever. Sometimes employees have talked with team members on the phone or through e-mail for months without knowing what their colleagues look like. It's great fun to actually see a colleague in the videoteleconference, and to be able to pick up the extra information conveyed through facial expressions, body language, hand movements, and the interaction among participants on one side of the camera.

For the ESL participant, videoteleconferencing is patently nonthreatening. In fact, it seems to work in his or her favor. Despite the sophisticated technology that makes videoteleconferencing possible, a videoteleconference is not the same as a meeting with everyone in the same room. The differences are what matter here.

For one thing, there is a slight delay in transmission, perhaps a bit like that encountered during a telephone conversation with someone calling from overseas. But it initiates a slight feeling of unreality, and there is often a bit of muddle at the beginning of the teleconference while everyone is getting settled and switching on the desired camera orientations. It's rather like sitting in a concert hall, listening to the orchestra tune up; you know that in a few minutes the action will begin. In the meantime, you hear: "Hello, can you hear me clearly?" "I only see one segment of your group; please switch on all three cameras." "Hi, Charlie, who's that sitting next to you just outside the range of the camera?" All this prefatory discourse between members at different centers makes for a fairly relaxed atmosphere. Even though high-level officers may be present, the formal chill of the executive conference room can't be maintained.

Because of the frequent false starts while participants check to learn if their comments are received clearly (they usually are), a hesitant speaker is unremarkable in the electronic conference. It is much more frequent in the electronic videoconference for participants to repeat their comments, raise their voices, and generally respond to what they believe to be the deficiencies of the technology. All this preoccupation with the technology does distract somewhat from the content of the meeting, but at the same time it deflects attention from any one participant. There seem also to be fewer instances of one participant dominating the discourse. The turf is subtly altered. The man or woman who speaks frequently, at length, and with enormous self-confidence in the conventional meeting room becomes noticeably less active when facing an electronically transmitted panel of colleagues working at an unfamiliar location. That means you have more opportunity to speak up if you wish to; at the same time there is less pressure to speak up if you don't wish to.

Videoteleconferencing is a powerful way of bringing a dispersed group of collaborators together at the same time for brief and manageable meetings. (There is always another group waiting to use the facility.) For the corporation, the enormous expense of installing a customized system is offset by eliminating the need for frequent air travel. At least that's the theory. Some videoteleconferencers so enjoy seeing their distant colleagues on screen that they develop an urge to meet them in person. In either case—on-screen meeting or stimulated travel— the technology helps you to understand your company better, meet more colleagues having the same specializations, and avoid location provincialism.

ELECTRONIC MAIL

Electronic mail (e-mail) is a form of collaborative communication that's available to far more employees than the luxury of videoteleconferencing. E-mail comes in a number of software packages and with varied configurations. It's not necessary to tell you here what electronic mail is because no doubt everyone reading this book is using some type of it: cc:Mail, QuickMail, Profs, MCI Mail, NotesMail, and so on. That fact alone indicates that the single greatest problem of collaborative writing or messaging through e-mail is that not all packages are compatible, although, the various software developers promise to work toward compatibility. Also, e-mail messages on a different e-mail system can be routed to a gateway that will deliver it to your e-mail system. But e-mail users quickly develop a sense of loyalty to whichever form they're familiar with. If the transparency of the messaging is disrupted by an awareness of communicating through an "alien" package, some of the flow of composition is lost.

Electronic mail offers the supreme advantage to all users of time convenience. Senders can relay messages when they have an inspiration or a break between tasks; receivers can access messages when they have a moment to read their mail. Further, colleagues can be included by the Send To command. Or they can be apprised of commented messages by the Copy To commands that include the original message plus the receiver's comments. And the Print command enables you to capture messages for a hard copy file.

Electronic mail as a communication genre is difficult to define. It's neither a memo nor a telephone conversation; it's somewhere in between. Its implications have not yet been fully probed, but it does have the potential for some damaging results. We all tend to message back and forth rapidly and quite informally by means of e-mail. We forget that our electronic remarks can be captured and archived. Everyone has heard stories about intimate electronic conversations that get disseminated to everyone in a company through pressing the wrong key. And everyone has heard worse stories about hard copies of e-mail messages being presented in court as evidence of slander, sexual harassment, racial discrimination, or breach of security.

Electronic mail is more rather than less advantageous to the ESL engineer or scientist. You can express professional ideas in almost shorthand syntax; nobody expects elegantly polished sentences in an e-mail message. Actually, you should be on guard about becoming too sloppy with electronic messaging. That's a piece of advice for *everyone* in the technical workplace. Everyone should also keep in mind that while the tone and intent of e-mail is closer to speech than to writing, the typed word doesn't carry the meaning markers that spoken language does. Consequently, avoid sarcasm and irony. Don't transmit jokes that may be misinterpreted. Double-check the tone of each e-mail message: We're more prone to allow emotion to enter an e-mail message than a memo. Be careful about intimacy; when we are messaging to a close friend we are at his or her mercy. E-mail files can be maintained a long time. And even when they've been erased, there are back-up files stored at a computer center somewhere.

We all love e-mail, especially when it comes equipped with a long menu of wonderful graphics. It provides a highly effective way of settling issues quickly. It is the ultimate tool for collaboration. But keep the elephant pits in mind.

ELECTRONIC NETWORKS

The Internet and, most recently, World Wide Web epitomize electronic communications. Whereas e-mail permits messaging between two colleagues who know one another, the networks open up communication among multiple travelers on the information highway. Newsgroups, bulletin boards, or discussion databases bring together strangers across the country and possibly around the world. These strangers share an interest in and access to electronic networks, in addition to topics of mutual interest.

After searching electronically through topics already established for discussion (or you can initiate a new topic), you can highlight a topic of choice and join any dialogue that interests you. It's a bit like suddenly having unknown collaborators anywhere in the world with whom you can exchange opinions, problems, questions and answers. People develop electronic friendships. Some correspondents even establish idiosyncratic identities. Discourse frequently strays from professional discussion; jokes are shared, arguments arise, insults are flung, and compliments exchanged.

Navigating the networks is so addictive that concern is now arising over just how productive all this electronic messaging is. As increasing numbers of employees become involved in time-consuming electronic dialogues, the watchdogs of productivity are beginning to question if all this interaction is relevant to the work for which staff members are being paid. Even the most dedicated workers can find themselves lured from a discussion on the grammar structure of a Creole language into a conversation about Caribbean cooking. Short of standing in front of a staff member's screen, there's no way for a supervisor to monitor if you are testing a syntax diagram or exchanging recipes.

Despite the enjoyable distractions available on local area and international networks, and everything in between, you can locate potential collaborators more quickly through networks than by any other means. If you find yourself stuck with a problem in the design of your experiment, you can send out an SOS that may be answered by someone working on the same problem somewhere else in the country. The networks truly afford the capability of uniting an international community of scholars and researchers. English as a world language for science and technology combined with the capabilities of electronic networks forecasts a new era of scientific collaboration.

12

ADDITIONAL

RESOURCES

At no time in the history of the United States has more assistance been available for immigrants. Many states offer public assistance to new citizens as well as indirect aid to those who are not yet citizens. In addition, church congregations, citizen groups, state bureaus, national societies, schools and universities all provide special services for newcomers. Care and concern for other people has been institutionalized to a degree not even approached in the past by private charities and religious organizations. Care for others is not restricted to new arrivals to the country. It extends to citizens who live in poverty, to those suffering from deadly diseases, to women with or without children, and to people belonging to minority races.

Corporate America has also institutionalized the trend. Companies routinely offer psychological counseling to their employees, stress management clinics, cost-free flu shots, wellness maintenance programs, health clubs, and more. In addition, employee training and education budgets include funds for tuition-free degree programs and in-house courses. Corporation facilities are made available for autonomous clubs like Bible study groups and Star Trek science fiction clubs. All these forms of company assistance pay off richly in terms of employee satisfaction. They also create company loyalty.

The purpose of this chapter is to make you realize that all this works on your behalf. You need to understand that seeking assistance and accepting benefits are social norms in the United States. It's not considered shameful to register for accent-reduction courses, to join ethnic or racial support groups, or to look for professional help for personal problems. An extraordinarily wide variety of resources is available. The *Resource Book* will bring only a few to your attention. This limited selection will guide you to the proverbial trough of water. You must decide to drink from it.

Toastmasters International

Local branches of Toastmasters International often hold their monthly meetings on company premises. These meetings are attended by both American-born members and those from other countries. Toastmasters meetings are run by each chapter membership with the purpose of helping members improve their public speaking skills. According to international president Jack Gillespie, "A Toastmasters club is a place where people learn the arts of listening, speaking, and thinking. Its mission is to provide a mutually supportive and positive learning environment in which members can develop communication and leadership skills, which in turn foster self-confidence and personal growth."

The meetings provide a forum for members to practice various forms of public speaking such as an "ice breaker," an extemporaneous presentation, a prepared lecture, or a briefing with graphics. Certain protocols are learned and practiced such as how to open a meeting, how to greet the attendees, how to close a presentation, and how to accept questions. For each presentation, one of the members serves as a timekeeper, thereby emphasizing the importance of tailoring presentations to fit into agreed amounts of time.

The Toastmasters organization, with headquarters in California, is over 60 years old. In addition to its time-tested formulas for helping members develop public speaking skills, the organization strengthens leadership qualities by means of a full roster of duties for each group officer. All officers learn the criteria of leadership at an annual Leadership University, a combined meeting of regional chapters held at a central location.

The membership of any one group or chapter is singularly egalitarian. For example, members of a group may include both technical and nontechnical employees, service personnel, and members of middle management. If near a military base, a group may have a mixed civilian and military membership. The size of each group is what you might consider "comfortable." Chapters tend to have memberships of about 20 to 25, and not everyone attends every meeting.

The nature of the club fosters friendly but professional behavior. If you attend a meeting as a visitor, you can see that members strive to project a courteous, supportive attitude toward one another. They seem aware that they have a mission to encourage one another in developing speaking and listening skills that will enhance their careers and enrich their lives. Luncheon meetings and occasional dinners add a social dimension.

Some companies offer meeting rooms and facilities like a podium, microphones, and presentation media for Toastmasters to use. Company sponsorship offers the convenience of meeting during lunchtime or directly after work without having to drive to a different location. If you think your colleagues would attend Toastmasters meetings and your company doesn't sponsor a Toastmasters group, ask the Human Resources Department (formerly known as the Personnel Department) to sponsor a chapter. Expenses incurred by a company sponsoring a group are so minor that they can't even be tracked, whereas the value of Toastmasters sponsorship to the company's image is significant.

For information on where to find a group near you or for information on setting up a new group, contact the Toastmasters International headquarters:

Toastmasters International
P. O. Box 9052
Mission Viego, CA 92690
Phone: (714) 858-8255
Fax: (714) 858-1207

Stress Management Programs

In the past decade or two, programs for managing stress have spread throughout corporate America. Large companies contract with external vendors to set up in-house programs for their employees. These vendors should be licensed social workers (LICSW) who are qualified to lead workshops on coping with stress. Usually a company will also provide an office for the social worker to use for private counseling sessions which are held in complete confidence.

Stress might be defined as the "reactions inside an organism when the demands exceed its ability to cope." Chronic stress at work might be caused by a conflict between demand and resources (money, people, expertise). Educators in public schools are frequently victims of this sort of stress creation. The International Labor Organization (a branch of the United Nations) reports that stress-related injury claims on the job have climbed from 5 percent of all occupational disease claims in 1980 to 15 percent in 1990. Stress certainly occurs as the result of a hostile management-employee atmosphere or a destructively competitive environment.

Stress can be caused by problems at home. Parents of rebellious teenagers, professionals trying to care for aged parents, partners with troubled relationships are all involved in stress-producing situations. Usually, a company supporting a stress management program will not distinguish between personal and job-related problems. A troubled employee is not able to work at his or her best level of achievement, so it benefits a company to provide help with getting the situation under control regardless of the causes of stress.

Stress management has special relevance for engineers and scientists from cultures where anxiety is traditionally kept buried. If you think about which of your friends and colleagues suffer from ulcerated stomachs, you'll be able to identify cultural backgrounds that inculcate repression of anxiety. Other physical manifestations of stress are high blood pressure and heart attacks. The competitive nature of corporate America induces high blood pressure. Because blood pressure is easily measured, you should use the services of your company's medical center to get a blood pressure reading. Keep it for a baseline. Return to the medical center to get your blood pressure checked every few months, and keep a record of its ups and downs. If it reaches a level of marginal concern, the nurse will alert you. Higher than that, and the company doctor can prescribe medication to reduce it.

Most stress mangement programs promote physical and attitudinal approaches to controlling reactions of stress. Although social workers are not authorized to prescribe medication, they can teach you techniques for managing your own reactions to stressful situations. Many tips for stress management exist. Here are only a few to help you reduce work-related stress.

TIP 1: Avoid trying to be a perfectionist. Strive to do the best you can under existing circumstances.

TIP 2: Take care of yourself. Get enough rest and eat well. Remember that mind and body work together.

TIP 3: Learn how to have fun. Recreation is as important as work, so schedule time for both work and play.

TIP 4: Understand that stress is based on your perception of something that you believe can harm you. See if you can change that perception by finding at least one aspect of that threat you can control.

TIP 5: Get regular exercise. Your body chemistry changes during periods of high stress and exercise tends to dissipate this effect.

TIP 6: Improve your appearance to promote good self-esteem. Should you lose weight or buy some new clothes? A new tie for a man or a pair of beautiful earrings for a woman can help.

TIP 7: Monitor your "self talk" to diminish pessimism. Change the subject if you find yourself thinking about how pressured you are at the office.

TIP 8: Develop a support system with colleagues at work that emphasizes mutual help and problem-solving instead of just exchanging complaints. Avoid people who complain all the time.

TIP 9: Make your office or laboratory pleasant. Can you arrange for more light, some attractive colors, and pictures you like? Some healthy green plants will do wonders.

TIP 10: Develop the habit of doing your paperwork immediately; don't let it build up.

TIP 11: Go out for lunch whenever possible.

TIP 12: Arrange a carpool, if possible, to minimize stressful commutation.

TIP 13: Learn to relax by using deep breathing exercises.

TIP 14: Set time aside to relax alone.

TIP 15: Practice meditation or yoga.[1]

Psychologists have noted that some people have what is called "psychological hardiness." These people are more resilient than others. You can develop some of the characteristics that have been noted in psychologically hardy people. Typically:

- They accept the fact that there are some tasks they can't do. They set limits for what they undertake. They don't apologize for what they can't do. They have learned how to say no.

[1] Herbert Benson's *The Relaxation Response*, New York: William Morrow, 1975, teaches a useful and easy form of meditation. It has been reissued (1992) as an Avon reprint by Random House.

- They don't need to be liked. By liberating themselves from the need to be liked, they eliminate an entire complex of stress-producing feelings.
- They have a fundamental faith in their own ability.

According to Dr. Robert Evans, a practicing psychologist at the Wellesley (Massachusetts) Community Agency, acquiring these attitudes *always helps*. He says that "people's ability to tolerate stress dramatically improves" when they adopt the self-protective attitudes listed here.

If you would like to find a stress management counselor, you might ask for recommendations from your company nurse. If you'd rather not work through a company-sponsored program, contact the National Association of Social Workers for a list of licensed members in your state:

National Association of Social Workers
750 1st Street NE, Suite 700
Washington, DC 20002
Phone: (202) 408-8600
Fax: (202) 336-8310

Multicultural Diversity Training

Multicultural diversity training, like stress management programs, has become increasingly available in corporations over the past few years. In fact, you, the ESL professional are not the target audience for multicultural sensitivity training. Rather, your American-born colleagues, and especially your American-born supervisors, are the employees for whom this training has been developed. It's another expression of the trend described at the beginning of the chapter whereby the majority population is being educated away from national provincialism.

Multicultural diversity training is not entirely based on philanthropic motives. Firm demographic data indicates that the American workforce is rapidly becoming multinational and multiethnic. If you hear references to Workforce 2000, a frequently invoked term, know that the phrase is code for the fact that by the turn of the century the minority worker will have become the majority. As someone from a foreign country, someone speaking a foreign language, and someone possibly exhibiting foreign behavior, you need to know that corporations across the country are supporting your inclusion into the mainstream.

Unfortunately, the consultants conducting multicultural training are rarely themselves representative of many diverse cultures. Typically, teams of one white woman and one black man conduct the workshops. In the United States today, being female still represents a minority gender in the workplace, while being African-American distinguishes the teacher as a member of a minority racial group. But American women and African-American men do not comprise a *multi*cultural cohort. Essentially, Americans are teaching Americans about foreign people with precious little input from the subjects of the seminars.

The field of multicultural training would be greatly enriched if professional men and women from overseas would become active in the training room. While multicultural diversity training is not a resource directed at you, we all would benefit greatly, directly or indirectly, if Indians, Pakistanis, Africans, Chinese, West Indians, Taiwanese, Italians, Cambodians, Venezuelans, Mexicans, Brazilians, Japanese, Bangladeshi, Afghanis, Poles, Puerto Ricans, and so on would start to conduct multicultural training sessions.

If you aren't ready to lead multicultural seminars, you can participate. Participation can take a number of forms. By just attending a course, you would be able to add insights that the American-born trainers would greatly appreciate learning. You might have to argue with the registrar that although you're not considered a member of the intended audience, you really want to attend. By volunteering to participate in a role-play during the course, you could bring invaluable information to the class. Your participation in role-playing would bring out attitudes and behaviors from far-away countries to which few Americans have had any exposure. Also, by suggesting how training courses could include more information about your culture or country, you can enrich them. You can't know what such courses lack if you don't attend them.

Finally, by doing some part-time consulting in diversity issues yourself, you can add genuine value to the technical workplace. Consulting will rapidly help you gain self-confidence. After all, you have more first-hand information about the outsider's position than anyone else. You will need to learn a few presentation techniques, but the models for conducting diversity seminars already exist. The best source for material on trainers, seminars, and materials is the American Society for Training and Development (ASTD), as it's widely known.

American Society for Training and Development
Box 1443, 1640 King Street
Alexandria, VA 22313-2043
Phone: (703) 683-8100
Fax: (703) 548-2383

Self-Assessment Tools: Personality Type Indicator

Americans at work are enrolling in cultural diversity seminars to learn more about working with you. How can you learn more about working with them? Or, more important, how can you learn more about yourself so that you can work successfully with others? The richest, most widely tested self-analysis instrument is the Myers-Briggs Type Indicator. Popularly known as the MBTI, this self-analysis tool has been steadily gaining nationwide respect. It's used by many U.S. Government agencies, by some military services, and by private corporations. It's even part of the curriculum at university schools of management. Although it exists primarily to help each individual better understand his or her own personality type, MBTI is now being used extensively for team building in the technical workplace.

The Myers-Briggs Type Indicator is designed to implement the personality theory developed by Carl Jung, a Swiss physician and psychologist. It provides a practical way to help you understand personal differences so that everyone can work together productively and you can remain comfortable with yourself.[2] It's an instrument designed in such a way that those who take it are forced to choose between multiple sets of binary preferences. The multiplicity of the choices builds up into a rather complex personality description. There is nothing simplistic about the results: 16 possible combinations of personality factors build in a reasonable level of flexibility. In fact, the flexibility of the self-assessment is such that if you retake it immediately, it can yield slightly different results. Further, retaking it over an interval of years or decades often yields even different results that track changes in lifestyle preferences. These shifts in results do not compromise the validity of the instrument; they strengthen its basis in reality.[3]

The 16 possible combinations are derived from four areas of definition: a person is either extroverted or introverted, intuitive or sensing, thinking or feeling, perceiving or judging. Remember, these are merely descriptors, and you describe yourself. The MBTI is not a test nor is it an instrument of judgment. The selections are not made by an outsider. The exercise is primarily for self-information. It's only in recent years that companies have seen its value for employee counseling and for team-building exercises.

The chart here displays the 16 possible combinations, followed by a key for the chart.

---

[2] Isabel Briggs Myers with Peter Myers. *Gifts Differing*, Palo Alto, CA: Consulting Psychologists Press, Inc., 1980, is a highly readable introduction to understanding the differences of human personality types.

[3] Isabel Briggs Myers and Mary H. McCaulley. Manual: *A Guide to the Development and Use of the Myers-Briggs Type Indicator*, Palo Alto, CA: Consulting Psychologists Press, Inc., 1993, offers good descriptions of the 16 types as well as many pages of statistical support for test reliability.

Key to the MBTI Chart

E=Extroverted
I=Introverted
N=Intuitive
S=Sensing
T=Thinking
F=Feeling
P=Perceiving
J=Judging

ISTJ	ISFJ	INFJ	INTJ
ISTP	ISFP	INFP	INTP
ESTP	ESFP	ENFP	ENTP
ESTJ	ESFJ	ENFJ	ENTJ

When the instrument is used in the corporate classroom, some typical MBTI seminar objectives include:

- Increasing self-awareness and confirming self-perception.
- Learning about differences in perception, judgment, and energy source.
- Appreciating the gifts and strengths of one's strengths and the strengths of others.
- Supplementing and augmenting those areas that do not come easily.
- Applying the knowledge gained about personality type.

A skilled trainer can offer a seminar for managers only in which the team-building properties of using the instrument are stessed. More advanced seminars can be conducted relating MBTI typing to Total Quality Management theory.

Seminars are taught only by trainers who have been certified through the Center for Applications of Psychological Type, Inc. (CAPT) or one of their affiliated agencies. Trainers must attend a week-long, eight-hour day course and pass a rigorous examination to become certified. The train-the-trainer centers are loosely affiliated with CAPT. Certification paperwork and supplies for testing are all obtained from a central source, thereby protecting the standardization of materials. Some trainers submit the data from their courses to the central database. More need to do so to keep the database up to date and relevant to today's workforce.

If you are interested in attending an MBTI seminar or in having your personality type analyzed, contact CAPT for information on how, when, and where:

Center for Applications of Psychological Type, Inc.
2815 NW 13th Street
Suite 401
Gainesville, FL 32609-2861
Phone: 800-777-2278
Fax: 800-723-6284
Internet: mary@capt.org

Other Self-Assessment Tools: Skills Inventories

Consulting psychologists and career counselors prefer their clients to take more than one test. Whereas MBTI is really a personality type identification tool, other tests exist that attempt to identify skills. The Strong Interest Inventory (SII) and the Campbell Interest and Skill Survey are two of these. There are others. All of them require that you select from lists of activities. In addition, you may be asked to rate yourself on a range of responses to hypothetical situations or on a range of personal characteristics. Both the Strong and Campbell tests organize answers into broad functional categories. For example, the Campbell categories are influencing, organizing, helping, creating, analyzing, producing, and adventuring. The final result is intended to guide you toward career choices that are likely to work for you and to warn you against those that you should avoid.

The SII works well when applied to homogeneous groups like electrical engineers or actuaries. As a widely used assessment of interests, the SII—like the MBTI—has a long history of research behind it. According to Dr. Mary C. Patrick, an organizational and educational psychologist based in Washington, DC, the SII is "an especially valuable tool in career planning, because its assessment of interest profiles is such an excellent predictor of occupational fit. As well, it provides a framework for organizing an individual's personal interests within the world of work."[4]

If you are already firmly committed to a profession, the SII can help you expand your occupational options. By taking one of the skills tests, you can uncover ancillary competencies. For example, in addition to your skill in engineering you might learn that you have teaching skills. These skills would enable you to teach engineering courses to undergraduate students in evening classes at your local college.

The SII derives its theoretical framework from Holland's Theory of Vocational Behavior (see Figure 12.1). Unlike the MBTI that has four basic binaries, Holland ascribes six basic personality types to humans:

[4] Mary C. Patrick. "A Good Look in the Mirror," *Contingencies*, Washington, DC: American Academy of Actuaries, May/June 1994.

R=Realistic
I=Investigative
A=Artistic
S=Social
E=Enterprising
C=Conventional

Rather than the MBTI cube, the Holland hexagon of types enables interpreters of this instrument to pair adjacent types, alternate types, and opposite types, creating 18 possible pairings in addition to the six primary types. When the complex analysis for each individual or for a group is completed, the subjects learn not only what they already suspect about themselves but also some startling information about what they need to do to supplement the critical competencies they already have.

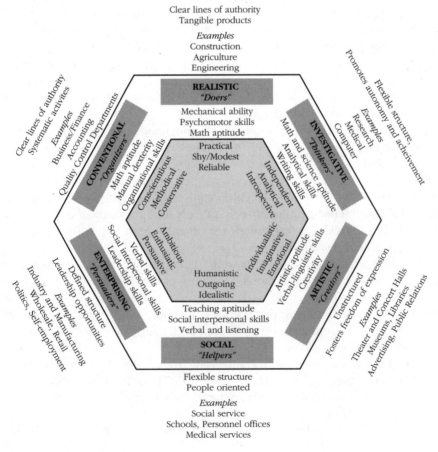

FIGURE 12.1   Holland's hexagon.

The question arises, "How useful are these tools for professional people who have been born into and nurtured by another culture?" It's only now, when increasing numbers of professionals from overseas are entering the United States workforce, that career counselors and corporate trainers must ask themselves this question. The highly organized coterie of MBTI practioners has already addressed the question; their answer is that Jung's types are universal. The database in Florida now includes data not only from foreign-born professionals taking the test in this country, but also results from tests administered in Canada, Mexico, France, China, Korea, and Japan. These instruments have been written in or translated into the languages of the indicated countries. Data to date, while relatively sparse, seems to indicate that the universality of Jung's analysis of personality types holds up under multicultural and multinational testing.

Some of the best work along these lines is being done in the Washington, DC, area. Helen Pelikan of Pelikan Associates is offering already-qualified trainers workshops on Successfully Applying the MBTI in Multicultural Settings, and Dr. Patrick has produced what might well be the first comprehensive summary of profile results comparing specific overseas samples to U.S. samples.

Your company might like to explore this data. Your affirmative action advisory group might find the international aspects of personality and skills profiles especially interesting. And you might look into the language aspects of converting American-grown tests into instruments for use overseas. In fact, providing language-sensitive translations could be a rewarding avocation for you as an ESL professional. You can begin your exploration near Washington.

Mary C. Patrick Associates
10301 Grosvenor Place
Suite 1701
Rockville, Maryland 20852
Phone: (301) 530-8750

Sources of Celebration

This chapter has asked you to venture beyond grammar, style, and writing training. It has urged you to go beyond improving speaking and listening skills. It has alerted you to resources for maintaining healthy attitudes, for examining your personal preferences and skills, and for helping you join your colleagues in supporting one another. In addition, you've picked up hints about ways of using your special status to improve your company's training program and even to earn money outside your regular job. All the resources mentioned, however, have been developed by other people. They simply await your patronage.

Ultimately, like everyone else, you'll have to devise your own strategies and learn how to depend upon yourself. If you have a family, they, of course, are your greatest source of strength. In any case, your motivations must come from within. Similarly, you'll benefit from devising your own system of rewards for accomplishments. You needn't wait for your company to present you with a certificate or a plaque. You can find more exciting rewards than these.

If you've worked through all the exercises in this book and resolved to explore additional resources, you owe yourself a reward for a job well done. What will it be? You are both granter and recipient. You can name your own prize! Think of "treats" to yourself as ways to celebrate each competency gained. These treats will also reinforce the good motivation you've already demonstrated.

Some examples of rewards you can grant yourself include a meal at a favorite restaurant, a bottle of good wine or fine cognac, or a new camera. Pretty new shoes or a beautiful blouse would remind you of your success in surmounting the article system, the verb system with its many peculiarities, or a pronunciation problem. Treating yourself and a friend to the ballet or a concert takes on additional value when you connect it to a personal accomplishment. It might be fun to throw a party. If your guests ask if they're helping you celebrate your birthday, you can answer that they're helping you celebrate your emancipation from fear of meetings!

In sum, if you can have fun at work as the new workplace philosophers recommend, and if you can observe causes for celebration as an ESL survivor, your life, will become much happier.

Ethics in the Workplace

The *Resource Book* has been written with the single purpose of helping you to help yourself. Most of the recommendations suggest mechanical types of activities to help you advance in your career. Grammar exercises, practical tips, document production guidelines, and suggested coursework are among the materials you've been encouraged to use.

The book at times may project a tone of cynicism. Certainly the Tips for Survival and Success that follow frankly reflect the realities of life in corporate America. What cynicism emerges results from my having been there. It's the result of intellectual interest that's been leavened by lessons learned on the job. These are not the lessons taught in corporate training courses or in college textbooks on technical writing.

Cynicism aside, my premise is that you can succeed in a competitive environment without knowingly damaging your co-workers and colleagues. It's sad that success in the workplace is sometimes built on the destruction of competitors. It's sad if any success has such a foundation, and it isn't necessary.

You can adopt rules of ethical behavior that transcend culture, nationality, race, or environment. Ethical behavior has universality. Perhaps the institutionalized aids that were discussed at the beginning of this chapter express an American yearning to perfect an ethical society.

If you observe officers, managers, or co-workers engaged in actions that will hurt the careers of their associates, don't think that it is "The American Way." It's not. Unprincipled computer hackers, selfish meeting hogs, and devious wheeler-dealers notwithstanding, the heartland of America is honest and helpful.

13

TIPS FOR

SURVIVAL

AND SUCCESS

Survival and success in the workplace are every worker's concern. Some employees develop "street smarts" early, while others remain unaware of how to make life in the workplace more pleasant for themselves. As an employee from overseas, you may have a special need for simple techniques to deal with day-to-day relationships at work. Your perceptions may be filtered through cultural assumptions that don't apply to your current situation.

Organization Charts

A good starting point for any employee is to get copies of organization (org) charts for the company, for the department, and for the project team. These charts will help you understand reporting relationships. If org charts don't exist for lower-level units, it's a good idea to sketch out your own, remembering to keep the charts up to date. Frequent reorganization is a hallmark of companies attempting to cope with the economic realities of the late twentieth century and to anticipate the economic verities of the new century.

Secretarial Staff

As companies turn from traditional hierarchical structures to more complicated matrix structures, reporting relationships can become confusing. These relationships often need clarification. An extremely valuable resource, often overlooked, are the secretaries who support technical professionals. Even though support roles, too, are changing radically, you'll find that secretaries and office administrators can help you understand the vertical, horizontal, and diagonal reporting relationships of a matrixed organization. They are often the people who convert the abstract notions of matrixing into concrete graphics. As a result, they have a firm grasp of the big picture, and can be allies in helping you untangle the intricacies of hierarchical, matrixed, and hybrid structures.

A Dozen Tips

The following short tips summarize some unofficial conventions of the professional work scene in the United States. They apply to for-profit and not-for-profit companies, think tanks, federal and state agencies, university and government-supported research centers, and, in general, any fairly large organization where engineers, mathematicians, computer scientists, physicists, and social scientists work. Some of these tips may seem self-evident, but younger employees, new employees, and those reentering the workforce may not have had practical experience with the circumstances involved.

APPEARANCE AND REALITY

You will discover that appreciation for your technical ability varies from supervisor to supervisor. The ideal supervisor recognizes an employee's technical merit, and will help to develop communication skills that may be deficient. However, many supervisors judge (and perhaps reward) on the basis of appearance. As a result, "hand wavers" often move up while the quiet competents run in place. To overcome this situation, you must develop the appearance side of your performance.

> TIP: Cultivate an appearance of professionalism while you develop your technical skills.

CRITICISMS AND COMPLAINTS

A conscientious employee recognizes flaws in technical or personnel decisions. If the suggestion box option isn't available, and you wish to address a flaw, you must interact directly with your supervisor. Unfortunately, supervisors sometimes view such an effort as an attack on their management judgment. Thus, communication skill is highly important. Lacking it, you can be seriously damaged by the exchange of ideas.

> TIP: Immediately follow a criticism or complaint (negatives) with a suggestion for correction or improvement (positives).

PRAISE OR BLAME

The most successful work relationships praise strengths. A few coworkers and supervisors can absorb negative feedback in a reasoned manner. But until you become powerful enough to find fault without a political backlash, it's a better survival technique to simply grin and bear it. Remember, managers are empowered to identify employee weaknesses, but unlike academia, employees (students) aren't in a safe position to bring management (faculty) weaknesses to a manager's attention.

> TIP: If you can't say something good, don't say anything at all.

TROUBLEMAKERS AND TEAM PLAYERS

The corporate workforce is simplistically divided into "good guys" and "bad guys." Bad guys are those who seem to interfere with the smooth operation of the daily process. Good guys are those who work well with their colleagues. While developing a professional image, work with your colleagues as often as possible. Academia, on the other hand, has greater tolerance for the lone contributor who is viewed as an asset rather than as a nonteam player.

> TIP: It's wise to cultivate the image of a team player in the corporate workplace.

NEGOTIATION STRATEGY

If you perceive that you've been overlooked for promotion, that you've been assigned inappropriate tasks, or that you've failed to receive a routine salary increase, don't threaten to quit. You might just "rattle your saber" at a time when your manager has been directed to reduce staff. You will have provided your manager with an excellent opportunity for accepting your resignation even if you didn't really wish to leave your job.

> TIP: Always negotiate for improved circumstances; never threaten to quit your job.

ENEMIES IN THE WORKPLACE

Having enemies in the workplace is almost unavoidable. There is bound to be someone jealous of your ability or irritated by your way of doing your job. You may never know who some of your enemies are. It's important, however, not to create enemies needlessly. Be alert about what you say to your colleagues and how you say it. Hurt feelings easily translate into hatred that may be acted on in the future.

> TIP: Workplace relationships are far more sensitive than most of us realize. Actively avoid making enemies in the workplace.

CELEBRATION

Without appearing to be manipulative, it's important that you celebrate the achievements of your colleagues. Good managers will see that this happens. If your manager doesn't, join your co-workers in creating appropriate celebrations.

TIP: Celebrate your colleagues' successes. (We discussed how to celebrate your own successes in Chapter 12.)

THE CIVIL SERVICE LESSON

Do you find it painful to work under your current supervisor or manager? If so, take a lesson from the nation's civil servants who know that sooner or later the director (manager, supervisor, or whatever) will be promoted or retire. The real survivors in the business and military worlds are those who stay in place, doing a good job and waiting for the tide to turn.

TIP: Your manager is more likely to be transferred than you are. You can outlast an incompatible supervisor. The next one may be a perfect match for you.

OUTSIDE JOB SEARCH

If you decide to search for a new job outside the company, don't quit your current job. Although arguments do exist for full-time job searching, placement experts advise that it's easier to get a new job if you already have a job. In other words, you're seen as more employable if you're already employed.

TIP: Remain in your job while you search for a new job outside the company. You won't be so desperate to take anything that becomes available.

BURNING BRIDGES

While employees from overseas may be less likely than those on familiar turf to engage in confrontation, the urge to burn bridges is universal. The employee who exits by denouncing a work program, a manager, or a company policy has no future of return. Careers take unexpected directions, and it's always useful to maintain friendly contacts.

TIP: When exiting a company or department, maintain friendly relations regardless of the exit circumstances.

MULTICULTURAL DIVERSITY

Many businesses today are offering multicultural sensitivity training to their managers and U.S.-born employees. Try to become comfortable with the idea that as an engineer or scientist from overseas, you're entitled to allowances for your cultural and linguistic distinctions. Be cheerful rather than apologetic about your status. With a pleasant attitude, you'll find many supporters in the workplace.

TIP: Avail yourself of opportunities designed to enhance your performance. As an ESL professional, you're eligible for special consideration.

Beyond Multiculturalism

After developing comfort with your status as an ESL professional, transcend your differences. You can do this in several ways. For example, describe some of your culture's holidays to your co-workers, or explain the distinctions of an overseas education. Also engage wholeheartedly in group activities so that you're seen as a totally integrated member of the general team.

TIP: Share distinctive cultural experiences with co-workers. Even more effective, be a totally integrated member of your project team.

APPENDIX:

THE ENGLISH VERB

SYSTEM

The English verb system is sometimes oversimplified by defining verb forms strictly on the basis of time. Instead, concepts like completion of action, progression of action, habitual action, temporary state, or permanent state are more helpful to the second language speaker. The following does not attempt to provide an exhaustive list of each tense's possible uses, but serves to help you think about tense in terms of meaning in preference to time.

Admittedly, efforts to describe some of the more complex tenses (such as the past perfect progressive and the future perfect progressive) are most easily accomplished in terms of linear time. And the English tense system does divide time into a very large number of segments that, in general, reflect Western perceptions of time as linear.

Here is the list of 12 tenses discussed in Chapter 5 of the *Resource Book*. These represent the tenses of the active voice. Older grammar books list a different set of 12 tenses: six active voice and six passive voice tenses, but no progressive.

English Verb Tenses

Simple Present
Present Progressive
Simple Past
Past Progressive
Simple Future
Future Progressive

Present Perfect
Present Perfect Progressive
Past Perfect
Past Perfect Progressive
Future Perfect
Future Perfect Progressive

Simple Present

COMMENTS

- You can identify tenses by means of certain markers: *ed, ing, will* or *shall, have* or *has, had,* as examples. The simple present tense is the least marked form.
- Of all the tenses, simple present is the one most characterized by a sense of timelessness; its action is neither past nor completed.
- The simple present has many uses; it is, perhaps, the most used of all the tenses.

EXAMPLES

Universal truths: The sun *rises* in the east. Water *freezes* at 32°.
Habitual actions: Rajeev frequently *questions* his professor's theories.
Characteristic (or fixed) action: Rajeev's printer *prints* poorly. His terminal *operates* slowly.
Historical present: Iago *lies* to Othello, and Othello *kills* Desdemona. (This artificial use of the present tense is largely literary.)

Present Progressive

COMMENTS

- The present progressive conveys a sense of indefiniteness. It describes actions that are not completed or actions in progress.
- Often, present progressive conveys a sense of temporariness or lack of permanence.
- The *ing* verb form is also sometimes used to express future time.

Examples

Act-in-progress: Carmen *is attending* a conference today.

Temporariness: Our photocopier *isn't working* right now.

Habitual actions: Carmen *is* always *complaining* about the food in the cafeteria.

Future expectations: Carmen *is coming* tomorrow to teach the class.

Simple Past

Comments

- Simple past usually refers to a single point in the past.
- It can refer to an action that took place over a period of time in the past. This reference to duration is not the same as past progressive.
- It can also refer to a habitual act that took place in the past.
- Simple past is sometimes used to soften a request. Used this way, it has no relation to pastness.

Examples

Single point in the past: Bhavani *retired* on the first of April.

Duration in the past: He *taught* aeronautical engineering for 20 years.

Habitual past action: As an intern, Juliana *spent* four hours at the lab every day.

Conversational softener: I *wondered* if I might borrow your dictionary.

Past Progressive

Comments

- Past progressive is never used by itself; it combines the past of *to be* plus an *ing* form.
- It's frequently used in complex (the syntax form) sentences because it tends to be relational.
- Past progressive can be easily replaced.
- It is a very limited tense.

EXAMPLES

Action in progress in the past: At 7:45 this morning, Andrew *was turning* on his computer.

Action in progress in the past (relational): I *was driving* to work when the van hit my car.

Action in progress in the past (simultaneous): While Andrew *was turning* on his computer, his secretary *was opening* the morning mail.

Note that it is easily replaced by simple past: While Frances *opened* the mail, Andrew *turned* on his computer.

Simple Future

COMMENTS

- In English, the verb proper isn't inflected to express futurity (as in French, for example). Hence, contemporary grammarians consider future tense a false tense.
- Whether structurally false or not, future tense is very useful.
- The tense markers are *shall* and *will*. The distinction between the two is less important than it was once held to be.
- If in doubt about which to use—*shall* or *will*—choose *will*. It's less stiff, less formal.
- The other way of expressing futurity is by using (*to be*) *going to*. Example: George *is going to read* his paper at the panel tomorrow.

EXAMPLES

Action to take place: Alim *will fly* out at 10 A.M. on Tuesday.

Contingency: I*'ll see* him in San Diego if I can get away.

Commitment: I *will arrive* there as scheduled.

Condition: If you go too, you *will find* us at the site office.

Prediction: This project *will not succeed*.

Future habitual: Alim *will manage* the San Diego site over the next few years.

Future Progressive

COMMENTS

- By adding *will be*, you add distance to the future time; you project a sense that an event may not happen.
- You do not use *will* or *be going to* in a future time clause introduced by some other time marker such as *before, after, when,* or *as soon as.* Example: Before I *leave* for the airport, I wish to call for my driver.

EXAMPLES

Action in progress at specific future time: The shuttle *will be landing* at 8:05 A.M. Friday.

Duration in specific future time: Our division *will be working* on the AWACs enhancement over the next two years.

The Perfect Tenses

All the perfects are relational. Each reported act has some relation to some other event.

Present Perfect

COMMENTS

- The present perfect relates to past events having relevance to the present or having results in the present.
- The present perfect looks at an act retrospectively. It's often used to refer to events that began in the past and last up until the present.
- You can often substitute the simple past without much change in meaning.

EXAMPLES

Past situation with present relevance: Barry *has* already *spoken* to the employees about the expected reduction in workforce.

Situation or act that began in past and lasts to the present: Roy *has been* an employee since 1959.

Past situation with results in the present: The word kludge *has become* part of our vocabulary, so we can now use it in our documents.

Recently completed action: Ron *has* just *briefed* the other officers about our research funds for the remainder of the year.

Present Perfect Progressive

COMMENTS

- This form combines the meaning of present progressive and present perfect.
- By adding *ing*, you give the verb such additional meanings as temporariness, or immediacy, or an ongoing condition.
- A hidden characteristic of *ing* is that it tends to personalize the verb.
- Note: There is an entire category of verbs—called stative verbs (start, begin, finish)—for which present perfect progressive cannot be used. Example: Our group *has been beginning* a new approach to software development.

EXAMPLES

Situation begun in past and continuing to present: Frederick *has been managing* the Heidelberg site for 10 years now.

Incompleteness of an action in progress: Lynn *has been working* on the software development program.

Temporariness of an action begun in past and continuing to present: Numerous virus protection packages *have been functioning* with varied degrees of success.

Past Perfect

COMMENTS

- Past perfect is another relational tense. It refers to an action completed in the past that has relevance to a different period in the past. In other words, everything is past.
- Be alert: Past perfect isn't necessary if the relation is expressed by another vocabulary item; however, it is absolutely necessary when nothing else explains the relationship. Compare: When Alice entered the cage, the lion *had eaten*. When Alice entered the cage, the lion ate.
- This tense is used more often in written English than in spoken English.

EXAMPLES

Action completed in past before some other past action: Ernie *had* already *pressed* the starter button before I could stop him.

In a clause relating to a past conditional action: If Megan *had read* the company's policies and procedures manual, she would know what to do.

Past Perfect Progressive

COMMENTS

- Past present progressive is used to express an action or habit taking place over a period of time in the past (that's the past progressive part) prior to some other past event. In other words, everything is past.
- The *ing* introduces a sense of motion even though all acts are completed.
- If used incorrectly, this tense can cause serious confusion in a technical document.

EXAMPLES

Past action prior to another past action: Ursula *had been transmitting* code for three days without rest, so her supervisor told her to take a few days off.

Interruption of a past event in progress by another past action: System Command *had been planning* a new launch until they learned that the project was aborted.

Future Perfect

COMMENTS

- Just as all the actions of the past perfect and the past perfect progessive are in successive stages of pastness, future perfect (and future perfect progressive) describes successive stages of future action.
- Future perfect is most useful when discussing a future action to be completed before some specific time. This is where you will see it used most frequently in documents like memos or monthly activity reports.

EXAMPLES

Future act or event preceding a more distant future action: My group *will have completed* its task before next year's deadline.

Future act to be completed before some more distant specific future action: Our senior administrative secretary *will have collated* our material by the time we must deliver it to the sponsor at 4 P.M.

Future Perfect Progressive

COMMENTS

- Like past perfect progressive, this is a tense that you will rarely use.
- This tense is restricted to expressing habitual action or action lasting over a period of present time. The action will continue into the future.
- The future time into which the present action extends is specifically expressed.

EXAMPLES

Habitual or durative action continued to specific future time: On October 15, I *will have been working* here for 10 years. *Will* you *have been living* here long enough by next June to qualify for citizenship?

BIBLIOGRAPHY

Akmajian, Adrian, Richard A. Demers and Robert M. Harnish. *Linguistics: An Introduction to Language and Communications*. Cambridge, Massachusetts: The MIT Press. Second Edition, 1988.

Azar, Betty Schrampfer. *Fundamentals of English Grammar*. Englewood Cliffs, New Jersey: Prentice Hall Regents. Second Edition, 1992.

Bénouis, Mustapha K. *Le Français Economique et Commercial*. New York, New York: Harcourt Brace Jovanovich, Inc. 1982.

Benson, Herbert. *The Relaxation Response*. New York, New York: William Morrow. 1975, and New York, New York: Random House/Avon. 1992.

Celce-Murcia, Marianne and Diane Larsen-Freeman. *The Grammar Book: An ESL/EFL Teacher's Course*. Cambridge, Massachusetts: Newbury House Publishers. 1983.

Covitt, R. "Some Problematic Grammar Areas for ESL Teachers," UCLA. Unpublished M.A. Thesis, 1976.

Crews, Frederick. *The Random House Handbook*. New York, New York: Random House. Third Edition, 1980.

Davis, Katie. *Sentence Combining and Paragraph Construction*. New York, New York: Macmillan Publishing Co., Inc. 1983.

Day, Robert A. *Scientific English: A Guide for Scientists and Other Professionals*. Phoenix, Arizona: Oryx Press. 1992.

Decker, Randall E. *Patterns of Exposition 8*. Boston, Massachusetts: Little, Brown and Company. 1982.

Gilbert, Judy B. *Clear Speech: Pronunciation and Listening Comprehension in American English*. Cambridge and New York: Cambridge University Press. 1989.

Gopen, George D. and Judith A. Swan. "The Science of Scientific Writing," *American Scientist*. vol. 78, no. 6, November-December 1990.

Graham Associates. *Effective Business Writing*. Washington, DC: American Management Systems, Inc. 1991.

Graham, Judith and Daniel O. Graham Jr. *The Writing System Workbook*. Fairfax, Virginia: Preview Press. 1995.

Huckin, Thomas N. and Leslie A. Olsen. *Technical Writing and Professional Communication*. New York: McGraw-Hill. 1983.

Huckin, Thomas N. and Leslie A. Olsen. *Technical Writing and Professional Communication for Nonnative Speakers of English*. New York: McGraw-Hill. Second Edition, 1991.

Jay, Frank (ed.). *IEEE Standard Dictionary of Electrical and Electronics Terms.* New York: The Institute of Electrical and Electronics Engineers, Inc. Second Edition, 1984.

Kaplan, Robert B. "Cultural Thought Patterns in Inter-Cultural Education" in *Towards Multiculturalism,* edited by Jaime S. Wurzel. Yarmouth, Maine: Intercultural Press, Inc. 1989.

Kirkpatrick, David. "Here Comes the Payoff from PCs," *Fortune.* March 23, 1992.

Lay, Mary M. and William M. Karis (eds.). *Collaborative Writing in Industry: Investigations in Theory Practice.* Amityville, New York: Baywood Publishing Company, Inc. 1991.

Markel, Michael H. *Technical Writing Situations and Strategies.* New York, New York: St. Martin's Press. Third Edition, 1992.

Masse, R. E. "Theory and Practice of Editing Processes in Technical Communication," *IEEE Transactions on Professional Communication.* March 1985.

Matthews, Candace. *Business Interactions.* Englewood Cliffs, New Jersey: Regents/Prentice Hall. 1987.

McCaig, Isabel and Martin H. Manser. *A Learner's Dictionary of English Idioms.* Oxford: Oxford University Press. 1986.

Michaelson, Herbert B. *How to Write and Publish Engineering Papers and Reports.* Phoenix, Arizona: Oryx Press. Third Edition, 1990.

Murphy, M. J. *Test Yourself in English Idioms.* London: Hodder and Stoughton. 1987.

Myers, Isabel Briggs and Mary H. McCaulley. *A Guide to the Development and Use of the Myers-Briggs Type Indicator.* Palo Alto, California: Consulting Psychologists Press, Inc. 1993.

Myers, Isabel Briggs with Peter Myers. *Gifts Differing.* Palo Alto, California: Consulting Psychologists Press, Inc. 1980.

Orion, Gertrude F. *Pronouncing American English* [a set of 16 audiotapes]. Boston, Massachusetts: Heinle & Heinle Publishers. 1988.

Orion, Gertrude F. *Pronouncing American English: Sounds, Stress, and Intonation.* New York, New York: Newbury House Publishers. 1988.

Patrick, Mary C. "A Good Look in the Mirror," *Contingencies.* Washington, DC: American Academy of Actuaries. May/June 1994.

Rathbone, Robert R. *Communicating Technical Information.* Reading, Massachusetts: Addison-Wesley Publishing Co., Inc. Second Edition, 1985.

Rice, Scott. *Right Words Right Places.* Belmont, California: Wadsworth Publishing Co. 1993.

Sabin, William A. *The Gregg Reference Manual.* New York: McGraw-Hill Book Company. Seventh Edition, 1994.

Skillin, Marjorie E. and Robert M. Gay et al. *Words into Type.* Englewood Cliffs, New Jersey: Prentice-Hall, Inc. Third Edition, 1974.

Snow, C. P. "The Two Cultures and the Scientific Revolution," *New Statesman.* October 6, 1956.

Spencer, Donald D. *Computer Dictionary.* Ormond Beach, Florida: Camelot Publications. Fourth Edition, 1993.

Superintendent of Documents. *U.S. Air Force Effective Writing Course.* Washington, DC: U.S. Government Printing Office. n.d.

Superintendent of Documents. *U.S. Government Printing Office Style Manual.* Washington, DC: U.S. Government Printing Office. 1984.

Ward, A. E. "Acronyms, Abbreviations, and Code Words," Bedford, Massachusetts: The MITRE Corporation, WP22424, rev. 3. July 1983.

Index

A

Abbreviation, 50
Abstract (of report), 12, 15, 52
Accent, 247
Accent inventory, 253–255
Accent reduction, 40, 252–260,
    285
Accessibility, 13, 16. *See also*
    Technical writing
    characteristics
Accuracy, 13, 16. *See also* Technical
    writing characteristics
Acronyms, 43, 49–54, 226
Active voice, 141, 144–148
Adult learner, 5
African languages, 74
Agreement (of subject, verb), 141–
    144
Alphanumeric, 50
Ambiguity, 228–230
America, American, 4, 131, 290,
    295–297
Apostrophe, 235
    in contractions, 235
    in possessives, 235
Arabic, 8, 14, 20, 97
Articles (part of speech), 73–79
ASTD (American Society for
    Training & Development),
    290

B

Babbage, Charles, 61
Brainstorming, 28, 266–268
Briefings, 246–248
Briticisms, 129, 131
Business English, 11
Business letters, 28, 29, 37–39
Bullets, 43–44, 48

C

Campbell Interest & Skills Survey,
    293
Capitalization, 46, 53, 237
Case, as inflection, 158, 159
Chinese, 97
Clancy, Tom, 215

Audience, 27, 209, 210, 217
    analysis, 210
    multiple, 209, 210, 211, 217, 269
    primary, 211, 217
    secondary, 211, 217
    single, 209
Auxiliary modals, 83–88
Azar, Betty, 79